Behold the Land

THE JOHN HOPE FRANKLIN SERIES IN AFRICAN AMERICAN HISTORY AND CULTURE

Waldo E. Martin Jr. and Patricia Sullivan, editors

Behold the Land

The Black Arts Movement in the South

James Smethurst

The University of North Carolina Press CHAPEL HILL

This book was published with the assistance of the Z. Smith Reynolds Fund of the University of North Carolina Press.

Set in Merope Basic by Westchester Publishing Services
Manufactured in the United States of America

The University of North Carolina Press has been a member of the Green Press Initiative since 2003.

Library of Congress Cataloging-in-Publication Data
Names: Smethurst, James Edward, author.
Title: Behold the land : the Black Arts movement in the South / James Smethurst.
Other titles: John Hope Franklin series in African American history and culture.
Description: Chapel Hill : The University of North Carolina Press, 2021. | Series: The John Hope Franklin series in African American history and culture | Includes bibliographical references and index.
Identifiers: LCCN 2020044269 | ISBN 9781469663036 (cloth ; alk. paper) | ISBN 9781469663043 (pbk. ; alk. paper) | ISBN 9781469663050 (ebook)
Subjects: LCSH: Black Arts movement—Southern States. | American literature—African American authors—History and criticism. | African Americans in literature. | Black nationalism in literature. | Black nationalism—Southern States—History—20th century. | African Americans—Southern States—Intellectual life—20th century.
Classification: LCC PS153.N5 S558 2021 | DDC 810.9/896073—dc23
LC record available at https://lccn.loc.gov/2020044269

Cover illustration: *Were You There* by Jim Alexander (African Liberation Day, Washington, D.C., 1972). Used by permission of the artist.

Portions of this book were published in different form in “The Black Arts Movement in Atlanta” in *Neighborhood Rebels: Local Movements for Black Power in America*, edited by Peniel Joseph (New York: Palgrave Macmillan, 2010); “Retraining the Heartworks: Women in Atlanta’s Black Arts Movement” in *Women in the Black Revolt*, edited by Dayo Gore, Jean Theoharis, and Komozi Woodard (New York: New York University Press, 2009); “Black Arts South: Rethinking New Orleans and the Black Arts Movement in the Wake of Katrina” in *Radicalism in the South Since Reconstruction*, eds. Christopher Green, Rachel Rubin, and James Smethurst (New York: Palgrave Macmillan, 2006); and “The Black Arts Movement and Historically Black Colleges and Universities” in *New Thoughts on the Black Arts Movement*, eds. Lisa Gail Collins and Margo Crawford (New Brunswick: Rutgers University Press, 2006).

In memory of Lorenzo Thomas

Contents

Acknowledgments

This project was a long time coming. As always, it is the result of the work of many hands, not the least the people who built the Black Arts movement in the South. Nevertheless, its flaws are strictly my own. I am grateful to the many people who contributed. As always, please forgive me if I have forgotten someone.

First, I would like to thank everyone who allowed me to interview them (in some cases more than once): Jim Alexander, Abdul Alkalimat, the late Amiri Baraka, John Bracey Jr., Pearl Cleage, the late Sam Cornish, the late Ebon Dooley, Levi Frazier, Esther Jackson, the late James Jackson, Michael Lomax, Alice Lovelace, the late John O'Neal, Kalamu ya Salaam, A. B. Spellman, Edward Spriggs, William Strickland, Ekwueme Michael Thelwell, the late Lorenzo Thomas, Askia Touré, Jerry Ward, the late Nayo Watkins, and the late Ahmos Zu-Bolton. Safe home to those interviewees who have passed since I interviewed them.

I am deeply indebted to the many people who answered questions, gave me leads, shared their research, helped me better understand Black art and Black Arts (and Black Power) in the South, read portions of this study, corrected me, and otherwise supported and encouraged me in ways large and small, including Nadia Alahmed, Quo Vadis Gex Breaux, Emahunn Campbell, Margo Crawford, Maria Damon, Doris Derby, Jonathan Fenderson, Elizabeth Rodriguez Fielder, Tanisha Ford, Henry Louis Gates Jr., Dayo Gore, Kiara Hill, Gerald Horne, Peniel Joseph, Kenny Leon, Kim McMillon, Catherine Michna, Kelli Morgan, Aldon Nielsen, Roscoe Orman, Howard Ramsby II, Eugene Redmond, Mona Lisa Saloy, Sonia Sanchez, Michael Simanga, Cherisse Burden-Stelly, Candy Tate, Jean Theoharis, Stephen Ward, and Komozi Woodard.

I am particularly grateful to the Schomburg Center for Research in Black Culture and its Scholars-in-Residence Program for its support of this project. Many thanks to Farah Jasmine Griffin, the director of the program during my time there. Thanks, too, to my fellow Fellows, Myra Armstead, Devyn Benson, John Perpener, Rashad Shabazz, and Rafia Zafar, for their community and invaluable comments on my work, and to my research assistant at the Schomburg, Melay Araya. And much gratitude to Aisha

Al-Adawiya for her generosity and making things happen while I was at the Schomburg.

As always, I want to acknowledge my past and present colleagues in the W. E. B. Du Bois Department of Afro-American Studies at the University of Massachusetts Amherst: Ernest Allen Jr., John Bracey Jr., Yemisi Jimoh, Amy Jordan, Anne Kerth, Agustin Lao-Montes, Toussaint Losier, Traci Parker, the late Femi Richards, Britt Rusert, Archie Shepp, Stephanie Shonekan, Manisha Sinha, Nelson Stevens, William Strickland, Esther Terry, Ekueme Michael Thelwell, Steven Tracy, and Robert Paul Wolff. As always, I am grateful to Tricia Loveland, the organizational heart of the Du Bois Department, for practically everything.

I want to acknowledge the help I received from the staffs of the W. E. B. Du Bois Library at the University of Massachusetts, the Amistad Research Center at Tulane University, the Auburn Avenue Library, the Woodruff Library at Emory University, the Mississippi State Archives, the Moorland-Spingarn Research Center at Howard University, the Beinecke Library at Yale University, the Schomburg Center for Research in Black Culture of the New York Public Library, the Spellman College Archives, and the Woodruff Library at Atlanta University Center.

I want to thank also the editorial and production staff at the University of North Carolina Press, especially Chuck Grench, Debbie Gershenowitz, Catherine Hodorowicz, and Dylan White. I am also grateful for the extremely helpful comments of the Press's two anonymous readers.

I owe many thanks to my family: William Smethurst, Ludlow Smethurst, Richard Smethurst, the late Mae Smethurst, Andrew Smethurst, Alejandra Ramirez, Katie Smethurst, Jacob Smethurst Rubin, Silvie Schlein, Thea Schlein, Rachel Lee Rubin, Jessie Rubin, Merle Forney, and Margaret Forney. Special thanks to Carol Forney.

Abbreviations Used in Text

AAA	Afro-American Association
ALD	African Liberation Day
ALSC	African Liberation Support Committee
AUC	Atlanta University Center
BARTS	Black Arts Repertory Theater and School
BPP	Black Panther Party for Self-Defense
CAP	Congress of African People/Congress of Afrikan Peoples
CBE	Center for Black Education
CIO	Committee for Industrial Organization/Congress of Industrial Organizations
COFO	Council of Federated Organizations
CORE	Congress of Racial Equality
CPUSA	Communist Party of the United States of America
CRC	Civil Rights Congress
DHU	Dillard History Unit
ERAP	Economic Research and Action Project
FAP	Federal Artists Project
FE	United Farm Equipment Workers Union
FST	Free Southern Theater
FTP	Federal Theater Project
FWP	Federal Writers Project
HBCU	Historically Black Colleges and Universities

IBW	Institute of the Black World
ILA	International Longshoremen's Association
ILWU	International Longshore and Warehouse Union
MXLU	Malcolm X Liberation University
NAACP	National Association for the Advancement of Colored People
NAC	Neighborhood Arts Center
NAG	Nonviolent Action Group
NOI	Nation of Islam
OBAC	Organization for Black American Culture
PDL	People's Defense League
RAM	Revolutionary Action Movement
RNA	Republic of New Afrika
SBCA	Southern Black Cultural Alliance
SCAW	Southern Collective of African American Writers
SCEF	Southern Conference for Education Fund
SCHW	Southern Conference for Human Welfare
SCLC	Southern Christian Leadership Conference
SDS	Students for a Democratic Society
SNCC	Student Nonviolent Coordinating Committee
SNYC	Southern Negro Youth Congress
SOBU	Student Organization of Black Unity
TABU	Toward a Black University
UAW	United Auto Workers Union
UNIA	Universal Negro Improvement Association
WPA	Works Progress Administration
YOBU	Youth Organization of Black Unity

Behold the Land

Introduction

> The future of American Negroes is in the South. Here three hundred and twenty-seven years ago, they began to enter what is now the United States of America; here they have made their greatest contribution to American culture; and here they have suffered the damnation of slavery, the frustration of reconstruction and the lynching of emancipation.
>
> —W. E. B. DU BOIS, *Behold the Land* (1946)

This study is essentially a cultural history that investigates the origins, development, maturation, and decline of this vital but understudied regional manifestation of the Black Arts movement in the southern U.S. from the early 1960s until the early 1980s. As in my earlier work on the Black Arts movement, a great deal of attention is paid to the local specificities and variations of African American culture and politics in different cities and sections within the South. However, unlike my earlier work, *The Black Arts Movement: Literary Nationalism in the 1960s and 1970s*, the organization of this book is fundamentally more chronological rather than simply geographical because the origin and evolution of Black Arts in different southern locales is even more intertwined than elsewhere in the United States.

Though this study grows out of *The Black Arts Movement* to a large extent, since my earlier book basically cut off around 1972, it mostly missed the apogee of Black Arts in the South in such institutions as the Southern Black Cultural Alliance (SBCA) and Atlanta's Neighborhood Arts Center (NAC). On the one hand, as I said in the introduction to my earlier book, I did not try to do a history of the entire movement since there was no way to pay the sort of attention to the regional manifestations of the movement that I thought necessary and keep the book to a manageable length if I attempted that sort of chronological coverage. On the other hand, I knew that, given what might be thought of as the uneven development of Black Arts in different regions, especially the South where the movement, the Free Southern Theater (FST) notwithstanding, peaked later and survived longer than in other areas, I missed some of the most consequential aspects of Black Arts. With further study of the full arc of the Black Arts movement, I became more and more convinced that even though Black Arts in the South had received the least sustained scholarly attention of all the major sections of the country where the movement flourished, it was perhaps the most consequential in its impact. It certainly was more successful in reaching the grassroots over the long term and left a more tangible local legacy than almost any other place with the possible exception of Chicago. Other than the inadequacy of my treatment of gender in *The Black Arts Movement*, my inability to examine the full range of the southern Black Arts movement, even if it was the result of unavoidable practical decisions, remains perhaps my largest regret about that project. This monograph, then, is among other things an effort to pursue a crucial aspect of Black Arts that I was unable to do in my first book on the movement.

The fact that Black Power and Black Arts existed and thrived in the South, as reported in, say, *Black World*, *The Journal of Black Poetry*, and *Black Theatre*, performed an essential ideological task for those movements. The South was central to almost every Black radical notion of African American identity and culture, both as, to quote Amiri Baraka in *Blues People*, "the scene of the crime" and as the ur-home of Black people in the United States or "the land" in the words of W. E. B. Du Bois and the Republic of New Afrika (with its slogan "Free the Land" and efforts to found a self-sufficient Black community ["Kush"] in the Mississippi Delta). Consequently, the movements in the North and the West could not have seen themselves issuing from, speaking to, and being for a liberated Black nation (or a nation in the process of freeing itself) without the whole infrastructure of Black Arts organizations, institutions, and events in the South. Finally, the movement in the South saw some of the most intense publicly supported institutionalization of African American art and culture of anywhere in the country. This inspired what are still some of the highest profile cultural events in the United States, including Atlanta's Black Arts Festival, Wake Forest's Black Theater Festival, and the New Orleans Jazz & Heritage Festival, as well as a host of smaller, more localized festivals, such as the Black August Community Arts Festival in Jackson, Mississippi.

Yet the Black Arts movement in the South still remains to a large extent terra incognita in scholarship on the upsurge of Black political and cultural activism in the 1960s and 1970s. There has been important newer work done by Margo Crawford, Catherine Michna, Candy Tate, and Kalamu ya Salaam (himself a major figure of the southern Black Arts movement), joining older efforts by Jerry Ward (another veteran of the movement), Lorenzo Thomas (a transplant from the North and Panama who also played an influential role in later southern Black Arts), and, frankly, me. Of course, much pioneering work was done by Black Arts critics and cultural historians during or immediately after the Black Arts era. The premier example of this is Eugene Redmond's *Drumvoices*, long the only book-length history of African American poetry with a heavy focus on Black Arts and tracing the geography of Black poetry and of Black Arts organizations and institutions of that era.[1] However, this new work is overwhelmingly focused on New Orleans, the Free Southern Theater, BLKARTSOUTH, and the journal *Nkombo*, with the exception of Candy Tate's groundbreaking but as yet unpublished dissertation on Atlanta's Neighborhood Arts Center (NAC).[2] The New Orleans–centered iteration of the southern Black Arts movement was crucial to the growth of a regional Black Arts movement, both in concept and in material terms, not the least because it became the linchpin of the most important regional Black Arts organization, the Southern Black Cultural Alliance (SBCA). As the poet, critic, and political activist Askia Touré observed, the SBCA was the largest grassroots Black cultural organization in the United States during that era—really, it was unique in its regional coverage. Still, New Orleans was only one locus of the southern Black Arts movement, if one of the most consequential. And with the exception of Salaam, most of this new scholarship (again, though excellent) is not much concerned with the influence of BLKARTSOUTH in the region outside of New Orleans other than Crawford's reflection of the impact of BLKARTSOUTH and *Nkombo* on the journal *Callaloo* (now and long one of the top U.S. journals in African, African Diasporic, and African American literary and cultural studies). Even in the case of *Callaloo*, at the time of its origin, it was based in Louisiana at Southern University in Baton Rouge and in the immediate geographical sphere of the New Orleans–based Black Arts movement.

Defining the U.S. South

So, to begin, what is the South? Where is the South? When was the South? Why was the South? These are all large questions for which I have provisional, evolving, historically contingent answers. The South is obviously a large geographical region with a diverse ethnic, religious, economic, topographical, and political profile—and, despite some stereotypes to the contrary, has always been so. It figures prominently in the cultural imagination of the United States even to this day. There are a number of widely circulated, sometimes competing, sometimes intersecting visions or versions of the South in which planters, "hillbillies," "rednecks," and alternately threatening, entertaining, and subservient Black people loom large—where the landscapes of Tara, Bourbon Street, Beale Street, Catfish Row, Mayberry, Dogpatch, and Hazzard (to name only a few iconic fictional and actual locations) overlay or are overlaid on each other. It is interesting in this regard to note how much the political crisis of fall 2013 around the funding of the federal government and the raising of the debt ceiling was cast by many commentators as a second secession by the southern states. Depictions of Donald Trump's supporters in the moment that I am writing these words often draw on the stereotype of the "hillbilly" and frequently implicitly or explicitly link the subjects of those representations to a certain "southern" style and mentality—even if talking about people in Michigan or Wisconsin.

There are certain truths underlying these popular culture images that are worth recalling. That is to say, without relying too much on the Old Left Marxist notion of base and superstructure, at heart the contours of the South are defined by a labor system from which grew much more. In short, the South—surprise—is chattel slavery. Of course, slavery existed as an institution in many regions of the United States (and had an economic and political impact on all U.S. regions), including, as Robert Rohmer has shown, in the Connecticut River Valley of New England, where I live.[3] Still, it is worth recalling the seemingly obvious fact that the South basically consists of those states in which the racialized labor system of slavery was both legal and at the heart of the economy of those political units until the end of the Civil War, which was initiated by the slave owners and their supporters in order to maintain that labor system.[4] While that fact and the origins of the Civil War are more or less settled in the history profession, popular debates about slavery and Southern (and U.S.) history have taken on a new life in the early twenty-first century, especially with the election of Trump. I say those political units because I would argue one of the things that make areas in which the African American population was small, such as portions of Appalachia, "southern" was that they were part of states in which the institution of slavery thrived. (There are some gray areas, so to speak, such as Delaware, in which slavery was economically unimportant but psychologically so consequential to white people that they refused to give up the institution during the Civil War even when the federal government offered financial compensation to slave owners.)

As a result, given the Enlightenment, Rights of Man liberal ideology that literally framed the founding of the United States, revolving around inalienable natural rights of life, liberty, and the pursuit of happiness and the opposition, or even dialectic, of slavery and freedom, it is not surprising that the philosophical, economic, legal, social, and cultural dehumanization (or subhumanization) of African Americans found its most intense manifestation in the South—really defined the South. Of course, as Harriet Wilson pointed out in *Our Nig*, "slavery's shadows fell even" in the North, also.[5] Arguments about whether U.S. slavery was a racial caste system that was in large part a result of very long-standing European, particularly English, prejudices against Africans has engaged historians for generations. Without getting into that sort of chicken-or-egg argument, I will say that whether or not the intensely, and one might even say insanely, racialized nature of slavery in the United States was an almost inevitable consequence of a deep English racism, it was certainly a necessary result once the system of slavery in which African-descended people were defined as uniquely enslaveable took shape and matured to solve the labor shortage problem of what became the U.S. South. Further, I would argue, without any great originality, that it was from this matrix that other structures of racial hierarchy, notably Jim Crow, issued, grew, and formed models for the understanding and adjudicating of race across the United States and beyond (as in the case of South Africa and the ways in which Jim Crow informed the creation of the edifice of apartheid).

The terms and concepts of free, freedom, and, of course, emancipation (that is, the process or the act by which one becomes free—or freer, anyway), juxtaposed against tyranny, slavery, and coercion, have a significant legal, political, cultural, and felt meaning for all in what would become the United States before, during, and after the American Revolution. However, they obviously have a particularly intense significance for those who were most viciously caught in the meshes of the fully developed system of chattel slavery, which is to say African Americans in the South. Their presence in huge numbers, their condition, and their work in this system were the most salient defining characteristics of what made the South the South—as well as what made African Americans "Negro" or "Black"—which is to say, among other things, a people with international connections. These terms contained (and contained within themselves) a multitude of often conflicting inflections or accents. A particular contest inhered to "emancipation" as a term referring to a large group or category of people in the sense of a people being freed versus the notion of a people freeing itself.

The second sense of emancipation as the process of a group or people freeing itself is in turn connected to another concept much used in the Black Arts/Black Power era, self-determination, in the Leninist sense of the right, even the obligation, of a people to determine its own political, social, economic, and cultural destiny, up to and including an independent polity if necessary. While Benedict Anderson may be correct in his estimation that nationalism and nation (much like race) are significantly imaginative acts (or a nexus of acts) with material consequences rather than any sort of natural phenomenon, there is nothing like a group of people linked to a particular territory or set of territories rebelling against an authority that in fact persecutes them or dominates them as a group for some purpose, be it political, socio-psychological, economic, or all of the above, to produce a sense of nationalism—as the American Revolution attests. As a result, it was almost inevitable that even if the terms *freedom*, *free*, and *emancipation* in the Black Arts and Black Power era did not have exactly the same valence as they had in the slave era, from very early on they set in motion ideas and practices—one might say an epistemology and symbology—that resonated in the Black Power and Black Arts era with their connection to self-determination, peoplehood, nationalism, and nation, particularly in the South. The South, then, is from its beginning defined not simply by racialized Black labor, but also Black struggle—something that was of primary importance to the Black Arts movement in the South as well as to the national movement.

When was the Black Arts movement? Generally speaking, most scholars would locate the movement in the period from around 1965 to about 1975. While those dates are useful, I'll state the obvious and say that in delineating the boundaries of any historical or cultural period—say, the Harlem or New Negro Renaissance—such periodization is provisional and subject to debate. In fact, as seen in my more specific discussion of the movement in the South, Black Arts is particularly hard to pin down historically—and not encompassed by the 1965 to 1975 temporal periodization. It is certainly possible to move the end date to at least 1985 in the South.

What was the Black Arts movement? Well, that, too, is a difficult question to answer in any concise way. One thumbnail that has been commonly used is that it was the cultural wing of the Black Power movement. However, one could just as easily say, and in fact I have, that the Black Power movement was the political wing of the Black Arts movement. That is to say that the movements are so twinned and joined at the hip that it is impossible, really, to tell where one begins and the other ends. In many instances both movements (if they are, in fact, distinct movements) were largely populated by politicized artists and political activists passionately interested in art and culture. Often they were both. In fact, activists, both "cultural nationalist" (most commonly identified with Maulana Karenga and his neo-Africanist Kawaida ideology) and "revolutionary nationalist" (often seen, somewhat narrowly, as embodied in the Black Panther Party for Self-Defense [BPP]), were not simply interested in art and culture but saw them as essential terrains or battlegrounds for the transformation of Black consciousness and the building of Black unity. Virtually all younger Black radicals were deeply moved by the thought and rhetoric of Malcolm X. His speeches, such as his frequently repeated question to Black people, "Who taught you how to hate yourself?," presented fundamentally cultural arguments. It was through culture, both popular and "high," that this white lesson in self-hatred was primarily transmitted. This cultural focus was nowhere truer than in the South where Kawaidaism and Marxist-cultural nationalist hybrids exerted great influence during the Black Arts era.

Another problem of definition is that Black Arts was so decentralized geographically and ideologically. The great strength of Black Arts, its grassroots character, makes it hard to grasp. Black Arts activities and institutions appeared in almost every community and on every campus where there was an appreciable number of Black people. Again, this grassroots dispersion was particularly true in the South where African Americans were (and are) a significant presence throughout the region, both in the cities and in the countryside—and where the vast majority of historically Black colleges and universities (HBCUs) were (and are) located. While there was communication and often cooperation between these various regional and local manifestations of Black Arts (workshops, theaters, bookstores, galleries, schools, poetry readings, concerts, dance companies, visual arts galleries, museums, journals, and newspapers), each community had its particular history, demographics, traditions, institutions, and so on.

Also, there was a tremendous ideological and aesthetic diversity within Black Arts and Black Power. Participants held a variety of political beliefs, ranging from revolutionary Marxism to versions of what was understood as the cultures and ideologies of traditional precolonial Africa, versions that could be strangely futuristic even as they invoked tradition. Often, again especially in the South, Black Arts and Black Power organizations and institutions were guided by amalgams of Marxism and cultural nationalism. While many of the groups of Black Arts and Black Power communicated with each other, read each other's publications, networked, and attended many of the same festivals, conferences, and events, there was also much disagreement and debate, sometimes to the point of violence. So if one is going to talk about Black Arts, then one has to try to look at the movement broadly and yet not smooth out its differences and complex relationships.

However, despite this range of often conflicting beliefs, Black Arts and Black Power activists generally shared a concept of African American liberation and the right of African Americans to determine their own destiny. There was usually some common notion of the development or recovery of an authentic national Black culture, often (though not inevitably) linked to some subset of existing African American folk or popular culture. In short, this culture was to be mass, revolutionary, and paradoxically traditional. Another common aspect of Black Arts, contrary to notions of it as anti-intellectual and antitheoretical, is a near-obsession with theory, both aesthetic and political, that would undergird, explain, and provide a way of evaluating this new Black art. Again, what was common was not the particular theories, which were often at odds, but an urge toward theory that addressed shared issues. Thus, in some respects, Black Arts might be understood as a set of discussions or debates around mutual concerns rather than a unified movement. However, it was a discussion or debate that was intended—to paraphrase Karl Marx—not simply to describe the world but to change it. And that debate did in fact set people in motion and bring about significant change—in the South as much or more than any region.

So, broadly speaking, what one sees in New York, Philadelphia, Boston, Detroit, Chicago, Los Angeles, San Francisco, Oakland, Berkeley, St. Louis, Washington, D.C., Cleveland, New Orleans, Houston, Durham, Miami, Memphis, Jackson, Atlanta, Nashville, and so on, is that there are ideological and institutional spaces in which young, and not so young, Black artists and intellectuals come together and organize, study, and think about what a new Black art (and a new Black politics) might be. The context for such thoughts is the new openings (and closures) in the world provided by such events as the founding of the United Nations, the Chinese Revolution, the Bandung Conference, Dien Bien Phu, the Cuban Revolution, the emergence of Kwame Nkrumah's independent Ghana, the murder of Patrice Lumumba, Malcolm X's calls for Black pride and political and cultural self-determination, Robert Williams's promotion of armed self-defense, the Montgomery bus boycott, and the 1960 Black student sit-in movement. These spaces were largely found in what remained of the formal and informal networks (study groups, bookstores, forums, lectures, educational associations, magazines, and so on) of the Old Left, networks that were often subterranean but nonetheless present in the Cold War South, and those of what might be thought of as the old nationalism of Garveyites, Pan-Africanists, and so on. These networks often moved through the surviving neighborhood arts centers and schools, settlement house galleries and theaters, and grassroots artists' workshops that were themselves so often the products of early twentieth-century leftist notions of art for the people as well as in new spaces opened up by the civil rights movement, the new nationalism, and the New Left.

Margo Crawford, one of the relatively few newer scholars of Black Arts to write extensively about the movement in the South, especially about the BLKARTSOUTH/*Nkombo* group in New Orleans, argues that the Black Arts movement epitomized what she terms "Black Post-Blackness," that is a concept of "Blackness" that both looks forward and looks back, that is concerned with group identity and cohesiveness *and* multiplicity, that is, Crawford suggests, a twenty-first century iteration of Amiri Baraka's notion of the "changing same." Oddly enough, the most common readings of "post-Blackness" (a phrase of which one of the coiners, Thelma Golden, suggested that perhaps what she really meant was "post-Black Arts movement") relies on a vision of Black Arts as articulating a relatively unitary and often prescriptive notion of Blackness and *the* Black aesthetic against which one could be "post," which is to be Black in new and multiple ways. So there is a productive sense that "Black Post-Blackness" as a hallmark of the actual Black Arts movement is set against Golden's idea of the movement. The rebellion against any Black Arts unitary aesthetics and ideology, of course, as Crawford argues, was not merely a "post" phenomenon offered later but was in fact a part of the Black Arts moment itself. For example, as Crawford notes, the leaders of BLKARTSOUTH often juxtaposed their sense of the multiplicity and fluidity of their project against what they saw as more reductive ideas of Blackness promoted elsewhere (usually Chicago and New York). However, while Crawford's observations here are extremely useful for getting a handle on BLKARTSOUTH, I would argue that though they resisted efforts to prematurely and narrowly define Blackness, the southern Black Arts activists, especially in BLKARTSOUTH, still felt the pressure of such definition and the sort of Black solidarity that they thought the political and cultural situation required, particularly in a region where the political challenges remained great and oppression was so raw. There is a sense that post-Blackness in the way that it is usually understood remains particularly problematic for people in the South even to this day, as in the 2018 governor's race in Florida where one candidate, Andrew Gillum, who tended to emphasize class over race in the campaign nevertheless felt compelled to utter in the face of often openly racist attacks on him by his opponent, "And the truth is, you know what? I'm black. I've been black all my life and as far as I know, I'll die black."[6]

Chapter Summary

Chapter One
Ancestors: The Popular Front, Black Nationalism, Bohemia, and Black Art in the South before 1964

This chapter traces the long foreground of radical Black art and African American cultural institutions in the South from the New Negro Renaissance in the 1920s through the Left political and cultural milieu of the 1930s and 1940s to the civil rights upsurge of the 1950s and early 1960s. It pays special attention to the Popular Front era of the 1930s and 1940s. This period saw the growth of Black or interracial community-based cultural institutions often affiliated with Popular Front political organizations, such as the People's Theaters of Richmond and New Orleans, as well as the emergence of historically Black colleges and universities as centers of socially engaged art. The first chapter also takes up the ways in which the new civil rights movement, especially the Black student movement and emergence of the Student Nonviolent Coordinating Committee (SNCC) in the early 1960s, refocused the attentions of Black artists and intellectuals on the South in a positive way, energizing and activating those who had long remained in the South, both on the historically Black campuses and in the community, as well as bringing South cultural and political activists who began to found new Black Arts institutions or revitalize old ones.

Chapter Two
Becoming Black, Becoming Southern: The Gulf Coast and the Rise of a Southern Black Arts Infrastructure

Chapter 2 takes up the movement of cultural and educational institutions in the Gulf Coast South from interracial civil rights organizations to more self-consciously Black institutions as the national Black Power and Black Arts movements took shape. Again, the most significant group in this regard is the FST in New Orleans. At the same time, groups of young African Americans began to set up new institutions. The chapter also considers how mostly young Black artists, intellectuals, and activists, who had gained entrée to various institutions that had previously been entirely or almost entirely reserved for white people found in these institutions lingering restrictions and not so transparent ceilings that moved them in a more nationalist direction. As the chapter traces, a key event in this regard was the separation of the writers and theater workshops of the FST from the theater and the formation of BLKARTSOUTH in New Orleans. Both *Nkombo*, the journal of BLKARTSOUTH, and the BLKARTSOUTH performance group tours helped inspire African American artists to form like groups from Texas to Florida, laying the basis of the Southern Black Cultural Alliance (SBCA).

Chapter Three
From Campus to Community: The Early Black Arts Movement in Atlanta

Chapter 3 takes up the increasing importance of Black Arts and Black Power in Atlanta and the movement of radical Black cultural initiatives from the campus to the community. This chapter describes the interrelated growth of the institutionalization of Black Arts with the growth of Black political power in Atlanta, particularly with the election of Maynard Jackson as mayor in 1973, and of the importance of the urban South in the national networks and organizations of Black Arts and Black Power. At the same time that Black southerners played vital roles in such national Black Power organizations as the Congress of African People (CAP) and the African Liberation Support Committee (ALSC), a network of local community-based Black Arts institutions emerged, often closely related to CAP and ALSC.

Chapter Four
Black Arts, Black Studies, Black University: Washington, D.C., Nashville, and North Carolina

Chapter 4, too, looks at the connection between Black Arts and Black Power on campuses, primarily those of HBCUs, and communities of the urban South in Washington, D.C., Nashville, and Durham, Winston-Salem, and Greensboro, North Carolina. It examines the central role of the arts in the emergence of Black Studies and notions of the Black university that found fertile ground in the cities of the upper South. While the attempts to create Black universities failed, they created a legacy and a network of

Black educational and arts projects that continue to this day in such institutions and events as the National Black Theatre Festival, founded by Larry Leon Hamlin of the National Black Repertory Theatre in Winston-Salem in 1989.

Chapter Five
The Southern Black Cultural Alliance, the Neighborhood Arts Center, and the Institutionalization of Community-Based Black Arts in the South

Chapter 5 lays out the further growth of a Black Arts network in the South with the emergence of the SBCA and its annual business meeting and yearly performance festival in different cities or on historically Black college campuses. It also delineates new ways in which Black Arts became institutionalized as African Americans gained new political power in southern cities, in large part due to an increased priority on the region by Black political and cultural activists nationally. One aspect of this new emphasis put on political and cultural organizing in the urban South was increased migration of Black artists and intellectuals to the region.

Conclusion
The Decline of Black Arts in the South, the Persistence of Black Arts in the South

The conclusion chronicles the decline of the movement, particularly with the disintegration of the SBCA and the depoliticizing of many of the arts events, institutions, and programs initiated by Black Arts activists. This decline issued largely from the conflicts that plagued the national organizations and networks of Black Arts and Black Power that could not help but affect a region that had become central to these organizations and networks. Also, as elsewhere, cuts and changes in funding for the arts on the national and local levels, combined with the decline in the organized base of Black Arts and Black Power, did much to undermine the southern Black Arts movement. Yet in other ways, many of the initiatives of Black Arts in the South and much of its grassroots constituencies survived to an extent unmatched anywhere in the United States except perhaps Chicago.

The conclusion ends with a meditation on the southern Black Arts movement and the debates about the historical meaning of New Orleans, its destruction by Hurricane Katrina (with human help), and the nature of its reconstruction—or lack thereof. In some respects the destruction or deformation of long-standing and vital Black neighborhoods by flooding and the so-called recovery in New Orleans are like speeded-up time-lapse photography versions of the obliteration of Black neighborhoods and Black commercial and cultural centers throughout the South (and elsewhere) that has been occurring since at least the 1950s and continues to this day from Houston to Richmond. What is the import of this destruction to historical and cultural memory, both symbolically and practically? These are debates of a particular moment but are also likely to be of considerable duration as the questions of cultural legacies of the 1960s and 1970s and the public support of the arts in the United States continue to generate political conflict in a highly polarized, if not downright terrifying, time.

Notes on Geographical Definition and Terminology

For the purposes of this study, my geographical definition of the South encompasses nearly all those states in which chattel slavery was still legal at the time of the Civil War plus the District of Columbia. So *the South* here encompasses such border states as Kentucky and Maryland and such cities as Baltimore, Louisville, and Washington, D.C. Obviously, such regional definitions are to some extent arbitrary. Border cities as gateways between regions, cultures, and even national states obviously have much in common with each other, regardless of which side of the border they might be on, whether one is speaking of the borders of the Mississippi River, the Ohio River, or the Rio Grande. One possibly questionable decision I made is not to include the "Gateway City," St. Louis—even though I discuss the "Gateway to the South," Louisville. As Clarence Lang points out, St. Louis has many southern features, and Missouri was a slave state until 1865. Like Lang, though, I came to agree with his approving quote of longtime Black activist and civil rights leader Margaret Bush Wilson that St. Louis was a "northern city with a southern exposure."[7] By contrast, Louisville strikes me as a southern city with a northern exposure. In the end, I decided that St. Louis Black Arts groups, notably the important Black Artists Group, interacted more with their counterparts in Chicago and elsewhere in the Midwest than the Black Arts networks of the South. If a scholar wishes to argue otherwise, I am willing to change my view.

The states I am calling southern are also, by and large, those states in which statewide Jim Crow laws and Black disenfranchisement were most intense—though cities that nearly everyone in the United States would consider southern—say, Memphis, Tennessee and relatively nearby Jackson,

Mississippi—could be quite different from each other in the practical application of Jim Crow laws. (For reasons having to do with the local features of the political machine of Edward "Boss" Crump, African Americans could vote in Memphis during the Jim Crow era, for example.)

Beyond a significantly shared, if somewhat locally variable, experience with slavery, Jim Crow, and the civil rights struggle against Jim Crow, one thing that distinguished the states and localities that I am terming southern is the density of HBCUs, which were centers of Black art and culture not present in other parts of the United States other than a handful of schools in Ohio and Pennsylvania. These schools provided the base for artists and activists who, first under the influence of the Popular Front and later more intensely in the Black Arts and Black Power era, inspired and interfaced with community activists to create grassroots southern arts initiatives throughout the region, many of which continue to this day.

When I use the uppercased *Communist*, I refer to the Communist Party USA (CPUSA) and its political and cultural circles. The lowercased term *communist* denotes Marxists in the Leninist stream who are not affiliated with the CPUSA. In that sense, many of the leaders of the Student Organization of Black Unity (SOBU) and the Youth Organization for Black Unity (YOBU) who later joined the Maoist Communist Workers Party were communists, but not Communists. Similarly, "*Socialist*" alludes to the Socialist Party and its circles as distinguished from the more general "*socialist.*"

I uppercase the term *Black* here for the first time (for me) in quite a while. I use it both to refer to African Americans and to Africans and African-descended people outside of the United States. I believe that this combination of nationality and internationalism is in keeping with the subject of the book. Also, to use the lowercased *black* in this moment seems to me to make a political statement that I would prefer to avoid. However, I do not capitalize *white*. I remain unconvinced that "white people" are in fact *a* people or complex of peoples. I largely agree with the late Noel Ignatiev that "whiteness" is an emblem of a systemic social power rather than a national or cultural identity.[8] I certainly believe that Black nationalism and white nationalism are two entirely different things, which is not to say that I might not disagree ideologically with various expressions of Black nationalism to one degree or another.

The term *cultural nationalist* has been deployed variously by scholars inside and outside African American Studies. Here I use it to primarily identify groups, institutions, and individuals that subscribed to the neo-African Kawaida ideology of Maulana Karenga and his US organization to one degree or another. The issue of the influence of Karenga and Kawaidaism is often difficult to parse. Unlike the ALSC, CAP, YOBU/SOBU, and the BPP, the US Organization did not have official branches outside of Los Angeles and San Diego. Karenga was not a national chairman, pope, or commissar. Even if he had the inclination (which he didn't), Karenga had no standing to throw Kalamu ya Salaam out of BLKARTSOUTH, for instance, because Salaam differed with him about the meaning of the blues and Black popular music. Rather, groups and individuals declared their general acceptance of Karenga's principles and thought. Still, it is crucial to note the widespread dispersion and utility of Karenga's Kawaida vision of a neo-African counterculture, with its seven principles (Nguzo Saba) of unity (umoja), self-determination (kujichagulia), collectivity (ujima), cooperative economics (ujamaa), purpose (nia), creativity (kuumba), and faith (imani). Again, the use of Kawaidaism varied flexibly from place to place. The South, for instance, saw some of the most creative amalgams of Marxism and Kawaidaism, particularly among activists in the upper South—though these activists, particularly the Drum and Spear group in Washington, D.C., also frequently embraced the "African Socialism" of Julius Nyerere's ujamaa ideology, a more distinctly socialist cultural nationalist, transethnic vision than Kawaidaism. (Karenga was certainly well-versed in Marxism, which was present below the surface in Kawaidaism in various ways, though.) However, Kawaidaism, often through Karenga's famous Green Book of his aphorisms and concepts (a conscious analogue to Mao's Red Book that was also used by many more openly Marxist Black radicals in the 1960s and 1970s), was a very teachable set of organizational and ideological principles with which one could anchor a new group or institution.

Finally, the term *nation* is generally used in the Marxist sense of "a people" descended from the Third International on the "National Question," a line that exerted tremendous influence on the Third World Marxism of Amiri Baraka and many southern radicals—indeed, also, on the positions of non-Marxist "territorial nationalists," such as the RNA.[9] This sort of Marxist nation is distinguished from the nation-state—though a central tenet of such Marxism is that nations have (or should have) the right to self-determination, including the ability to form a nation-state, though not ruling out the possibility of a multinational state. The term can get a little murky when trying to parse the distinction between a nation and a national minority in this school of Marxist thought. (Basically, a nation occupies a more or less contiguous territory while a national minority does not—hence the Comintern and CPUSA notion that African Americans in the

"Black Belt" of the South constituted a nation while those in the urban ghettoes of the North and West did not.) Also, while this Marxist notion of a nation with a common language, economic life, territory, psychology, and so on intersects with older Black nationalist ideas, it also conflicts with the common Black nationalist sense of Africans and African descendants everywhere as being a people—or, as Maulana Karenga and Kawaidaists would say, Africans (or "Afrikans") on the continent and in the diaspora. Both the Third International/Third World Marxist sense of a Black nation or people and the Black nationalist/Pan-African vision of nation and people coexisted in the thinking of many Black radicals discussed here, even in that of quite a few people who considered themselves Marxists, such as those connected with People's College and YOBU/SOBU in the South. It might be worth noting that though such nations may be, after Benedict Anderson, imagined communities, those imaginings had and have tremendous power and material consequences.[10]

CHAPTER ONE

Ancestors

The Popular Front, Black Nationalism, Bohemia, and Black Art in the South before 1964

Like any other political or cultural movement, the Black Arts movement in the South has a long, almost infinitely extendable foreground. One could trace a southern "long Black Arts movement" back before the New Negro Renaissance and the Garvey movement (which had their southern manifestations), the "Women's Era" of the turn of the century, Reconstruction and the creation of HBCUs in the South that taught literature and eventually established theater and applied arts departments, and the antebellum cultural offering of the Black folk in the slave South and Black abolitionists of the North to the expressive culture of the first Africans to come off the slave ships at Jamestown in 1619. If, as Amiri Baraka observed in *Blues People*, the disembarking African prisoners were not singing "The Saint James Infirmary Blues," they no doubt were strengthened and consoled by music, stories, poetry, prayers, and so on.[1] In fact, one might even go back before disembarkation, as Sterling Brown did in his introduction to one of the famous "From Spirituals to Swing" Popular Front concerts in 1937 in which he argued that the origins of masking in African American culture could be traced back to the Middle Passage and the differing cultural expressions of the enslaved Africans above and below deck.[2]

The Southern Popular Front and the Origins of the Black Arts Movement: SNYC and *Freedomways*

However, while keeping this very long foreground in mind, a more immediate and crucial antecedent of the Black Arts movement in the South, one which in some important ways remained a living presence in the Black Power/Black Arts era, is what might be thought of as the extended Popular Front of the 1930s and 1940s. The public manifestations of the southern Popular Front had, with a few notable exceptions, been crushed during the Red Scare of the late 1940s and 1950s in a wave of repression following the Progressive Party presidential campaign of Henry Wallace in 1948. Nevertheless, the networks and sensibilities engendered by the southern Popular

Front, particularly as expressed in the interface between HBCUs and community-based Black political and artistic efforts, persisted, especially in larger southern cities, such as Houston, New Orleans, and Atlanta.

The Popular Front nationally has often been considered, rightly, an integrated movement led by an integrated but predominantly white CPUSA with an integrated but mainly white leadership. However, in most of the South this situation was reversed. The Popular Front and the CPUSA there were far blacker than in the North and the West with a leadership that was significantly African American. The Communist Left in the South had a deep engagement with African American culture and radical traditions, including Black nationalism and Christianity, as well as a closer relationship with Black and white Socialists than was generally true in the North, prefiguring the cooperation and cross-pollination of different Left and nationalist strains in the region during the Black Power/Black Arts era. For example, the leftwing Highlander School in Tennessee was born out of the collaboration by a Socialist, Myles Horton, and a Communist, Don West, and featured such collaborations throughout its history. In fact, with the decline of Garveyism and the Universal Negro Improvement Association (UNIA), the Popular Front became the most viable space for building radical African American institutions with a bent toward Black self-determination in most of the South.

The significant influence that this pre–Cold War southern Left exerted on the development of U.S. politics and culture outside as well as inside the region is a topic only hinted at by scholars, for the most part, but not really examined. This sort of hint can be found in Robin Kelley's observation in *Hammer and Hoe* that the political soil that the Communist Left plowed in Alabama in the 1930s and 1940s yielded a crop that may have been stunted by McCarthyism, but that nonetheless surprised some civil rights workers who came South expecting to find nothing but barren ground—though other civil rights organizers, such as SNCC's Bob Moses, were more aware of this inheritance as they drew on a network of Old Left contacts during their initial organizing efforts.[3] So it is worth outlining some cultural legacies of the Popular Front in the South, sketching a few of the ways in which the southern Popular Front influenced the Black Arts movement in the South and beyond.

Young Black radicals in a variety of Popular Front organizations, particularly the Southern Negro Youth Congress (SNYC), promoted politicized African American arts and literature in the South during the 1930s and 1940s in ways that had lasting consequences. As with the militants of the later

SNCC and the Black student movement of the 1960s, some of these SNYC activists had lived most or all of their lives in the South to that point, some had been born in the South but had moved elsewhere with their families during the Great Migration, and still others were almost entirely new to the region. Some were graduates of HBCUs; some were alumni of predominantly white colleges and universities; and some had little formal education.

The Cold War devastated the Popular Front in the South. This, of course, was true of all the regions in the United States, but in some places pockets of Left influence and Left-led institutions remained (e.g., the International Longshore and Warehouse Union in the Bay Area and the Packinghouse Workers Union in Chicago). However, almost all the institutions of the Popular Front, with a few important exceptions, were crushed by federal, state, and local government harassment as well as vigilante violence. Even those that survived in one form or another, like the Southern Conference for Education Fund (SCEF) and its newspaper the *Southern Patriot* and the Highlander School, suffered serious losses. This environment of legal repression and violence forced many of the higher profile Popular Front activists, especially relatively open CPUSA members or supporters, to leave the region—or to move to a different part of the South from where the base of their activities had been. However, these transplanted activists drew on their earlier experience to help create new political and cultural institutions and organizations, such as the journal *Freedomways*, that in turn facilitated the creation of new radical African American initiatives in the South. These institutions also helped build financial and other sorts of material support for those initiatives from outside the South, where fundraising was always difficult—at least until African Americans began to win control of the governments of southern cities and exert influence in local and state public arts funding apparatuses. Also, many less prominent (or less openly connected to the Communist Left) rank and file participants in the networks of the Popular Front remained behind in Black communities and on HBCU campuses and often stayed in contact with those who were forced to leave.

When one considers the Popular Front and its impact, one is always faced with the issues of periodization and whether one is speaking of an era or an approach to political work, culture, and so on. The official policy of the Popular Front arose from the response of the Communist International to the Nazi rise to power in Germany in 1933, the subsequent smashing of the Communist Party of Germany (the largest outside of the U.S.S.R. at the time), and victories of fascist or semifascist movements throughout Europe and ended with the German-Soviet Nonaggression Pact in 1939. However, the Popular Front style of work and engagement with mass popular culture, both as aesthetic resource and critique (often simultaneously), as well as with folk and national traditions of the people (and peoples) largely characterized the Communist Left long past 1939.

In the U.S. South, where the CPUSA was largely (and often overwhelmingly) Black in most places, this style involved a new level of positive adoption, adaptation, and alliance with the institutions, rhetoric, music, literature, and beliefs of the Black church, given the centrality of the church and the cultural practices associated with it in nearly all African American communities there. It also entailed a new appreciation for secular Black expressive culture, particularly popular and folk music, as a medium for struggle for "Negro liberation," social progress, and the fight against Fascism (which was seen as closely allied with Jim Crow segregation and the Klan). In terms of personnel, there was a network of activists and artists that included people closely affiliated with the CPUSA at one time or another, such as James Jackson, Esther Cooper Jackson, Louis Burnham, Dorothy Burnham, Edward Strong, Augusta Strong, Margaret Walker, Charles White, and Elizabeth Catlett, and others whose political sympathies were on the left but whose organizational affiliations are less clear, such as Hale Woodruff, John Biggers, Marcus Christian, and Samella Lewis (a visual artist and art historian who studied with Elizabeth Catlett at Dillard University in the 1940s).

Though, again, the official period of the Popular Front as an international Comintern strategy ran from about 1935 to the end of 1939, the Popular Front approach to political organization, iconography, and aesthetics characterized the domestic work of the Communist Left in the United States far beyond 1939, particularly in the South. For example, the names of the leftwing Abraham Lincoln School in Chicago, Jefferson School of Social Science in downtown Manhattan, and George Washington Carver School in Harlem continued to stake symbolic claims to U.S. democratic icons and democracy Popular Front–style in the 1940s and 1950s, despite moves left and right in the larger international Communist movement. Some of the most important examples of such claims in the South, such as John Biggers's 1953 Houston mural *The Contribution of the Negro Woman to American Life and Democracy* and the naming of the *Southern Patriot* took place long after the official end of the Popular Front.

The Left-led SNYC became a linchpin of radical African American art and literature in the South, particularly outside of the campuses of HBCUs. SNYC was proposed at the first national meeting of the National Negro

Congress in 1936 in Chicago. The 1937 inaugural meeting of SNYC in Richmond drew 500 delegates from a wide range of political, civil rights, labor, community, religious, and fraternal organizations. Leaders of SNYC included native southerners such as Virginians Esther Cooper Jackson and James Jackson and Alabaman Sallye Davis (mother of Angela Davis), children of the Great Migration such as Edward Strong (born in Texas and raised in Michigan), and northern transplants such as Harlemite Louis Burnham (born in Barbados but raised in New York) and Brooklynites Dorothy Burnham and Augusta (Jackson) Strong who had come South basically out of the CPUSA, the Young Communist League, and the Left-led National Student Movement. SNYC interacted with other Popular Front and progressive organizations. These included the Southern Conference for Human Welfare (SCHW—an interracial organization that had a strong African American presence), the Popular Democratic Party in South Carolina, the People's Defense League in New Orleans, and Congress of Industrial Organizations (CIO) unions (particularly such Left-led affiliates as the Mine, Mill, and Smelter Workers, Food, Tobacco, and Agricultural Workers, United Cannery, Agricultural, Packing, and Allied Workers of America, National Maritime Union, United Office and Professional Workers, International Longshoremen and Warehousemen, and United Furniture Workers), and even some American Federation of Labor locals (particularly Black-led locals of the International Longshoreman's Association and the Brotherhood of Sleeping Car Porters.). This southern Popular Front political network also included civil rights workers, educators, ministers, and others in institutions and organizations that were not leftwing as such but open to the politically and economically democratic goals of the southern Popular Front. It is worth noting that while some might consider the ideology and ideals of the Popular Front to be essentially "liberal" or "reformist" and a retreat from a more consistent and principled revolutionary politics, the push for democratic labor rights, political rights, educational opportunity, and access to public resources that included African Americans on the basis of full equality was, in fact, a radical move in the South that demanded a fundamental transformation of society in the region. As during the era of the civil rights movement, such efforts also entailed enormous personal risk on the part of political activists, risking violence both from the state and from racist vigilantes.

SNYC headquartered itself in Birmingham, the premier industrial center in the South and a comparative southern stronghold of the CPUSA, particularly among Black steelworkers, miners, and sharecroppers in northern

Alabama. It was active from Virginia to Texas. The initial administrative center of the CPUSA in the South lay not too far to the north in Chattanooga, where the Communist regional newspaper, the *Southern Worker,* was edited from 1930 to its demise in 1937.[4] In 1939, SNYC organized what may have been the first off-campus southern African American visual arts show, in Birmingham, Alabama. It helped initiate two radical theaters, the People's Theatre in Richmond and the People's Theatre in New Orleans. The New Orleans theater staged Langston Hughes's revolutionary "poetry-play" *Don't You Want to Be Free?,* a play that Hughes would repurpose for the civil rights era and that would be staged by the FST as part of its first touring season in 1964. The SNYC-sponsored Puppet Caravan Theatre, which numbered the poet Waring Cuney (an early innovator of blues poetry along with Langston Hughes and Sterling Brown during the New Negro Renaissance) among its members, toured the South, presenting plays on voter registration and labor rights to farmers and farm laborers, anticipating the tours of the FST twenty years later. The SNYC published poetry in their journal *Cavalcade* and featured such poets as Langston Hughes and Sterling Brown at their events. SNYC also operated three cultural/educational/recreational centers in Birmingham, modeled on Harlem's Popular Front Carver School.[5]

Despite contradictory images of the South as both the fount of African American culture and an artistic backwater, the Left African American arts scene supported by SNYC largely mirrored what was going on elsewhere in the country. The Black Left, particularly those artists and activists in and around the CPUSA, all across the United States were instrumental in the founding or strengthening of cultural institutions and the staging of arts events from Los Angeles to Harlem: art shows, galleries, theaters, concerts, poetry readings, study groups, schools, artists' workshops, and so on. However, though SNYC worked closely with liberal and radical white southerners in the CPUSA, SCHW, League of Young Southerners, CIO, and other organizations, it was dedicated to the idea of building Black political and cultural institutions run by and for African Americans with an intensity that was unmatched anywhere—except perhaps in Chicago. It also reached out to prominent Black political, educational, and cultural leaders within and beyond the South, including W. E. B. Du Bois (who made his famous "Behold the Land" speech at the 1946 SNYC Columbia Youth Legislature in Columbia, South Carolina) and Dillard University president Albert Dent (father of the key southern Black Arts figure Tom Dent), forming a network of contacts that survived the demise of SNYC to a significant extent.[6] As Erik Gellman notes, SNYC and the Black Popular Front in the South not only held an internationalist vision of the Black liberation struggle in the South but increasingly foregrounded international connections and alliances, particularly with anticolonial independence organizations and activists from Africa and Asia, anticipating similar ideological and material moves by southern Black Arts activists. For example, Esther Cooper Jackson attended the first World Youth Festival organized by the newly formed World Federation of Democratic Youth (an international late Popular Front organization) in London as a representative of SNYC. It was at that 1945 festival that Jackson met W. E. B. Du Bois, as well as a host of anticolonialist leaders from Africa and its diaspora.[7] This meeting set the stage for Du Bois's "Behold the Land" speech the next year and for a relationship with Du Bois that would last the rest of his life, as well as Jackson's later connection with Du Bois's second wife, Shirley Graham Du Bois, a bond that had important consequences for the founding of the journal *Freedomways*.

Cold War repression and internal struggle led to the dissolution of the SNYC in 1949 and the relocation of many of its leading activists and many of the most public leaders of the southern Popular Front outside the region, especially after the anti-Red hysteria following the Wallace presidential campaign in 1948. Quite a few, including James Jackson, Esther Cooper Jackson, Louis Burnham, Dorothy Burnham, Augusta Strong, and Edward Strong, eventually ended up in Philadelphia or New York, where some almost immediately became involved in Paul Robeson's new newspaper *Freedom*, which, like the SNYC's *Cavalcade*, was a Black Left political publication with a strong interest in culture. In fact, if one was going to look for an antecedent African American publication most closely parallel to *Freedom* in its interests and editorial policies, it would almost be certainly be *Cavalcade*. This should not be surprising since Louis Burnham became the managing editor of *Freedom*.

Freedom also fell victim to McCarthyism in 1955—as did nearly all the major Black institutions and organizations of the Communist Left, including the National Negro Labor Council and the Civil Rights Congress. Almost from the moment *Freedom* folded, Louis Burnham and Edward Strong began to imagine its replacement with another journal that would combine progressive domestic culture and politics with the radical internationalist spirit of liberation exemplified by the Afro-Asian Conference in Bandung, Indonesia, that same year. They drafted and circulated a prospectus of such a journal in the mid-1950s.[8] These efforts were initially unsuccessful. However, with the rise of a new activist civil rights movement, some diminishment in McCarthyism in the late 1950s, and the continued growth of what

Black radicals increasingly called the "Bandung world," Burnham, now a columnist for the Left *National Guardian* (itself a product of the Henry Wallace campaign and the late Popular Front), saw an opening for a new politically engaged Black cultural journal. Burnham's idea was that the journal would provide an outlet for emerging Black artists (many of whom joined the Black Arts movement) as well as for somewhat more established cultural activists, such as Alice Childress, John O. Killens, Lorraine Hansberry, W. E. B. Du Bois, Shirley Graham Du Bois, Margaret Burroughs, Elizabeth Catlett, and others who had been a part of the *Freedom* circle and other progressive Black cultural institutions. The idea was to provide a venue for politically engaged literature, art, and social commentary, giving older and younger artists a vehicle for linking their work to the liberation struggles at home and abroad. This project came to fruition in 1961 with the journal *Freedomways*.

While the genesis of *Freedomways* was in the North (and its editorial office was always in New York City, though its editors were scattered around the globe), the network of activists, artists, and intellectuals who formed the core of its staff and supported it had largely coalesced in the South. The nucleus of activists with whom Burnham first discussed the journal consisted largely of former leaders and supporters of SNYC: Edward Strong, Augusta Strong, Louis Burnham, Dorothy Burham, Shirley Graham Du Bois, W. E. B. Du Bois, and Esther Cooper Jackson. The new journal that became *Freedomways* in many respects continued the leftwing, anti-imperialist, anti–Jim Crow culturally oriented project of *Freedom* within the new context of the civil rights movement, particularly after the rise of the sit-in movement and the resulting Black student movement, as well as the successes and failures, the revolutions and counterrevolutions of the African, Asian, and Latin American anticolonial and anti-imperialist movements and emerging nations. It was, however, conceived as less of a newspaper in the vein of *Freedom* and more of a journal that combined scholarship and political and cultural analysis, and a strong focus on the arts, much in the mode of early editions of *The Crisis* under W. E. B. Du Bois's (and Jessie Fauset's) editorship in the 1910s and 1920s, but in a more openly Left way. While *Freedomways*, too, was an internationalist journal (and had an abiding interest in Harlem and the South Side of Chicago), it featured an even closer connection to the South and the southern Black freedom movement than had *Freedom*, utilizing the network that the Jacksons, the Burnhams, the Strongs, et al., forged in SNYC.

Burnham died before the first issue of *Freedomways* appeared in 1961. However, before he died, he hired his SNYC comrade Esther Cooper Jackson, who now lived in Brooklyn with her husband, CPUSA leader James Jackson, and her family.[9] Esther Cooper Jackson became the managing editor of the journal, holding *Freedomways* together with her critical intelligence, organizational skills, and sheer determination for more than two and a half decades through political ups and downs, ideological disputes, and many changes of editors. With the death of Louis Burnham (and Ed Strong before him), there was considerable doubt as to whether the journal could and should go on. However, W. E. B. and Shirley Graham Du Bois emphatically insisted on the importance of the new journal. With their backing, Esther Cooper Jackson demonstrated the sort of organizational ability and resolution that maintained *Freedomways* for so long and built a larger network of supporters, raised money, and recruited an editorial board. Shirley Graham Du Bois was the initial editor of journal. Since Graham Du Bois was living in Ghana by the time the first issue of *Freedomways* appeared, much of the practical functioning of the journal fell on Jackson and the collective of older Popular Front veterans she recruited, such as John Henrik Clarke and Augusta Strong, and younger Black leftists, such as Jean Carey Bond, whose husband, architect J. Max Bond, was a cousin of Julian Bond.

Freedomways lasted for twenty-five years, providing an internationalist perspective, a strong emphasis on the arts, and a deep sense of the history of Black radicalism reaching back at least to the nineteenth century. As Burnham, Strong, and its other initial supporters intended, the journal provided a vehicle that linked different moments and venues of Black radicalism with the liberation movements of the Bandung world. It also provided a bridge between the Black liberation movement in the South and the new, often nationalist Black radicalism in the ghettos and the Black communities of the South.

While often critical of African American nationalism, especially more separatist notions of Black nationalism, *Freedomways*—conceived, organized, and run entirely by African Americans, though publishing work by non–African American writers—was often much more sympathetic to nationalism and the principle of African American self-determination than has sometimes been allowed in the wake of Harold Cruse's bitter critiques of the CPUSA and its cultural circles in general and of *Freedomways* in particular.[10] Certainly, Esther Cooper Jackson (more so than her husband, interestingly) and the board of the journal were on the whole far more open to the thinking and work of Black Power and Black Arts activists than were most of the remaining national institutions and leaders of the CPUSA—though it is also true that other Black Communists and former Communists still active on Left, such as Richard Durham, Christine Johnson, John O. Killens, John Henrik Clarke, and William L. Patterson, cooperated with and even played leading roles in Black nationalist organizations and institutions, such as the Nation of Islam's newspaper *Muhammad Speaks* and the University of Islam and Malcolm X's Organization of Afro-American Unity as well as the Free Huey campaign of the BPP.[11]

In the spirit of SNYC, Jackson and the editorial board believed in the importance of building and maintaining *Freedomways* as an African American–led institution. They were adamant that the staff and editors, including all of the editorial board, be Black. Perhaps ironically given Harold Cruse's criticism of the journal, this stance caused conflict with some important intellectuals and leaders within the CPUSA, including the historian Herbert Aptheker, leading some to actually charge the journal with being Black nationalist despite the fact that the journal did accept contributions by non-Black authors—though, again, the position of James Jackson and others associated with the journal within the CPUSA no doubt protected it to a considerable degree.[12] In fact, while the journal published critiques of the more separatist and what were seen as the more adventurist tendencies of different strains of Black Power, though often in the vein of a sort of critical support, it is fair to say that as the 1960s wore on, the dominant ideology of even the poets, fiction writers, and other artists associated with the magazine, such as John O. Killens, Ruby Dee, Ossie Davis, Tom Dent, James Baldwin, Alice Walker, Shirley Graham Du Bois, and Tom Feelings, was—as John O. Killens remembered the late Lorraine Hansberry in 1979—basically "Black nationalist with a socialist perspective."[13]

Like many Black artists and intellectuals who came of age in the Left of the 1930s, 1940s, and early 1950s and published in its pages and/or served as contributing editors, *Freedomways* sought to educate readers about the historical arc of Black radicalism, even as they linked the Black radical past to the new moment of civil rights and international liberation. To this end, the journal frequently showcased older Black (and sometimes sympathetic white) writers (and often older poems of these writers), such as Margaret Walker, Langston Hughes, Claude McKay, Naomi Long Madgett, and Sterling Brown, as well as older visual artists such as Charles White, Elizabeth Catlett, Romare Bearden, Ollie Harrington, and Jacob Lawrence. At the same time, it undertook to alert readers to the new currents in Black art and politics, including various stripes of Black nationalism, printing the work of younger literary and visual artists such as Mari Evans, Paule Marshall, Sarah Wright, Tom Dent, Tom Feelings, Nikki Giovanni, David Henderson, Calvin Hernton, Audre Lorde, Sonia Sanchez, Haki Madhubuti, Askia Touré, and Alice Walker, as well as following and reviewing the efforts of a broad ideological and aesthetic spectrum of new Black artists and institutions, particularly in the South. For example, *Freedomways* was one of the first journals to pay attention to the efforts of the FST to build an indigenous southern Black theater that would reach a mass audience in the cities and rural areas of the region. When considering the new Black radical journals that appeared or were refitted ideologically at more or less the same time as *Freedomways*, such as *Liberator* and *Negro Digest*, none paid as close attention to the South as *Freedomways*.

Through its wide range of contacts among older and younger activists, the journal was able to bring together an incredibly wide range of Black artists, intellectuals, political organizers, and politicians in its pages and at its events, again recalling the sort of networks that SNYC built. One instance of this range can be seen in the 1968 centennial celebration of W. E. B. Du Bois's birth under the auspices of *Freedomways* with a seemingly unlikely sponsor list that included the CPUSA's National Chairman Henry Winston, NAACP's Roy Wilkins, Cleveland's mayor, Carl Stokes, Muhammad Ali, Martin Luther King Jr. (who delivered his notable speech about "our irrational, obsessive anti-communism" there), Ella Baker (whose work in the NAACP during the McCarthy era involved identifying Communists for expulsion), Julian Bond, James Foreman, and Septima Clark. Sponsors also included artists as varied in aesthetics, media and genre, ideology, and age as Amiri Baraka (then still LeRoi Jones), James Baldwin, Harry Belafonte, Ossie Davis, Ruby Dee, Dizzy Gillespie, John O. Killens, Jacob Lawrence, Odetta, J. Saunders Redding, Paul Robeson, Margaret Walker, and Charles White. It is hard to think of another institution that could have put together such a celebration even in the late 1960s—though one could see it as a forerunner to such united front Black Power events as the 1970 CAP Convention in Atlanta and the 1972 Black Political Convention in Gary, Indiana.

Young nationalist writers who were key figures in the formation of the Black Arts movement, such as Madhubuti and Touré, published in *Freedomways* well into the 1970s. *Freedomways* had close and reciprocal relationships with many of the younger Black artists and institutions of the Black bohemia of the Lower East Side in the early 1960s. Not only would many of these artists go on to be important figures in the Black Arts movement of the Northeast, but others, especially Tom Dent, A. B. Spellman, and Lorenzo Thomas were key in building the Black Arts infrastructure in the South. Members of the proto-Black Arts Umbra Poets Workshop, particularly Dent (who had known Esther Jackson from childhood through the contacts that SNYC had made with his father, Albert Dent, president of Dillard University), Calvin Hernton, and David Henderson (a native Harlemite who later toured with the FST) regularly attended *Freedomways* events and published in the journal.

Likewise, Jackson and others in the *Freedomways* circle supported Umbra and frequented Umbra readings, fundraising parties, and so on. Similarly, artists closely linked to the journal mentored some of the best-known younger Black writers—as in the relationships between Madhubuti and Margaret Burroughs (herself a longtime contributing editor of the journal) and between John Killens and Nikki Giovanni. Close *Freedomways* associates Sarah Wright and Calvin Hicks initiated On Guard for Freedom, a group of Black artists, intellectuals, and activists based on the Lower East Side that included Amiri Baraka and was an important forerunner of the Black Arts Repertory Theater and School (BARTS) in Harlem. And, as the key New Orleans Black Arts organizer Kalamu ya Salaam notes, the *Freedomways* book column of Ernest Kaiser, a research librarian at the Schomburg Library in Harlem and veteran of the postwar institutions of the Harlem cultural Left, such as *Harlem Quarterly*, was considered by many of the younger artists to be a vital annotated compendium of new African American writing in the 1960s (and 1970s and 1980s).[14]

The journal also featured a wide range of visual art from leading older and younger artists who donated their work to the journal, including Elizabeth Catlett, Charles White, Romare Bearden, Ollie Harrington, Jacob Lawrence, Tom Feelings, and Hugh Harrell. In short, again despite critiques of the journal by Harold Cruse and others influenced by him, the journal both served as a model of what a radical Black political and cultural journal that embodied the principle of self-determination might be (even for artists and activists hostile to the CPUSA and their sense of its old-fashioned Eurocentric Marxism) and practically supported the work and institutions of younger Black artists and intellectuals. As Erik McDuffie points out, *Freedomways* was more than a journal; it was an intellectual community in which Black radical women played central roles and were instrumental in furthering a leftwing Black feminism that was in many ways an evolution of Black Left thought of the 1940s and 1950s.[15] Another way of putting it might be that *Freedomways* was a crucial instrument in maintaining the intellectual and political community forged by the Black Popular Front even after many in the community had left the CPUSA, connecting that community to the new Black radicalism of the 1960s and 1970s, and providing younger Black radicals a greater depth of historical perspective and experience as well as practical expertise.

The Southern Popular Front and the Origins of the Black Arts Movement: New Orleans and the Idea of Ancestry

As a hub of Black Popular Front political and cultural activity in the South, New Orleans provided a useable Black radical past in politics and the arts. Southern Black Arts activists in the 1960s, especially Tom Dent, sought out and honored this past as evidence of the continuing importance of New Orleans and the South to contemporary Black politics and culture beyond the almost mythic era of the birth of jazz and the blues as musical forms in the late nineteenth and early twentieth centuries. Unlike Buddy Bolden, Black Popular Front era writers and artists like Marcus Christian and Octave Lilly still walked the streets of New Orleans. Like many southern cities, it had a long history of racist violence and Black resistance to Jim Crow. It was, after all, the site of the signature case of Black civil disobedience and legal action against the Jim Crow system, leading to the Supreme Court's *Plessy v. Ferguson* in 1896, as well as of the brutal, racist "Robert Charles riots" in the summer of 1900, both still living memories in the early Popular Front era. Jazz pianist and composer Jelly Roll Morton (Ferdinand Joseph LaMothe) recalled the riots in his 1938 recordings for the Library of Congress.[16]

As in Birmingham, Richmond, and Memphis, Popular Front efforts in New Orleans centered on labor organizing, largely of Black workers, and on Black civil rights, both in opposition to Jim Crow and in support of African American enfranchisement. The major Popular Front organization in New Orleans was the People's Defense League (PDL), based in the Black communities of Center City anchored by Dryades Street (where the FST would later be based and conduct its workshops) and led by Ernest Wright and Zachary Ramsey II. Wright was a lawyer and SNYC activist who led a successful organizing drive of clerical workers at Black insurance companies, setting up a local of the Left-led CIO affiliate, the United Office and Professional Workers in 1940. After working for the CIO, Wright devoted himself to being a fulltime organizer for the PDL. Ramsey came from a family of NAACP leaders, Garveyites, and labor activists.[17] Cooperating with the CPUSA, progressive unions, and civil rights organizations (including the local affiliate of the NAACP, which had shifted to a much more militant and grassroots-based local leadership during this period), the PDL used a variety of lobbying and direct action tactics, including marches and boycotts, to successfully gain jobs for Black workers, combat police brutality, and register Black voters in the face of racist violence and jailings by the police and vigilantes, without any sort of protection from the federal government. For example, the PDL led a march of an ideologically and organizationally varied group of over 5,000 people on the registrar of voters, gaining the right to vote in primaries for African Americans for the first time since the triumph of Jim Crow.[18] In this and other actions, the PDL mirrored the successful tactics of the "Don't Shop Where You Can't Work" campaigns led by a de facto alliance of leftists and nationalists in northern cities, but with the aim of combining Black political rights already available in the North with Black economic rights, as was often the case in the early civil rights movement.

The Black Popular Front in New Orleans distinguished itself in the depth of its commitment to recording, analyzing, and celebrating the history and cultural life of everyday African Americans in Louisiana and the South. Of course, to some degree such efforts characterized the work of the Popular Front practically everywhere. However, few, if any, places in the South displayed the sustained work in such scholarly and cultural activities during the 1930s and 1940s as New Orleans, due in large part to the Louisiana affiliate of the Federal Writers' Project (FWP) of the Works Progress Administration (WPA, renamed the Work Projects Administration in 1939).

Like other projects of the WPA's Federal Project Number One, such as the Federal Theater Project (FTP) and the Federal Artists Project (FAP), if not precisely an institution of the Popular Front, the FWP was a vehicle for Popular Front art and artists and scholarship across the nation, at least in those states and cities where the Left was strong. The FWP was particularly important for African American writers. Prior to the FWP, very few Black authors ever made a living solely or primarily through their writing for any length of time. Much of the relatively well-paying commercial writing work that sustained many white authors, such as writing screenplays in Hollywood, was simply not available to African American writers to any significant degree. The only Black author to really earn his living through his writing in the period immediately before the FWP was Langston Hughes, who wrote in an enormous variety of media and genres (though not, to his disgust, for the movie industry) in order to make ends meet. Thus, the FWP supported many Black writers who had already achieved a certain measure of critical success or who would later go on to achieve significant literary reputations, including Richard Wright, Margaret Walker, Zora Neale Hurston, Ralph Ellison, Arna Bontemps, Sterling Brown, Robert Hayden, Fenton Johnson, Chester Himes, Willard Motley, William Attaway, Claude McKay, Katherine Dunham, and Waring Cuney. For the first time in the history of the United States, relatively large numbers of Black writers (and theater workers and visual artists) were paid a more or less living wage to pursue and develop their craft, writing local histories and descriptions of Black communities, collecting oral histories, and producing studies of Black folklore. Many of these writers, particularly Margaret Walker and Ralph Ellison, found the interviews they did on FWP assignments to be invaluable resources for their later fiction and poetry.

This celebration and investigation of the history, folklore, arts traditions, language, and so on of nonelite Americans, as opposed to the great man theory of history, can be seen as bedrock features of the cultural work of the Popular Front (or what Michael Denning famously termed the Cultural Front) and characterized the work of the various Federal Arts Projects, even where the organized Left was weak. However, as noted before, in cities and regions where the Left, especially the Communist Left, was strong, the character of the FWP and the other Federal Arts Projects took on a distinctly Popular Front cast.[19] In those states, the struggle to make sure that Black writers and artists got hired by the FWP, the FTP, and FAP was generally more successful than elsewhere.

Where the Left had less influence, fewer Black writers and artists were hired. Also, in such states far less attention was paid to African American culture and history (and when some attention was paid, the result was often a farrago of racist stereotypes). Sterling Brown, the FWP's "editor of Negro affairs" based in Washington, D.C., spent much time combatting racial discrimination in employment in the different state projects and issuing guidelines for the respectful treatment of African Americans, and protesting racist accounts of Black character and culture, with varying degrees of success.

The number of African Americans hired by the FWP differed wildly from state to state, especially in the South. Many state projects in the South hired virtually no Black writers. One exception was the Louisiana Writers' Project, particularly in New Orleans. The head of the Louisiana project was the white journalist and fiction writer Lyle Saxon, a longtime New Orleans bohemian who had been a significant figure in the artistic counterculture of the French Quarter in the 1920s that also included a young William Faulkner and Sherwood Anderson. Saxon was an early promoter of the careers of Jean Toomer and Harlem Renaissance visual artist Richmond Barthe.[20]

In his role at the Louisiana Writers' Project, Saxon's most notable accomplishment was the establishment of a "Negro unit," the Dillard History Unit (DHU), based at the HBCU Dillard University in 1936. The DHU was supervised by Dillard history professor Lawrence Reddick, who was succeeded by poet and printer Marcus Christian after Reddick left Dillard to become curator of the New York Public Library's Schomburg Collection of Negro Literature in 1939. The DHU employed a team of Black writers, artists, and researchers, including such Black Left writers and artists as painter and printmaker Elizabeth Catlett, poet Octave Lilly, and poet and novelist Margaret Walker as well as the historian Benjamin Quarles, who studied the history and culture of African Americans in Louisiana. The DHU's most significant product was the 1,200-plus page *The Negro in Louisiana*, on which Marcus Christian continued to work long after the end of the Louisiana Writers' Project in 1942. *The Negro in Louisiana* argued for the essential contributions of African Americans to the economy, arts, speech, and folklore of Louisiana. It also struggled against both sentimental plantation images of slavery and false characterizations of the alleged horrors of Reconstruction, emphasizing Black agency and continued resistance to the slave system in ways that anticipated Margaret Walker's landmark 1964 novel *Jubilee*—a novel with roots in the 1930s. (Walker spent much of her childhood in New Orleans and was a veteran of the FWP in Chicago and New Orleans.) One important aspect of the DHU was its relative autonomy and Black leadership, an extremely unusual situation among the Writers' Projects in the South. Of course, ultimately the DHU answered to white authorities, especially Saxon. However, unlike, say, the situation in the Florida Project, where Zora Neale Hurston reported to the considerably younger, white, and much less experienced and qualified in terms of the field of folklore Stetson Kennedy (even though Kennedy was himself a leftist who was inclined to let Hurston do what she wanted in her gathering and writing of folklore), the immediate supervisors of the DHU were Black.

While some DHU activists, such as Walker and Catlett, had been drawn into the organized Left outside of the South before their tenure on the project (though, again, Walker had spent most of her youth in New Orleans and Alabama), others like Christian and Lilly were veterans of the Popular Front political and cultural scene in New Orleans during the 1930s and 1940s in such groups and institutions as the FWP, PDL, SNYC, Left-led CIO unions, and the militant Depression-era leadership of the local NAACP. Lilly, who spent most of his working life with People's Life Insurance, had been part of the executive board of a very activist branch of the NAACP in his hometown of New Iberia, Louisiana in the early 1940s until legal (and extralegal) harassment, violence, and death threats by the sheriff's department and vigilantes forced Lilly and other leaders to leave New Iberia in 1944.[21] Lilly returned to New Orleans where he had gone to college at Dillard and worked on the DHU. While the demands of Lilly's working life at People's Life caused a hiatus in his writing during the 1940s, 1950s, and early 1960s, the murder of Martin Luther King Jr. galvanized his literary career in the Black Arts era, when he published a book of poetry and had poems in such journals as *The Crisis, Freedomways, Negro Voices,* the *Louisiana Weekly,* the *Pittsburgh Courier, Negro Digest/Black World,* and *Nkombo.*

Marcus Christian's poetry, a body of over 1,200 pieces written over a long career reaching back to the New Negro Renaissance, focused on African American working-class communities. It drew on Black vernacular diction and rhetorical forms to depict local police brutality, racism, and Jim Crow as well as to render southern Black responses to national and international events, such as the Italian invasion of Ethiopia in 1935 and the Supreme Court's 1954 *Brown v. Board of Education* decision. Christian worked at many jobs in his life, from chauffeur to professor at the University of New Orleans. During much of the 1940s and 1950s he was a librarian at Dillard and then ran his own printing company. He was for decades the literary editor of the *Louisiana Weekly,* one of the oldest Black newspapers in the Deep South.

Christian corresponded with prominent Black Left writers in the 1930s, including Langston Hughes, and became acquainted with Lyle Saxon during that decade. Saxon championed Christian's work (unsuccessfully) to major publishers, hired Christian to the Louisiana FWP, and later promoted Christian to head DHU after L. D. Reddick left. Christian continued to work on *The Negro in Louisiana* after the end of the DHU, in part supported by a Rosenwald Fellowship. He was later, like many of his generation, a critical supporter of Black Arts, deeming it insufficiently aware of the history of Black political, literary, and artistic efforts in the South. Christian softened this judgment after being honored by Tom Dent and BLKARTSOUTH as a crucial cultural and political ancestor. He, too, published in *Negro World/ Black Digest.*

One important cultural consequence of the FWP, the DHU, and the Black Popular Front in New Orleans was that it made available an idea of ancestry (to quote the title of Indiana Black Arts poet Etheridge Knight's poem about his family in Mississippi), or a usable past for the activists associated with the FST, BLKARTSOUTH, and the SBCA in the 1960s and 1970s (and beyond) in New Orleans.[22] As will be taken up at some length later, Tom Dent in particular sought out Christian, Lilly, and other writers and artists of the Popular Front era in New Orleans, much as he did in New York, and promoted them to the younger Black Arts activists of the city as important exemplars of an indigenous New Orleans (and southern) Black radical literary and intellectual past (and present). In fact, it was artists, scholars, and activists of the DHU, such as Benjamin Quarles, who made Dent aware, even as a child in New Orleans where his father was president of Dillard, that a serious Black intellectual, artistic, and scholarly life not only was possible but actually existed and thrived.[23]

The Southern Popular Front and the Origins of the Black Arts Movement: The Popular Front and HBCUs

As the poet, playwright, and educator Sonia Sanchez has observed, African Americans in the South emerged from slavery not in a spirit of bitterness but of building, creating (sometimes in concert with sympathetic white people) a wide range of religious, educational, economic, fraternal or sororal, and cultural institutions aimed at advancing and consolidating Black citizenship and promoting Black political, economic, and cultural power.[24] While many of these institutions did not survive the onslaught of Jim Crow segregation, disenfranchisement, and racist terror of the "Nadir" of the late nineteenth and early twentieth centuries, others, including new HBCUs, which were overwhelmingly concentrated in the South and the border states, continued (and continue) to function. In some ways, the HBCUs, like the Black churches, were strengthened in purpose and resolve by the ascendancy of the Jim Crow regime, even though the domination of segregationist politics in the region also presented a complex and often hostile political environment that the HBCUs and their administrations had to negotiate.

The administrations, and sometimes even the student bodies, of HBCUs have often been accused of being essentially conservative, hierarchal, and accommodationist throughout the twentieth century and beyond. There is no doubt truth to these charges in varying degrees, depending on the period and the institution in question. Nevertheless, many HBCUs were centers where the different strands of Black radical thought and practice intertwined, exposing students to a range of revolutionary ideas and traditions that were not available on the campuses of most predominantly white institutions. In part, this was because of a willingness to hire leftist and nationalist faculty members whom the vast majority of what might be thought of as historically white schools would not touch, especially in the Cold War era. And, in part, it was because an international student body drawn from Africa and its wider diaspora, especially the colonies and former colonies of the United Kingdom, as well as all the regions of the United States made available a range of political and social thought and cultural practices on a very personal level that simply did not happen at other institutions of higher education.

And if HBCUs were often characterized by autocratic, paternalist administrations that attempted to restrain the more radical elements of their faculty and student body (something that was also true of the vast majority of predominantly white schools in the 1950s and 1960s), they were willing to hire and retain radicals with roots in the Popular Front (or even earlier moments of Black radicalism) on their faculty in a time when such people were being fired or blacklisted, so to speak, at predominantly white colleges and universities. This, in turn, not only allowed many of these radicals to mentor young Black activists and artists (or future activists and artists), as was the case with John O. Killens and Nikki Giovanni at Fisk and Sterling Brown and Amiri Baraka and A. B. Spellman (and later Kwame Ture and the militants of the Nonviolent Action Group/SNCC) at Howard, but also gave these radicals an institutional base from which important Black Arts and proto–Black Arts initiatives were launched in alliance with younger Black cultural and political militants. While Margaret Walker at Jackson State, John O. Killens at Fisk, and Sterling Brown at Howard all had difficult relationships with their university and department administrations and sometimes colleagues, as will be discussed in subsequent chapters, they were all able to mentor younger Black artists and initiate institutions and events with major regional and national consequences for the development of Black Arts and Black Studies. One might add here that administrators at HBCUs were almost universally opposed to Jim Crow and sympathetic to the goals of the civil rights movement, if sometimes against or uneasy about direct action tactics. The same could not be said about administrators, or even the faculty, at many predominantly white schools in the 1950s and 1960s.

Though HBCUs had long been centers and incubators of Black art in the United States, providing employment for African American artists and professional training for Black artists and arts educators, the training of artists and the production of art, music, theater, and literature took on a greatly increased importance at many high-profile HBCUs during the 1930s and 1940s. Many of the artists hired to create or revamp HBCU literature and arts departments and programs were Black (and white) leftists who communicated their aesthetic sensibilities, engagement with social issues, drive to connect with local Black communities, build institutions that bridge the gap between town and gown, and so on to their students. Consequently, while Black colleges and universities were not radical institutions, and were often under tremendous political pressure to rein in radical faculty and students who actively challenged Jim Crow, they nonetheless became major hubs of the Popular Front in the South—and showed a willingness to hire and retain leftist faculty even after the onset of the Cold War, employing people who would have been political pariahs elsewhere in higher education. This willingness made these HBCUs important bridges between the Popular Front and Black Arts, providing some institutional continuity between different generations of Black radicals.

Atlanta distinguished itself in the sheer number and geographical clustering of its HBCUs. While the origins of Clark College and Atlanta University (AU) lay back in Reconstruction, it was in the Jim Crow era that they, along with the other schools of University Center (Morehouse College, Spelman College, and Morris Brown College) really took off, becoming among the most prominent Black institutions of higher education. By the 1930s all these schools were located in the West End of Atlanta near the Black working-class neighborhood of Vine City. Spelman, AU, and Morehouse formally affiliated with each other in 1929, joined by Clark a decade later. These mergers after the hiring of John Hope as AU's president in 1928, gave the schools of AUC an even higher profile in local, regional, and national African American cultural and intellectual life.

In general, the political and economic white elite of the city preferred to manage race relations through a paternalistic consensus and cooptation rather than direct repression during most of the twentieth century. However, at times the city was wracked by spasms of extreme racist violence, often by vigilante groups, such as the Black Shirts and the Ku Klux Klan, not under the control of civic, social, or economic authorities. The most infamous was, no doubt, the Atlanta Riot of 1906, in which dozens were murdered and many Black businesses in the Black business district centered on Decatur Street destroyed by white mobs. Atlanta also saw episodic government repression of attempts to challenge the Jim Crow order, as in the arrest of Black Communist organizer Angelo Herndon in 1932 for his work among the unemployed and his subsequent trial in which he faced the death penalty for "attempting to incite insurrection."[25]

As the state capital, Atlanta also featured considerable conflict between the local municipal government and state government (which was generally far less inclined toward accommodation than the city authorities) as to enforcement of segregation laws—and variation in the relative willingness of different branches of government to tolerate organized dissent against segregation. The mid-1940s also saw the repeal of the poll tax and the end of whites-only primaries, leading to a great increase of Black voter registration, particularly in Atlanta where African Americans were a third of the population. This gave African Americans a significant political leverage in Atlanta, if limited within the confines of Jim Crow and anticommunism. However, it also galvanized white voters to replace the liberal governor Ellis Arnall with the arch-segregationist Eugene Talmadge (who died before he could assume office and was replaced by his son Herman, another segregationist who eventually went on to a long career in the U.S. Senate). The push and pull between Black advances and white backlash became a hallmark of Atlanta and Georgia politics through the election of local segregationist icon Lester Maddox as governor in 1966 to the Fulton County "tax revolts" of the 1990s. The tug of war between city hall and the statehouse, too, characterized the politics of Atlanta in its relation to the state of Georgia throughout the Black Arts and Black Power era—and long after.[26] The contradictions between city and state government and between paternalist cooptation and the potential for direct and even violent repression complicated the situation of the HBCUs in Atlanta, which answered to both state and local officials in significant respects, and the ways in which administrators, faculty, and students could maneuver.

While there was (and has long continued to be) a serious town-gown split between the schools of AUC and the Black working-class neighborhoods that adjoined them, the 1930s witnessed the beginnings of Black cultural initiatives rooted on the campuses that reached out into the neighborhoods. The visual artist Hale Woodruff was hired by the new AU in 1931 to launch a greatly ramped up program in the fine arts.[27] Woodruff encouraged his students to paint subjects in the Vine City and other nearby Black neighborhoods as well as in the rural communities of North Georgia. This focus on workers, small farmers, and sharecroppers led to Woodruff and the circle of artists he mentored becoming known as the "Outhouse School" because of their penchant for including privies in their social realist renderings of rural Black life. Woodruff's program became a major beachhead of the Popular Front in the South and made Atlanta a hub for Black visual artists. It essentially became the regional center for the training of Black visual artists and arts educators who in turn went on to do likewise at other historically Black colleges and universities across the South. Woodruff also launched the AU Annual Exhibition of African American artists, beginning in 1942 and lasting until 1969. The Annual Exhibition became the premier show of African American artists in the United States, often highlighting such Left artists as Charles White, John Wilson, and Elizabeth Catlett—all of whom, especially Wilson and Catlett, would have a direct impact on Black Arts era writers and artists. Woodruff also worked with the WPA's Federal Arts Project, directing the painting of a four-part mural, *The Negro in Modern American Life*, at a local junior high school as well as murals at the AU School of Social Work. Finally, he was a member of the faculty of AU's People's School, a progressive adult education program founded in 1942 that offered a wide range of free classes to the Black community.[28] The People's School was a model for Black Power/Black Arts/Black Studies higher education programs and institutions, notably People's College in Nashville and Atlanta. Another participant in the People's School was W. E. B. Du Bois, whom John Hope brought back to AU in 1934. In 1940, Du Bois founded what was arguably the leading Black intellectual journal of the time, *Phylon*, there.

In 1934, a member of the Spelman faculty, Anna Cook, established AU's Summer Theater, which would put on four plays in six weeks during the summer break. While the majority of these plays were by European and white American authors, Cook attempted to stage at least one show by a Black playwright each summer. Sterling Brown, Owen Dodson, and Baldwin Burroughs were among the prominent figures who worked in the Summer Theater. Burroughs went on to teach at Spelman and direct the Summer Theater himself, becoming a central figure of Black theater in Atlanta for decades. Cook continued to direct the Summer Theater even after she left for the historically Black Hampton Institute (also an important node of radical Black visual art) and then Howard University.[29]

Many of the more leftwing artists and intellectuals, including Woodruff and W. E. B. Du Bois, left Atlanta in the mid- to late 1940s. The pressure of the deepening Cold War particularly intensified in the South with Henry Wallace's presidential campaign at the head of the Progressive Party ticket in 1948.[30] For example, Birmingham Commissioner of Public Safety Theophilus "Bull" Connor arrested Wallace's vice presidential running mate Glenn Taylor (and all the other white people present) as he spoke to the final convention of the SNYC in May 1948. The arrests were ostensibly for violating Jim Crow laws segregating meeting halls but were actually part of Connor's campaign against the CPUSA and its allied organizations. SNYC did not recover from this repression and ceased operations the next year. Connor shepherded the passage of a 1950 ordinance outlawing membership in the CPUSA within city limits. While the Birmingham anticommunist ordinance was overturned by the federal courts, the CPUSA ceased to exist as an organized force in Alabama politics by mid-decade. The Red Scare in Atlanta was less heavy-handed than in Birmingham but quite severe nevertheless. For example, Appalachian poet, educator, and activist Don West, one of the founders of the Highlander School along with Myles Horton, was driven from Oglethorpe University in 1948, in part for his efforts in the Wallace campaign. The House Un-American Activities Committee held high-profile hearings in Atlanta in 1958, using those hearings to red bait the civil rights movement However, despite the collapse of the CPUSA and nearly all late Popular Front organizations, many of the less formal networks and associations remained. Even after Hale Woodruff left Georgia, he maintained contact with Atlanta University, painting the six panels of the mural *Art of the Negro* there in 1950–1952.

The impact of the artists and arts programs of the AUC schools reached beyond the immediate Atlanta area. Woodruff painted a group of murals at Talladega College, a historically Black school in Alabama, at the end of the 1930s, publicly showing them in 1940. These murals can be seen as emblematic of the different dimensions of Black Popular Front radicalism. Some of the murals were clearly in the spirit of honoring the founding and contributions of Talladega College in ways that might be seen as relatively timeless celebrations of campus-supported art. However, Woodruff's famous Amistad Murals, also part of the group, were in keeping with the popular democratic struggle strain of the Black Popular Front. It is also hard to look at the panel of the actual shipboard rebellion showing the captive Africans overpowering and preparing to slaughter the slave ship's crew and not see a militant action of revolutionary self-determination in the spirit, again, of the Haitian Revolution. To paraphrase Robert F. Williams, the militant NAACP leader from Monroe, North Carolina, during the 1960s (and his subsequent radical radio broadcasts and journalism from Cuba and China), one might retitle the panel *Mutiny on the Amistad* as *Negroes with Machetes*. It is certainly possible to see more of a popular democratic iconography in the subsequent court scene. Even here, though, it is important to note that it is the chief of the rebels, Singbe, who is literally in the forefront with his arms implacably folded and a stern and proud expression on his face and not his white attorneys Lewis Tappan and John Quincy Adams, leaving no doubt about the real leader of the struggle.

In short, one is presented with a revolutionary history with Black people (and Black workers, one might add) in the leadership of a multiracial and multiclass alliance that provides to or provokes in the audience a certain historical knowledge and consciousness. The Amistad Murals also provide a way of examining and understanding the bases of how history is represented or written and to what ends that history is deployed. The murals raise the issue of what happens when you put African Americans at the center of the field of history, to paraphrase Mary Helen Washington's 1997 presidential address at the American Studies Association's annual meeting.[31] In fact, one might say that a hallmark of much Black Popular Front art, both North and South but especially in the South (as seen in the work of the DHU as well as here), is precisely devoted to this notion of putting Black people at the center of U.S. history and the writing of U.S. history. What this also meant and continued to mean was putting the Black South at the center of such history. One consequence of this was a historical consciousness and representation of history in southern Black Arts work that was more intense than in most other locales of the United States.

Like Woodruff, Elizabeth Catlett was a catalyst of what might be thought of as an artistic Black Popular Front in the South, first at Dillard University in New Orleans and later at Hampton Institute in Virginia. She never had the institutional power or base in the United States as had Woodruff or John Biggers (one of her mentees). She nonetheless was an inspiring teacher and, indeed, a motivator for African American artists in a wide variety of media and genres from the 1930s to her death in the twenty-first century. A prime example of her Black Popular Front work is *The Negro Woman* series of linoleum cuts that she initially created in 1946 and 1947 for the Communist cultural journal *Masses and Mainstream* (a descendant of the recently defunct *New Masses* but with a more purely arts focus) while in Mexico studying at the Left workshop of visual art Taller de Gráfica Popular.[32] What is perhaps most obvious about the series is the presence of what one might now call an intersectional analysis in which we see Black women as workers (both urban and rural), mothers, educators, and political leaders, who face "the triple oppression" of race, class, and gender as articulated in theoretical writings by Black women Communists, most famously Claudia Jones, as well as in the work of both male and female Black radical artists.[33] Of course, for these artists and activists, "triple oppression" was not simply a term of analysis but also a sort of call to action. One might see these works as the direct ancestor of the Black feminist strain of Black Arts and Black Power, as seen in, for instance, Toni Cade Bambara's collection of short stories *Gorilla, My Love* (1972) and novel *The Salt Eaters* (1980), both products of the southern Black Arts movement.

The series consists of fifteen cuts, three featuring well-known historical figures (Phillis Wheatley, Harriet Tubman, and Sojourner Truth); eleven with unnamed Black women laboring, studying, organizing workers, suffering from Jim Crow in the South, enduring gross discrimination in the North, and playing music; and one with the full body of a Black man who has been lynched (and the dangling legs of three other lynching victims). There is a particular focus on the faces of the Black women, often with one woman foregrounded in the company of other Black women, creating a dynamic, one might say dialectical, relationship between the individual and the collective, that, as will be noted further, characterizes the cuts as a whole. Interestingly, in the one cut featuring lynched Black men, entitled "And a special fear for my loved ones," the focus is on the trunk of the body and the dangling legs, not the face. As in Hughes's Popular Front play *Don't You Want to Be Free?* (1938) and in John Biggers's Houston murals, it would appear that the cuts are bifurcated into those that essentially document the present and others that represent a vision of the past, a history. However, again, the presence of the overtly historical figures of Wheatley, Tubman, and Truth suggests that Black women laboring in the present are historical actors in a continuum stretching back, at least, to the slave era.

The series not only posits a counter-history to that of the mainstream history profession but also revisits and revises notions of what might count as historical evidence, and what events might be significant. This anticipates the sort of new social history that would only gain real traction in the U.S. academy under the pressure of Black Studies (and other manifestations of "ethnic studies") and the sort of culturally inflected labor history from below most closely associated with E. P. Thompson and such U.S. devotees of Thompson as David Montgomery and Herbert Guttman, former Communists who never abandoned the Left. One might say that Catlett honors and invokes the revolutionary and Popular Front icons of Tubman and Truth (with the interesting inclusion of Wheatley who was rarely present on Black Left lists of revolutionary Black ancestors) while complicating what might be seen as a great woman theory of history. What one sees, then, is not simply a litany of heroines but a more dialectical relationship between leadership and the grassroots in which the familiar icons are placed in the context of and on a par with everyday Black women and in which there is a dynamic interplay between the individual and the collective.

Like Atlanta University, Hampton Institute in Virginia, where John Biggers enrolled in 1941, was a beachhead of the Black cultural front in the South. At Hampton Biggers encountered and was deeply influenced by a white Left refugee from Nazism, Viktor Lowenfeld, who became his primary mentor. He was also guided there by Charles White and Elizabeth Catlett, both closely connected to the CPUSA and sharing Woodruff's commitment to representing in public art accessible to working-class African Americans the struggles of urban and rural southern Black communities as well as what might be considered iconic moments and figures of the Black revolutionary tradition. Lowenfeld, White, and Catlett all encouraged Biggers to see his art not as individual expression but as voicing a collective African American culture of struggle: "I began to see art not primarily as an individual expression of talent, but as a responsibility to reflect the spirit and style of the Negro people."[34]

Much like Woodruff had earlier at AU, John Biggers came to Texas in 1949 to found and head a new art department at the historically Black Texas Southern University, located on the southern edge of the overwhelmingly African American Third Ward, a center of Black life in Houston for many decades. (It is where Beyoncé Knowles grew up.) When Biggers ran the Texas Southern Art Department during the 1950s, 1960s, 1970s, and 1980s, not only did aspiring Black artists from across the South come to that campus to learn their respective crafts and to be trained as teachers, they were encouraged and provided opportunities to actively engage the grassroots in Black neighborhoods such as the Third, Fourth, and Fifth Wards. The photographer Earlie Hudnall recalls coming to study at Texas Southern from Hattiesburg, Mississippi, in 1968. Not only were students challenged to match the high standards of work promoted by Biggers, the TSU arts faculty, and other students, but also he and fellow photographer Ray Carrington were able to get Model Cities program jobs photographing working class Black communities through TSU.[35] In other words, Biggers directly mentored the generation of young African American artists who would be the mainstay of the Black Arts Movement in Houston and elsewhere in the region drawing significantly on his own education in the southern Popular Front at Hampton Institute and elsewhere.

However, Biggers's impact on young Black artists was not only pedagogical and institutional but also through his work. His murals painted in public spaces and in Black institutions in Houston from the early 1950s to the 1980s display his journey from the Popular Front to Black Arts. What is fascinating about Biggers's murals is that the seeds of Black Arts, with a deep engagement with an African diasporic spirituality and sensibility, are clearly visible early on and that Biggers's Popular Front artistic origins, with close linking of a local class-based perspective with the international, never really disappear.

Of course, to a considerable degree, the nature of each mural commission significantly influenced its content and ideological stance. One of Biggers's early commissions in Houston was the 1953 *The Contribution of Negro Women to American Life and Education* at the Blue Triangle YWCA. It has a slightly cubist emphasis on planes and angles, compressing a range of stories from slavery to the Jim Crow era into a sort of historical mosaic, much as Diego Rivera did in his Detroit History of Industry mural and as Charles Alston often did in his murals. As in the work of his mentor Catlett, one once again sees the presence of a vision in which Black women are workers (both urban and rural), mothers, educators, and political leaders who face the triple oppression of race, class, and gender articulated by Claudia Jones and other Black Communists. One also notices in Biggers's work, as in that of Catlett and the efforts of Black Popular Front artists in a wide range of media and genres, the linkage of everyday people with more familiar icons, most prominently Harriet Tubman and Sojourner Truth (again, also featured in Catlett's Negro Woman series).

History of the International Longshoremen's Local 872, a commission from Local 872, a Black local of the International Longshoremen's Association (ILA) is also clearly in the Black Popular Front vein. (The mural is now located in the ILA Local 24 union hall where it was relocated after the merger of Black and white longshore locals in 1983.) As in New Orleans, despite the racism and corruption of the national leadership and the undemocratic structure of the national union, the Jim Crow segregation of ILA locals in many ports allowed Black stevedores in Texas to run their own locals and promoted the growth of a progressive African American leadership of the Black ILA local in Houston. So the 1957 mural that Biggers painted in the 872 union hall was, like Woodruff's *Amistad* series, clearly within the Black Popular Front public art tradition in which Woodruff, Catlett, Charles Alston, Charles White, and Jacob Lawrence worked. Again in a slightly cubist mode, dignified and hardworking Black longshoremen labor in the foreground of the mural while militant strikers are being urged on by a Black orator in the background. One might find it hard to believe that such a militant, Black pro-struggle mural could exist even in an African American union hall in a conservative Jim Crow Texas city in the depths of the Cold War when northern-based radical Black institutions like the National Negro Labor Council and the journal *Freedom* had collapsed. That it did exist might cause us to rethink some of our assumptions about the Cold War era.

As a result of a greater engagement with African culture, art, and politics, Biggers's work gradually moved away from his Popular Front social realist mode toward what might be thought of as an Africanist magical realism rooted in West African folklore and style, as seen in the 1966 *Birth from the Sea,* commissioned in 1964 by the W. L. Johnson Branch of the Houston Public Library in Sunnyside, an old Black neighborhood in southern Houston. However, even in *Birth from the Sea* one does not simply see a Black Venus rising on a half shell as might be predicted from the name. Instead, in many respects the mural is as organized around labor, particularly fishing and the processing of fish, as it is culture, though it is not likely that Biggers would separate labor and culture. In short, the Popular Front lingers. And it is also worth noting that the seeds of this mythic rendering of Black women in white and water, drawing on Black Christianity and the traditional African deities, particularly the Yoruba Yemoja, is already present in the 1948 *Sharecroppers.* Of course, this is also a reminder that social realism was not so much a style, but an ideological stance in which Left artists try to render both concrete everyday realities and the larger forces beneath those particular details by whatever means and methods they deem necessary.

As will be discussed in the final chapter, Biggers, through his work as both artist and educator at TSU, not only had a big impact on the development of Black artists and cultural institutions in Houston (and the South as a whole) during the Black Arts and immediate post–Black Arts era but continued to stimulate and influence the creation of new Black cultural institutions, really until the present moment. Rick Lowe, the key figure in the founding of one the most prominent post–Black Arts cultural institutions, Project Row Houses in Houston's Third Ward, pointedly cites Biggers's work and sense of the purpose of art and arts institutions as a key inspiration.[36]

Louisville, the Popular Front, and Black Bohemia

Quite a few southern cities, including Birmingham, New Orleans, Houston, Galveston, Miami, Tampa, Richmond, and Memphis, had been significant beachheads of the late Popular Front in the South in the 1940s. However, Louisville, the self-proclaimed "Gateway to the South," was one of the few where an important organization with its roots in the Popular Front, SCEF and its newspaper the *Southern Patriot,* survived. SCEF was headquartered in New Orleans, home of its longtime executive director James Dombrowski. However, its dynamic field secretaries Anne Braden and Carl Braden were based in Louisville, where SCEF relocated its main office in 1966 with Dombrowski's retirement.

The Bradens, who met as leftwing journalists and union activists, were much persecuted in the 1950s, particularly for their part in the nationally famous Wade case that stemmed from the efforts of a Black family to buy a house in the Louisville suburb of Shivley in 1954. Andrew and Charlotte Wade with the Bradens as intermediaries were able to buy a house, which was soon blown up by racists. While none of the actual bombers were identified or tried, the Bradens and other local activists were accused of aiding the Wades as part of a communist plot and charged with sedition. Carl Braden was sentenced to fifteen years in prison and served eight months before being released after the Supreme Court ruled against the state sedition laws. The cases against the other accused were dropped. The notoriety of the case and McCarthyism generally isolated the Bradens and SCEF—Carl Braden was forced to testify at one of the 1958 House Un-American Activities Committee hearings in Atlanta. Nevertheless, by the 1960s, particularly with the rise of the Black student movement and SNCC, the Bradens and SCEF were increasingly able to participate in local and regional politics, particularly in the West End.

The West End of Louisville included neighborhoods that housed a large portion of the city's Black community. While sections of it were almost entirely Black, as a whole it was still somewhat racially mixed even after white flight in the 1950s and 1960s. The West End neighborhood of Russell immediately proximate to downtown Louisville had grown into the Black commercial and entertainment center of the city by the 1940s, following the pattern of other southern cities during the Jim Crow era with Black business districts adjoining the central white retail, financial, and political centers. Like other Black commercial hubs, especially in southern cities, urban renewal buffeted Russell in the 1950s and 1960s. Nevertheless, the West End, particularly Russell, became the epicenter of Black art initiatives in the 1950s and 1960s drawing on Louisville's Popular Front survivals and a growing Black bohemia and offering a fertile ground for later Black Arts institutions.

Louisville was also a focal point of one of the most militant and leftwing of the CIO unions, the United Farm Equipment Workers (FE). Both Carl and Anne Braden worked for FE in the late 1940s. Local 236 of FE successfully organized Black and white workers at International Harvester's Louisville plant in 1947. The local promoted one of the most radical, egalitarian, antiracist stances of any major union in the United States. FE, along with other Left-led unions, was expelled from the CIO in 1949 as Communist-dominated, and Local 236 was eventually absorbed into the United Auto

Workers Union (UAW). However, the Louisville International Harvester local of UAW long remained a bastion of militant, anti–Jim Crow trade unionism in the South.[37]

One consequence of Louisville's continuing history of struggle for Black civil rights that was in part a legacy of the Popular Front era and the uneven application of Jim Crow under the pressure of this continuing struggle was that the University of Louisville (then a city-supported public college) desegregated much earlier than most predominantly white southern colleges and universities. The city removed the color line at the University of Louisville when it dissolved the Black Louisville Municipal College in 1951, before even the public schools were integrated in 1956. The desegregation of the campus had contradictory effects. On one hand, Black students were able to attend the university and access its considerable resources in arts education. At the same time, there were still relatively few Black students and almost no Black faculty as only a single Black faculty member (the sociologist Charles Parrish, who had ties to the late Popular Front and the Highlander School in Tennessee) from Louisville Municipal was retained at the University of Louisville. Consequently, the Black students in literature and arts programs were isolated at the school in many respects and were inspired by this isolation to build or participate in community-based Black cultural institutions, initially in a bohemian mode.

A key figure of the early Black bohemian milieu of Louisville was visual artist, poet, and musician Ted Joans. With the possible exception of poet Bob Kaufman, Joans epitomized Black bohemia in the 1950s more than any artist in the United States—so much so that he himself performed and parodied that image in his "rent-a-beatnik" efforts in New York City at the end of the 1950s and beginning of the 1960s. Joans's youth is shrouded in a sort of self-mythologizing that rendered his self-presentation a mode of his art, much like Kaufman. (Joans claimed to have been born on a riverboat, for instance.) Joans was born in Cairo, Illinois, and grew up in Illinois, Indiana, and Kentucky, including Louisville. He spent about four years in Louisville at the end of the 1940s and the beginning of the 1950s, roughly at the same time as the Popular Front's apogee in the city.[38] During this time Joans managed a Black movie theater in the Russell section of the West End, where he would host what one artist would later describe as "happenings," which is to say mixed media and genre performances of music, poetry, theater, and visual art, events that Joans reproduced on a more elaborate scale at the Brown Derby, a bebop stronghold in Russell, and Dave's Palm Room, another leading jazz club in Russell. Joans also organized and led a club devoted to bebop at the Chestnut Street YMCA, a Black branch of the Y founded in Russell in 1914.[39] When Joans departed for New York City (first to Harlem, then Greenwich Village) in 1951, he left behind a legacy of Black bohemian spaces in Louisville that was well remembered and seen as a continuing inspiration by the city's African American artists during the Black Arts era and after.

One important town-gown connection in Louisville during the 1950s was between the community-based Louisville Art Center (now Louisville Visual Art) and the art department of the University of Louisville. Quite a few of the arts faculty at the university taught classes at the Louisville Art Center's School of Art, as there was an agreement between the two institutions that enabled students at the School of Art to use the university's art facilities. Many younger Black artists of the 1950s and 1960s, such as Bob Thompson, Sam Gilliam, Kenneth Clay, and Robert Douglas, took classes at the Art Center as well as at the university.

However, Thompson, Gilliam, Clay, and Douglas found the overwhelmingly white milieu of the School of Art and the university to be alienating. By 1959, they began Gallery Enterprises as a discussion group/gallery space in the rear of the Brown Derby club in the Russell neighborhood as a way of building community, much like the sort of "happenings" that Ted Joans organized at Dave's Palm Room and the Brown Derby ten years earlier—again, a model of which these artists were well aware:[40]

> I suggested that if there was an announcement of a mural contest to include the other artists who "hung out" at Dave's Palm room, his intent to peak [*sic*] the interests of that younger crowd might be better served. McCarroll was also aware of the popularity of the artists and the excitement they generated around them. He agreed to the idea in hopes that the younger crowd might come to watch and enjoy themselves in the process. Thus, the goal that McCarroll had sold Leake on in order to be hired as his manager and minor partner had been achieved. When I told Sam and Ken about either a contest or a collective mural at the Brown Derby, it was decided that a larger meeting was necessary. We had at least two meetings, the second one at the Brown Derby, Bob Carter and Bob Thompson was [*sic*] also at the meeting. Instead of talking about the mural, Sam began again talking about his favorite subject, the significance about how all great changes

in art in the last hundreds years come out of group movements. The night he helped me select works for the Hite Scholarship Committee he talked about art movements.[41]

Between 1959 and 1961, Gallery Enterprises not only presented programs in the Brown Derby (and later a space above the Brown Derby) but also at the Chestnut Street YMCA and churches, community centers, such as at the Plymouth Settlement House (founded in Russell in 1917 for the Black community of the West End), and parks, setting a precedent for the presentation of art in grassroots public spaces that would remain influential long after the end of Gallery Enterprises in 1961:

> During the summer of 1961 we begin thinking and planning a "Happening" in a city park. We decided that Central Park in the heart of downtown Louisville was the perfect place. On August 16, 1961, we gave the first festival in a Louisville park probably in the 20th Century. We raised funds for prizes for first, second and third place in the professional art category. Also we offered a children's and amateur art contest. We sponsored a classical concert and a Jazz performance. The Milfred Reed players performed two acts from Baldwin's "Blues for Mr. Charley," but Doug Ramey the director of the Carriage House Players refused to do scenes from Shakespeare. Only after we refused to help him with his posters and sets as we had been doing for years, did he agree. Doug Ramey's players were so well received along with all of the other components of our "Happening," he was inspired to go it alone thereafter. He began receiving financial support and now Shakespeare in Central Park is history.[42]

The surviving networks and infrastructure of the Popular Front in Louisville, particularly the SCEF circles in which Ann and Carl Braden moved, were also important in the development of African American arts groups and initiatives as well as to the radicalization of neighborhood-oriented organizations, such as the West End Community Council. As the Red Scare lessened and the Black student movement grew in the South in the early 1960s, the Bradens and SCEF became less politically isolated with the emergence of younger activists on whom anti-Communism had less purchase than on their elders. Not only did the Bradens give material support to the new Black arts (and Black Arts) efforts, they also passed on basic organizing skills:

> However, what would become important for the Louisville Art Workshop creation and me is the other type of learning experience and

> opportunity the position as Organizer gave me. Ann Braden was a member of the West Community Council, but she and her husband Carl Braden also operated the organization, SCEF, Southern Conference Educational Fund and its home office was in Louisville at 3225 West Broadway. My estimation of SCEF's purpose is that it was a holdover from the Populist movement of the late thirties and involved in organizing the poor whites and blacks throughout the South in order to help them improve their lives economically and socially. A main focus was their publication that exposed the meager conditions and injustices which helped in some way to organize the South across racial lines to oppose whatever forces identified as hindrances to their well-being. Along this line the Bradens worked with established groups as well as create [*sic*] new ones. They held meetings in Louisville with the Community Organizers and other leaders or interested persons. At this meeting, they offered the use of their off-set printing press to create and distribute pamphlets, posters, announcements, etc. Also, they offered lessons in the use of the press beginning with the photographing camera, making ready art copy, developing the negatives, burning the negative on to off-set plates and printing the material and folding it if necessary. Because of the conversations that Fred and I were having about starting another art group, I saw this type of information as valuable to such an endeavor if the opportunity arose. While some of the other Organizers and group leaders took advantage of this opportunity offered by SCEF, others did not.[43]

Douglas also noted how the Bradens, particularly Carl, provided not only practical resources and instruction about basic organizing skills but also political education:

> Carl Braden and I often discussed the larger social and political issues. Although I had insisted since art school that the subject of my art should present and reflect the "Negro people," Carl made me aware of more specific possibilities by giving me my first copy of the 1934 Yenan Conference on Art, a booklet on what is revolutionary art. Moreover the pamphlet suggests how practitioners of the expressive art forms, i.e., music, dance, theater, and visual art might use their art to liberate a colonized or an oppressed people. The two basic concepts simply stated were to extol the virtues of the people and expose the enemies of the people. This was a startling revelation to me because of my tendency to paint Black people when most of my colleagues were

> either painting whites or people not identifiable of any group. In all fairness to most of us, this period of my professional art training, like theirs, was bombarded by the Abstract Movement and the propensity, even the necessity, of young professionals of all persuasion to seek, to court or to cajole the mainstream art world's acceptance. I began to realize that my dilemma and perhaps that of would-be artists like myself was linked to DuBois' [*sic*] double consciousness, that of how to be a productive citizen in the United States and also be Black or African and still have meaning and be accepted as a person and a professional artist. The Yenan Conference concepts on art also made me aware the main thrust of the goal of Gallery Enterprises, if not mainstream acceptance, it was to combat the mainstream denial of not only those of us who were Black, but also the young aspiring professional artists. This amounts to a class struggle for the strategic resources which is the patrons for the arts, individual buyers, galleries or museums. Those already in control of such resources do not want to share them unless on their terms. At that time none of us was aware of deeper, fundamental or sublime cultural reasons for art, only that we wanted acceptance from some source in order to be practicing artists making a living from our products. So I realized very slowly that if my artistic creations are not of value to America's mainstream art world, it should be of value to me and those like me. In order for this to happen it must address my needs and the needs of those like me. Thus I committed myself increasingly to producing artistic creations that either extolled the virtues of the poor and Black people or I would expose in some way those who are against Black [people] and thus keeping them poor.[44]

In that way, the Bradens played much the same sort of role as such older leftists as Charles and Margaret Burroughs in Chicago and Richard Moore and Esther Cooper Jackson in New York in mentoring and encouraging young Black radical artist-activists.

As the 1960s wore on, urban renewal increasingly hollowed and ultimately destroyed the old Black commercial and cultural hub of Louisville around W. Walnut Street in Russell. To a considerable degree, commerce in the West End never really recovered—not unlike the situation of many of the old southern Black business and cultural districts from Claiborne Avenue at the back of the Tremé neighborhood in New Orleans to the Jackson Ward section of Richmond, Virginia. The center of such Black commercial activity as there was in Louisville migrated farther south in the West End to the Parkland neighborhood, which became the focal point of Black Power in the city.

Black Nationalism in the South before the Black Arts Movement

The civil rights movement in the South has long been associated with an integrationist, nonviolent paradigm, such figures and organizations as the Deacons for Defense and Robert F. Williams notwithstanding. It has been and continues to be held up as a model of proper Black protest, critiquing other modes of Black radicalism and resistance from the civil rights era itself to the Black Lives Matter movement and angry responses to police violence and unequal justice in Black communities in the twenty-first century. However, the South also has a long tradition of Black nationalism and militant self-defense. On a certain practical level, African Americans in the South emerged from slavery in a burst of religious, fraternal, educational, political, and economic institution building, establishing a tradition of communal self-reliance that was in many respects intensified by Jim Crow, especially with regard to religious, economic, fraternal, and educational institutions, providing fertile ground for Black nationalism. As poet, playwright, political activist, and BLKARTSOUTH veteran Kalamu ya Salaam remarked, Black people in the South knew they could run businesses, primary and secondary schools, colleges, and so on, because they had already done that successfully, making nationalist visions of separate Black economies and states and other polities plausible on the grassroots level.[45] While this was true of other regions, especially the Midwest, nowhere was the theory and practice of Black self-reliance deeper than in the South. After all, while one might consider the educational philosophy of Booker T. Washington and the Tuskegee Institute in Alabama as one of accommodation to the Jim Crow system, at least publicly (privately, Washington's beliefs and actions about Jim Crow were quite different), it was also all about southern Black economic autonomy and power, making it one of the founts of modern Black nationalism from the Garvey movement on. This aspect of the Washington legacy continued to exert a strong influence in the South long after Washington's death.[46]

New Orleans, in particular, had a long tradition of organized Black nationalism, one that was closely tied to the culture and concern of the Black working class in ways that prefigured the sensibilities of the Black Arts movement there. The Garvey movement and the Universal Negro Improvement Association (UNIA) left a deep impression on New Orleans in the early twentieth century. With a membership of several thousand and many thousands more supporters, the UNIA of New Orleans was the undoubted center of Garveyism in the South. Centered in the working-class Black communities upriver from the French Quarter and downtown, the Garvey movement in New Orleans was more concerned with the day-to-day struggles of Black people in the city and labor issues, particularly among workers along the docks, than was generally the case in the North. As in other southern ports, the ILA was segregated into Black and white locals.[47] The UNIA in New Orleans had a close relationship to the Black-led local of the ILA. The vice president of the New Orleans division of the UNIA was also a leader of the Black longshoremen's local, and the UNIA met in the longshoremen's union hall before building their own Liberty Hall in 1926. The UNIA, anticipating similar efforts in the Black Power and Black Arts era, supported a medical clinic serving the uptown Black communities and provided other sorts of social services to Black New Orleans.[48] The New Orleans division of the UNIA also had an unusual (at least compared to its counterparts in New York and many Northern cities) engagement with local Black grassroots culture, sponsoring its own jazz band, the Holy Ghost Band, and holding popular "Red, Black, and Green" dances at Liberty Hall, featuring the Holy Ghost Band and other local jazz/marching bands.[49]

The UNIA declined as an organizational force in New Orleans during the 1930s, as elsewhere, but its energy and militancy was passed on to other Black movements. Though the CPUSA and its circles and the Garveyites (and other Black nationalists) often had a contentious relationship, there were also some much more positive interactions between the Left and the nationalists in New Orleans. In part, this was no doubt due to the unusually deep concern with organized labor by New Orleans Garveyites. Many Black CPUSA members and Popular Front activists in New Orleans, including Ernest Wright, were former Garveyites or from Garveyite families. The CPUSA (and Comintern) position on the "national question" that posited African Americans in the "Black Belt" South as a "nation" with the right to self-determination and in the Northern cities as a "national minority" with the right to full equality gave Black Communists with a nationalist bent considerable latitude in the 1930s and 1940s—though the degree to which the CPUSA saw "Negro liberation" as a "national question" and how it understood Black nationalism in the Popular Front era (and after) varied during these decades. As with SNYC, which was very active politically and culturally in the city, though Black Popular Front activists worked closely with white radicals and progressives, their primary focus was on building Black political and cultural organizations and institutions, often in conjunction with nationalists.

Not only were Black Communists in New Orleans often veterans of the UNIA and other nationalist groups and retained many ideological and practical traces of their former affiliations, but some nationalists in the 1940s, 1950s, and 1960s were also veterans of the CPUSA and the Popular Front who brought their engagement with Marxism and Left institution-building into their nationalist activities. Audley Moore (later known as Queen Mother Moore) had been an active leader of the CPUSA in Harlem during the 1940s. After breaking with the CPUSA in the early 1950s over what she saw as its retreat from the "national question," and "Negro liberation," Moore came back to her native Louisiana (like Octave Lilly, she was born and raised in New Iberia and later moved to New Orleans before her sojourn in Harlem). Despite her rupture with the CPUSA, she retained many associations with Black Left networks for a considerable period.

When Moore returned to New Orleans, she organized the nationalist Universal Association of Ethiopian Women and Sons and Daughters of Ethiopia, which held meetings in the building of the People's Defense League. These organizations were both educational and activist, organizing and agitating against lynching, the Jim Crow legal system, and police violence. Though these organizations were relatively small, the meetings dealing with the legal system and policing attracted dozens of people, a significant number for a radical Black nationalist organization in the South during the 1950s. Moore relocated to Philadelphia, a major waypoint between North and South for the civil rights movement, in order to promote her organizations. She became a major proponent of Black self-determination and an architect of the movement for reparations for slavery. In Philadelphia, Moore mentored Muhammad Ahmad (Max Stanford) and the emerging nationalist political and cultural circles centered on the Revolutionary Action Movement (RAM) and the Muntu Group, which also included poet, playwright, and critic Larry Neal, musician, poet, and critic James Stewart, playwright Charles Fuller, and critic, journalist, and educator Playthell Benjamin. These groups in turn would be instrumental in establishing a larger Black Power and Black Arts network, including BARTS in Harlem. While Moore was and long continued to be extremely critical of the CPUSA, she remained in touch with the network of contacts she developed during her time in the party and saw Marxism as an important analytical tool for understanding the oppression of African Americans.[50]

Like New Orleans and Virginia's Tidewater region (another area where the UNIA intertwined with Black longshoremen and seamen in the ILA and the National Maritime Union), Miami was a major center of Garveyism in the South. However, it differed from other hotbeds of southern Garveyism in that its primary base was not among the native-born African American population of the city. Instead, Garveyism found its most fertile soil among Black immigrants from the Caribbean, particularly the Bahamas, who labored as farm workers and in service industries in and around Miami and formed a slight majority of the Black community in the city—though the leadership of the local UNIA chapter was often non-Caribbean.[51] In spite of a relatively small number of supporters among southern-born African Americans, the UNIA claimed a membership of more than a thousand during its Miami heyday in the first half of the 1920s, mostly in the predominantly Bahamian community of Coconut Grove—though many UNIA activities were also held in the largely non-Caribbean Black community of "Colored Town" (now Overton).[52] Not surprisingly, given the immigrant base of the UNIA in Miami, its members were extraordinarily concerned with issues of the African diaspora as a whole. Though, as Claudrena Harold persuasively argues, the UNIA and its supporters tended to chart a course between accommodationism to Jim Crow and radicalism, a number of its leaders and members publicly affirmed and organized armed self-defense as a strategy for combating Klan and other racist vigilante violence that was endemic in Miami in the 1920s, going so far as to organize a self-defense unit that drilled in a public park.[53]

As was the case in New Orleans and elsewhere, leading Black participants in the CPUSA and the Popular Front in the 1930s and 1940s were veterans of the Garvey movement. They were active in the labor movement, especially Transport Workers Union Local 500, Shipbuilders Local 59 of the Industrial Union of Marine and Shipbuilding Workers of America, and the Laundry Workers Union. The Civil Rights Congress was also a prominent later Popular Front organization locally. (The Miami CRC affiliate was the largest in the South and the dominant civil rights organization of the city in the late 1940s and early 1950s.) The 1948 Henry Wallace campaign for President received more votes there than anywhere else in the South. Wallace attracted 12,000 to an outdoor rally in a city of less than 250,000. James Nimmo, formerly a very active Garveyite leader and an organizer of the

Laundry Workers Union, was the most prominent Black supporter of the Popular Front—though later he broke with the CPUSA and testified as a friendly witness before the House Un-American Activities Committee. Nimmo promoted CPUSA activities in Overton and campaigned for the Transport Workers Union among the Black porters, cleaners, and cafeteria workers of Pan American Airlines, who made up about 10 percent of the membership of the Left-led Local 500. Like the Garveyites, the CPUSA and the later Popular Front of Miami strove to promote diasporic and hemispheric connections, so much so that the FBI became obsessed with the Popular Front in Miami as a "Red" hotbed of both Black rebellion in the South and Communist intrigue in Latin America. While the institutional infrastructure of the Communist Left in the community and in the labor movement was crushed by federal, state, and local repression aided by Klan violence and anti-Communist efforts within the CIO, particularly the Transport Workers Union, in the early 1950s, both Garveyism and the Popular Front remained living memories in South Florida.[54]

As Lorenzo Thomas points out, the McCarthy era not only affected the Left but also various sorts of identities and ideologies deemed in some way deviant or un-American.[55] Nevertheless, even during the depths of the Red Scare, Black nationalist organizations arose and projected an increasingly visible profile. The Nation of Islam (NOI) established numbered mosques in Atlanta, Georgia; Richmond, Virginia; Miami, Florida; Charlotte and Durham, North Carolina; and Columbia, SC; and unnumbered groups in Birmingham, Alabama; Jacksonville and Pensacola, Florida; Louisville, Kentucky; New Orleans and Monroe, Louisiana; Orangeburg, South Carolina; Memphis and Nashville, Tennessee; Dallas and Houston, Texas; and Lynchburg, Martinsburg, Newport News, Norfolk, and Portsmouth, Virginia by the middle 1960s.[56] The profusion of NOI groups in Virginia, especially in the port cities of the Tidewater, is particularly notable, if not entirely surprising, since those areas were also previously hotbeds of Garveyite and Popular Front activity, particularly among African Americans in the longshore and maritime industries. The FBI surveilled the NOI and concluded that, as far as they knew, NOI only had about 600 southern members (out of a national membership of 5,000, according to the Bureau) showing that the Nation of Islam held little appeal to African Americans in the South. Still, the fact remains that the NOI was a public presence throughout the region despite the constant threat of government repression and vigilante violence. And, as Ernest Gaines suggested in the 1983 novel *In My Father's House*, set in Louisiana after King's assassination in Memphis, the influence of Malcolm X, Elijah Muhammad, and the NOI in the South, as elsewhere, extended far beyond the actual membership.[57]

The legacy of the Popular Front, Black nationalism, and other forms of Black radicalism in the South is complicated and sometimes hard to trace. As mentioned before, few Left-influenced institutions in the South survived the Cold War and the often violent assault on the organized Left and organized nationalism. Many of the artists and activists who spearheaded the southern Black Popular Front left the region—and sometimes the country. Those writers and artists who did remain, such as Margaret Walker, Octave Lilly, and Marcus Christian, kept a relatively low profile politically during the Red Scare, and, in the case of Lilly and Christian faded into relative obscurity and/or inactivity even locally until Tom Dent (recreating the sorts of relationships he had had with Esther Cooper Jackson and *Freedomways* in New York) sought them out after returning to his native New Orleans.

However, the work that Popular Front artists and activists did in the South in such institutions as SNYC, PDL, the arts departments and institutions of HBCUs, and so on, inspired and prefigured the notions of how artists should relate to the community that marked Black Arts literature and visual arts. Even though many of the leading figures of the southern Popular Front left the region due in many cases to Cold War pressures, they took with them the lessons, the style, and the dedication to Black institution building developed in the Popular Front generally and often the CPUSA specifically and influenced by the continuing legacy of various iterations of Black nationalism (especially Garveyism) in the region. They created institutions, especially *Freedomways,* that not only supported the Black Arts upsurge of the 1960s and 1970s but provided models of how new institutions might be created and might be run, drawing on different generations of geographically and ideologically diverse Black radicals.

CHAPTER TWO

Becoming Black, Becoming Southern

The Gulf Coast and the Rise of a Southern Black Arts Infrastructure

By the early 1960s, the South was the terrain of the most vibrant and diverse grassroots Black political activity in the United States, ranging from direct action nonviolent protest to actual armed self-defense and what was arguably the first urban uprising of the 1960s in response to a series of 1963 Klan bombings in Birmingham, including the infamous attack on the 16th Street Baptist Church.[1] As many commentators have noted, Cold War pressures forced the so-called mainstream of the civil rights movement to genuflect before Cold War anticommunism, with some civil rights leaders obscuring or jettisoning any open Left connections or pasts, at least in the earlier phases of the movement. At the same time, remnants of the circuits and the networks of the Old Left played important roles in building the new civil rights infrastructure. For example, E. D. Nixon, one of the architects of the Montgomery bus boycott, had been a member of the advisory board of SNYC. Rosa Parks, too, had a long association with Left institutions and activists, including the Highlander School and Esther and James Jackson, leaders of SNYC and later, in James Jackson's case, of the CPUSA. Also, the southern movement drew back into political activity Black artists and writers, some in the region (many on the campuses of HBCUs) and some outside of it, who had been active in the Popular Front in the South and elsewhere, but had distanced themselves from their previous commitments. As noted in the previous chapter with respect to the emergence of *Freedomways*, these artists and writers saw the civil rights movement as a new space in which they could engage a politicized and increasingly militant mass Black audience.

As the 1960s began, a little more than half of U.S. African Americans lived in the South, still more than any other region. The southern Black population was increasingly urban, though larger numbers of Black people lived in rural communities than in any other area of the United States, particularly in the "Black Belt" that had been dominated by the production of cotton and other staple crops. The Great Migration to urban centers in the North and the West as well as those of the South that flowed with renewed strength after the entrance of the United States into World War II continued apace through the postwar era and the rise of the Cold War into the 1960s. Coupled with "white flight" to new suburban developments, this drastically shifted the demographics (and politics) of many U.S. cities (southern as well as northern) and set the stage for successful Black mayoral campaigns in such cities as Gary, Cleveland, Detroit, Newark, Atlanta, Birmingham, Richmond, and, ultimately, Chicago and Philadelphia in the 1960s, 1970s, and 1980s—all campaigns with links to Black Power and Black Arts and, if one looked deeply enough, older sorts and circuits of Black radicalism, particularly that of the Popular Front. The migration also helped maintain personal, community, and institutional ties between Black people in the South and those in the cities of the North and West. As was the case earlier in the century, these ties linked particular parts of the South most intensely to certain northern and western cities or sets of cities (e.g., Louisiana and Texas to Los Angeles and the cities of the Bay Area; Mississippi, Louisiana, Alabama, west Tennessee, and Arkansas to Chicago and Detroit; the southeastern coast to the Boston-Washington corridor). These connections basically followed old railroad routes even if the newer migrants were more likely to come by car or bus than train. Many young Black people who grew up in northern and western cities in the 1940s and 1950s found themselves spending time with grandparents, aunts and uncles, and other relatives in the small-town South during their summer vacations. For those in southern cities, the relationship was often even closer as families moved back and forth between the country and the city. Some metropolises, especially New York and Los Angeles, drew migrants (especially those with artistic ambitions of one sort or another) from across the South as well as the rest of the country and, especially after the major 1965 change in U.S. immigration quotas, Africa and its diaspora outside the United States.

At the beginning of the 1960s, few colleges and universities in the South other than HBCUs admitted Black undergraduates. Even as the decade wore on, while desegregation and the at least nominal integration of many historically white schools presented challenges to HBCUs, 75 percent of Black undergraduates in the South still attended HBCUs in 1965—and 60 percent in 1970.[2] Given the significantly increased graduation rate of Black high school students in the South during the 1960s, the enrollments of HBCUs actually increased during the 1960s even when historically white schools began admitting African Americans.

As noted in the previous chapter, while the bulk of students at HBCUs came from the South, these schools drew, as they long had, Black undergraduate and graduate students from all regions of the United States as well as from Africa and its diaspora, especially the colonies and former colonies of the United Kingdom. The HBCUs also were often refuges for radical faculty members of various stripes who were otherwise unemployable elsewhere, even if these scholars and artists generally had to downplay their radicalism or approach it indirectly. In short, one could see many HBCU campuses as a demographically and ideologically pan-African environment. Various currents of African American thought, culture, and politics as well as of Caribbean and African anticolonialism and the ideas of Bandung World political, cultural, and economic development mixed in formal and informal contexts among students and sometimes even in the curricula. Also, as masses of Black students (and grassroots southern Black communities) became involved in the struggle against Jim Crow and for Black political and economic power, more space was opened for the expression of different and often interlocking kinds of Black radicalism by faculty members, and the increased hiring of such faculty, even if those students and faculty found themselves in conflict with college and university administrators.

With the decline of more community-based Black art projects and institutions after the collapse of the Popular Front in the late 1940s and 1950s, the presentation and performance of what might be thought of as Black "high" art, at least at a higher level of reputation and accomplishment, were often confined to HBCU campuses in much of the South, though community people often attended plays, concerts, art shows, and so on, on those campuses.[3] However, major genres of Black popular music, especially gospel and R&B (including various types of the blues), were produced and recorded in such southern music industry hubs as Memphis, New Orleans, Houston, and Muscle Shoals, Alabama, for a mass, significantly southern, Black audience. Contemporary jazz remained a substantial presence in New Orleans despite being overshadowed in the public imagination by more nostalgic recreations of early New Orleans jazz, often for white tourist audiences. Tom Dent and other New Orleans Black Arts participants often cited the work of such contemporary jazz musicians as pianist Ellis Marsalis Jr. and clarinetist Alvin Batiste as evidence of a dynamic, creative Black culture that rivaled that of any other city. Other jazz musicians, notably the banjo player and guitarist Danny Barker, whose career embraced a huge spectrum of jazz from early New Orleans jazz and the brass band tradition to bebop (and beyond), were seen to embody almost the entire arc of Black music in New Orleans. New Orleans was also a national fount of R&B as seen in the record sales of such local musicians as Professor Longhair

(Henry Roeland Byrd), Antoine "Fats" Domino, Irma Thomas, the Dixie Cups, and Johnny Adams.

One of the most important developments for the emergence of Black Arts (and Black Power) was the rise of the Black student movement in 1961 and the formation of the Student Nonviolent Coordinating Committee (SNCC). The civil rights movement had previously been to a large degree a series of comparatively discrete campaigns, demonstrations, and actions in which national organizations, such as SCLC, CORE, and the NAACP joined with local people to work toward a relatively finite end. SNCC and the more grassroots iterations of CORE, especially in Louisiana, established much more permanent campaigns, projects, and field offices in rural Black communities and (eventually) urban Black communities.

One crucial aspect of the Black student movement and SNCC was its "just do it" philosophy. That is to say, while these students respected some older Black leaders and activists, such as James Lawson in Nashville, King in Atlanta, and Ella Baker, Bayard Rustin, and Sterling Brown in Washington, D.C., they did not wait for approval or direction, but acted more or less as what they saw the situation demanding. This sort of approach that respected and even sought out elders but did not pause for approval by some established authority exerted a great influence on Black Arts approaches to building organizations and institutions. Also, as SNCC and other civil rights groups established more or less permanent civil rights schools, newspapers, singing groups, theaters, and so on designed to reach Black (and to a lesser extent white and Latinx) people beyond the campuses of HBCUs, the beginning of a southern Black Arts approach and of a Black Arts sensibility began, taking up and deepening where the Black Popular Front left off.

New Orleans, Civil Rights, and the Rise of a Community-Based Black Arts Network in the South

Beginnings of movements are always hard to pinpoint, but one possible starting point for the Black Arts movement in the South (and, indeed, a seminal moment for the movement nationally) was the establishment of the FST at Tougaloo College in 1964 after earlier discussions about the need for a theater that could serve the burgeoning civil rights movement in Mississippi and elsewhere in the Deep South, making it among the first of the Black Arts or proto–Black Arts theaters. At the very least, the theater was a prime exemplar of a move from civil rights to Black Arts, from Negro to

Black, from serving the folk of the Black South to being emphatically southern in a Black modality. At the same time, the activists of the FST saw their experience in the South as formative in their desire to engage the experience of Black people in the entire United States systemically: "We both felt bound by the apparent contradiction between the poet and the person. We claimed to be playwrights and poets; yet the political facts of life presented by the situation we first learned of in the South called for a life of useful (political or economic) engagement. How could we remain true to ourselves and our own concerns as artists and at the same time remain true to our developing recognition of political responsibility?"[4]

The FST's founders, John O'Neal, Doris Derby, and Gilbert Moses, had come to the Deep South to work in the civil rights movement with a considerable background in theater and the arts and in the movement elsewhere. O'Neal, a native of Mound Bayou, Illinois, had decided that he wanted to be a playwright by the time he graduated from Southern Illinois University-Carbondale in 1962. He had also become deeply involved in the Black student movement inspired by the sit-in of four North Carolina A&T students (planned by a group that included women from Bennett College) at a Greensboro, North Carolina, Woolworth's in 1960. O'Neal helped initiate the Student Nonviolent Freedom Committee, basically a Carbondale SNCC affiliate, in 1961. He was also active in more explicitly Left groups, such as Fair Play for Cuba and SDS, and began a lifelong interest in Marxism.[5]

After his graduation and a 1962 Student Nonviolent Freedom Committee/SNCC campaign against the segregation of public facilities in Cairo, Illinois, that attracted national attention (using SNCC leader James Foreman's "Segregation in the Land of Lincoln" slogan as a rallying cry), O'Neal found himself conflicted about the direction of his life. He was unsure whether he should move to New York City to pursue a theater career or go South to be on what he saw as the civil rights front lines. New York seemed to him (as to most theater workers) both the center of the commercial mainstream theater and the new American avant-garde. The Living Theater's production of Jack Gelber's 1959 play *The Connection* with its mixed media avant-garde approach to a real social situation and a deep interaction between dramatic performance and jazz improvisation particularly excited O'Neal during a visit to New York.[6] O'Neal opted to go South, seeing the struggle there as the most important thing happening in the United States. He worked in various SNCC projects in Georgia and Mississippi before joining Doris Derby, an artist from New York with interests in many media and genres, on the SNCC Literacy Project based at Tougaloo College near Jackson, Mississippi.

In late 1963, O'Neal and Derby met Gilbert Moses, a native of Cleveland and participant in the famous theater program at Karamu House there. Moses had acted off-Broadway in New York, giving him an impressive status in the eyes of O'Neal. Moses came South to work on a movement newspaper in Jackson, the *Mississippi Free Press*. Practically on meeting, O'Neal and Moses (who shortly became roommates) were deep in argument about whether tragedy (O'Neal) or comedy (Moses) was the highest form of theater, initiating the sort of productive, if complicating, conflict that characterized their relationship in the FST.[7] However, it was Derby who pushed the trio to actually form the FST, suggesting that the South was the key locale for a meaningful Black theater:

> It was late one night in the small, cluttered, smoke-filled apartment that Gil and I shared. Doris, Gil, and I had talked way past midnight and the smell of the meal we'd shared had long since turned stale. But oh so passionately did we still carry on about art and the theatre we thought *ought* to be—the theatre we wanted to work in.
>
> It was long after two A.M. when the heady conversation came to a pause. Simply and profoundly, Doris broke the heavy silence. "Well, if theatre means anything anywhere, it certainly ought to mean something here. Why don't we make a theatre?"
>
> The three of us passed a silent, open-mouthed gaze around the room. I don't know how long we sat like that before it was settled. In that quiet moment, the Free Southern Theater (FST) was born.[8]

Derby also made the point that theater was particularly powerful aesthetically because it was a form in which all the sorts of art in which the trio was interested (dramatic performance, music, poetry, visual art, and dance) could be combined:

> And the theater—we thought of the theater as the vehicle or the housing for the other arts. So, we could have plays that, you know, had music and dance, and I would do the dance group, and we'd have, we'd need to have the art, you know, the stage and the backdrops and all of this. And so, we said, "Well, let's write something," you know. And so, we wrote why we wanted a free southern—a theater, and we called it a "Free Southern Theater" because we wanted to take the plays out to the rural areas, go around and perform out in the cotton fields or in the churches. You didn't have a whole lot of community centers, just in certain places, you know. If there was one big grocery store,

> like gigantic grocery store, we could have a play in there. You know, it's like wherever you can have a place where people can congregate, outside or inside.[9]

Derby, Moses, and O'Neal's discussions about forming a movement theater combining grassroots agitation, community cultural access, and avant-garde aesthetics took concrete form as they became involved with a 1964 Tougaloo College Drama Workshop production of *Inherit the Wind*, which Moses directed. Within a few months of this production, the workshop morphed into the FST, which the founders essentially saw as an arm of SNCC and its campaigns. The general division of labor had Derby as a visual artist managing set design, Moses in charge of directing and training the actors, and O'Neal running production and the organizational needs of the theater.[10]

In 1964, the FST moved to New Orleans in part to to have access to greater material resources for a Black theater than were then available in Jackson. One of these resources was Richard Schechner, a young white professor at Tulane University and editor of the *Tulane Drama Review* (later renamed *The Drama Review* or *TDR*) who had been the college roommate of Moses's brother at Oberlin College.[11] The initial idea in recruiting Schechner to the FST was that his connection to the larger mainstream theater industry, the theatrical avant-garde, and the academy through *TDR* would give the FST an increased ability to attract foundation funding, theater workers, sponsors, and bookings, especially the bookings outside the Deep South that were crucial to FST's fundraising efforts. Though the results of FST's initial applications for money from major foundations were disappointing, Schechner's theatrical skills and his ability to serve as a buffer or mediator between Moses and O'Neal (who frequently disagreed about repertoire, production values, aesthetics, the need for fundraising activities, and just about everything) made him invaluable to the theater. While O'Neal would characterize his relationship with Moses as "productive conflict," Schechner helped keep the conflict from overwhelming the productivity.[12] The commute between New Orleans and Tougaloo was too difficult for Schechner to maintain on a regular basis, necessitating the move to New Orleans if he were to continue to play an active role.[13]

Schechner's link with *TDR* did not result in the level of fundraising and institutional support that O'Neal and Moses envisioned. As O'Neal remarked, the lack of funds was a constant threat to the FST's ability to carry out its regional goals.[14] Still, Schechner's role in FST led to *TDR* becoming an important conduit through which Black Arts theater first reached a larger public and, indeed, a medium through which the national movement conceptualized itself. For example, the landmark *TDR* "Black Theatre" issue (Summer 1968) contained not only O'Neal's "Motion in the Ocean: Some Political Dimensions of the Free Southern Theatre" but also Larry Neal's landmark essay "The Black Arts Movement," which essentially named the movement as a national formation alongside and inextricably linked to Black Power.

Beyond the value of allowing Schechner's daily participation, Moses and O'Neal saw New Orleans as having a larger Black middle class who might patronize a socially engaged African American theater—though this advantage was to a certain extent illusory because New Orleans's long economic decline that began to be apparent in the 1960s limited such patronage. In fact, O'Neal later considered the move from Jackson to be a mistake on the financial as well as political level despite the fact that he remained in New Orleans long after the end of FST. The desire of some of the founders, especially O'Neal, to attract high-level theater workers from outside the South, principally New York, to the FST was seen as more realizable if the troupe were based in New Orleans rather than in what some from outside the region (and even some in it) might consider the rural hinterlands, especially as far as the theater was concerned. Not only was New Orleans perceived as more urban and urbane than Jackson, but also as a place where the theater could have a little relief from the constant police harassment in Jackson while serving the movement. As Denise Nicholas recalled,

> When we moved the theater to New Orleans at the end of the first summer, we had been threatened, harassed. Our members had been, not been arrested but taken down to police headquarters in Jackson. Gilbert and John and then eventually Tom Dent and Richard Schechner out of New Orleans decided that it would be better to try and run this theater from New Orleans so we could live like human beings and not be afraid all the time and tour back into Mississippi. It would be a little freer environment to work in so we moved the theater to New Orleans at the end of the summer, 1964.[15]

O'Neal and others also saw the removal from the frontlines of the SNCC campaigns and from SNCC territory (the dominant civil rights group in most of Louisiana at the time was CORE) as a plus since it allowed the theater to focus on questions of craft in a way that was difficult under the pressure of day-to-day political work in which writing, rehearsal, and the technical work of staging a production could be almost endlessly deferred.[16]

This view was not universally shared by the FST's founders, though, as Doris Derby refused to make the move to New Orleans, largely because she felt that the theater should have stayed on the grassroots movement frontlines in Mississippi.[17] Instead, Derby remained with the SNCC Literacy Project and later worked in the Black cooperative movement and other Black cultural and educational projects based around Jackson, Mississippi, particularly the Poor People's Corporation's Liberty House on Farish Street in Jackson (with branch stores in New York City). Such craft cooperatives have not often been considered part of the Black Arts movement. Their primary purpose was to promote Black economic self-sufficiency. In the case of Liberty House, the goal was to provide rural African Americans in Mississippi an alternative to sharecropping. It did not achieve its economic goals—the Jackson store closed in 1972, though a New York store survived until 2017.[18] Still, Liberty House had a film production arm and sold books by such Black Arts publishers as Broadside Press as well as crafts. Not only can Liberty House be seen as a direct ancestor of Cooperation Jackson in the twenty-first century but also as an institution that connected grassroots African American craftspeople and expressive cultural traditions with urban Black Arts constituencies, making manifest the Black Arts ideal of everyday people as artists in the African American tradition, much as the FST-BLKARTSOUTH would do in its performances.

In New Orleans, the FST quickly became more like a professional traveling repertory theater. However, it came to be plagued by a number of contradictions that characterized it over the rest of the decade. In large part, these contradictions grew from the FST leaders' very different notions of what the theater (and drama in general) should be and what it should do—to some degree continuing the arguments of Moses and O'Neal that arose from their first meeting. Some of the debates within the FST, such as to what degree (if at all) and in what capacity white people should take part in the theater, mirrored similar debates in the civil rights movement itself throughout the nation, but especially in SNCC and CORE.[19]

Other contradictions were more particular to FST. The group took seriously the notion of serving a mass southern African American constituency. Yet its members were, for the most part, young Black and white theater workers from the North. O'Neal went to New York regularly to recruit promising Black actors to the FST. Since the FST National Board of

Sponsors was filled with prestigious names—such as James Baldwin, Harry Belafonte, Theodore Bikel, Ossie Davis, Ruby Dee, and Langston Hughes—a number of New York actors were willing to go South to work with the FST for a time as a sort of career stepping-stone as well as an expression of their political commitments. But few would stay away from New York or Los Angeles and the dreams of larger mainstream acting success for very long, especially as roles began to open up for Black actors on stage, movie screen, and television—success that such FST veterans as Moses, Denise Nicholas, and Roscoe Orman did, indeed, find.[20]

Money, too, was a persistent issue. Some saw John O'Neal as overly concerned with fundraising, suggesting that the theater mount its productions with whatever resources were at hand. O'Neal saw financial stability as a key element of the sort of institutional equilibrium that would allow the FST to survive.[21] In time, a certain schism would open up between O'Neal and the main touring unit of the FST and the local people who made up the members of FST's workshops over the question of fundraising and how much money was actually necessary—though it is fair to say that the FST had multiple and somewhat fluid factions within it that energized as well as disrupted it.

The FST also saw itself as having multiple and somewhat dissonant missions. One was to present drama that directly addressed and supported the campaigns of SNCC, CORE, COFO, SCLC, the NAACP Youth Council, and other civil rights organizations in the South. Another was to showcase work by contemporary Black playwrights, such as Ossie Davis's *Purlie Victorious*. Yet another was to expose poor and often rural African American audiences to serious modern drama like Samuel Beckett's absurdist classic *Waiting for Godot* (apparently at least in part chosen due to Moses's search for the sort of comedy that could connect with Black existential realities in the Jim Crow South).[22] The generically mixed repertoire that resulted frequently puzzled, provoked, and/or stimulated its intended core audience. Still, while some commenters, then and later, emphasized the mystification of rural Black audiences encountering the work of Samuel Becket, it is worth noting that the great Mississippi civil rights leader Fannie Lou Hamer defended that choice, explicating the meaning of *Waiting for Godot* for rural Black Mississippians.[23] Denise Nicholas, who was married to Gilbert Moses and an FST actress before her television and film career in Los Angeles, recalled,

> Well, we were all kind of, you know I mean even people, we were—I was in the audience you know backstage and I never, I mean the play

always gave me problems of course. It's supposed to give me problems but Fannie Lou Hamer stood up in the church and she said, she led the discussion. She said, "Well, I guess we know something about waiting don't we?" Everybody said yes ma'am, yes we do. And then from there opened up the discussion because in the play a character has a rope around the neck of one other character and then we started talking about slavery, we started talking about the incident, the rope being not only around the neck of the person who is the slave but in the hand of the enslaver is also, is also a kind of prison. So we, we talked, we had this incredible discussion with people who barely had a sixth grade education. So it flew in the face of everything, of every assumption that people have about people not having a formal education which was what Gilbert knew was going to happen anyway. He knew from the beginning that the theater, the images, the language, the physicality of it would open doors in people's minds that they didn't necessarily need to read a lot of books to get to. They didn't have to. They could go into that room without being college educated if, if it's presented in a way that they emotionally and spiritually can tie, can tie into, which they did over and over and over again.[24]

Like many early Black Arts theaters, such as BARTS and the Studio Watts drama group and the Watts Repertory Theatre in Los Angeles, FST programs also frequently featured the performance of formally innovative poetry, such as the verbal collages of David Henderson, a veteran of the Umbra Poets Workshop in New York who toured with the FST in 1967. Such use of poetry was a common feature of many Black Arts theaters in the South (and elsewhere). From the perspective of trying to engage local people with little or no training in theater, reciting poetry had the virtue of being a form of verbal performance that was a relatively simple method for untrained young (and not so young) people to begin to learn the fundamentals of performance in a way they found satisfying.

The conditions in which FST performed, especially in its shows in rural communities, had a profound impact on its aesthetics and general sensibilities. For one thing, such presentations on the civil rights frontlines were extremely risky. There was always the possibility that sheriff's deputies or vigilantes might violently interfere with the performances. Simply getting from one venue to another was extraordinarily dangerous for the FST members as well as for other civil rights workers in CORE, SNCC, and the Council of Federated Organizations (COFO), an umbrella organization of civil rights groups in Mississippi. It took a special commitment to reach out to Black audiences in the rural and small-town South. As Kim McMillon notes in the section of her dissertation on the women of the Black Arts movement that discusses Doris Derby: "What makes this theatre company notable is the willingness of the participants both on stage and in the audience to lay down their lives in the fight for equal rights and justice for all."[25]

The conditions under which the FST first performed in the field also helped instill an improvisational practice. This practice was dictated not simply by the improvisational aspects of African American expressive culture and avant-garde theater in a general sense, but also by the not-infrequent intervention of audience members in performances. As has been often observed, working-class African American audiences, whether in church, at musical performances, movies, or plays, rarely simply watch—they actively respond. Nowhere was that truer than in the rural South. At FST performances in the countryside, audience members would sometimes join in. O'Neal recalled one show where a man from the audience stood in the middle of the stage virtually the entire play without moving, serving as a sort of silent witness. Consequently, the group always had to be prepared for such an event and alter its actions accordingly.[26]

The FST was also seriously devoted to the development of a new repertoire, new actors, new playwrights, and new directors rooted in the local Black community, as well as the Black communities of the South generally. It instituted a playwrights' workshop and a writers' workshop in which the participants were almost all local. However, the FST also continued to import many of its key personnel from up North, especially New York, rather than relying on local people whom the workshop trained.[27]

Since the theater and its workshops were based in New Orleans and the workshop members were city people, the plays and other writings that emerged from the workshop necessarily had an urban sensibility and a citified voice that were somewhat at odds with the original rural focus of the FST. Not surprisingly, when the workshops of the FST set up their own touring groups, their performances were more often in cities and their audiences residents of Black communities of the urban South. Consequently, the groups, institutions, and networks that emerged out of the later FST primarily arose in cities and served urban constituencies in the first place, not the rural folk who were the initial focus of the FST. Of course, having said that, it is important to note that the boundary between city and country, between "the ghetto" and the rural "Black Belt" was often very permeable and quite ambiguous.

As Black Power began to emerge as a visible if not completely coherent movement, and as other Black Arts theaters (especially BARTS) gained a national prominence, the FST, too, took on a much more nationalist character, dropping from its repertoire the dramas by white modernist and postmodernist playwrights, and thinking of itself much more as a Black theater than a civil rights movement theater. Nevertheless, some of the other contradictions remained, such as whether to maintain the theater as a relatively elite professional group with actors and directors drawn for the most part from the North, especially New York, or to become a genuine community or regional theater committed to producing the work of local people and casting nonprofessional urban Black southerners in principal roles.[28]

A pivotal event for the growth of the Black Arts movement in the South was the 1965 return of Tom Dent to his hometown of New Orleans—a city in which he had not really lived since he was a teenager. Dent had been the chief instigator of the seminal Umbra Poets Workshop in New York City's Lower East Side that also included David Henderson (who toured with FST), Calvin Hernton, Ishmael Reed, Lorenzo Thomas (who would later migrate South to Houston), and Askia Touré (who worked in SNCC's Atlanta Project for a time, and who would return to Atlanta in the 1980s).[29] In New York, Dent was also active in such Left-influenced African American organizations of artists and intellectuals as the Harlem Writers Guild (among whose members numbered Maya Angelou, Lonnie Elder III, John O. Killens, Abbey Lincoln, Paule Marshall, Julian Mayfield, Louise Merriwether, Douglas Turner Ward, and Sarah Wright) and On Guard for Freedom (a Left-nationalist group whose participants included many of the young Black writers, visual artists, musicians, and intellectuals of the Lower East Side, including Wright, Amiri Baraka, Calvin Hicks, Harold Cruse, Archie Shepp, and A. B. Spellman). Through his connections in New Orleans (where his mother was a concert pianist and his father president of Dillard University) and in New York (where he had worked for the NAACP Legal Defense and for the Black newspaper the *New York Age*), Dent knew an enormous number of African American intellectuals, artists, educators, civil rights leaders, and political activists of all sorts of ideological and aesthetic stripes from Thurgood Marshall to Malcolm X to CPUSA leader James Jackson (and Jackson's wife Esther Jackson, the managing editor of the journal *Freedomways*) to Langston Hughes. He also sought out and was acquainted with what Lorenzo Thomas calls a Black "underground of unknown artists" "of storefronts, basements, and brownstone stoops on a summer night" both in New Orleans and New York as well as nationally across the United States.[30] This interest in conversation and community with older and younger Black artists, in addition to his skills as a listener, served Dent well as a builder of artists' groups and workshops. As Thomas recalled in a poem for Dent, "Discovering America Again," Dent was a sort of radical Black flaneur and keen listener who sought out all manner of Black artists, activists, and street savants:

> Someone has walked this way before,
> My friend
> Who was my friend
> A man who spoke with people
> Who asked you questions
> So that you could breathe[31]

O'Neal, on one of his recruiting trips to New York in early 1965, encouraged Dent to return home, regaling Dent with stories of the FST's work. The urging of O'Neal (and Dent's family) to come back to New Orleans found a responsive listener in Dent. Dent had become tired of the tribulations of living on New York's Lower East Side as heroin flooded the neighborhood, as well as of the intense conflicts within the early Black Arts movement in New York that, for example, tore apart BARTS in Harlem that year. These conflicts resulted in the hegira of many other leaders of the movement, such as Amiri Baraka, Sonia Sanchez, and Askia Touré, as they sought to escape the turmoil and internecine violence that reached its apogee with the shooting of Larry Neal by members of a deranged faction of BARTS. Dent was also familiar with the work of the FST through Doris Derby whom he had dated for a while after being introduced to her by Andrew Young in New York.[32]

Dent brought South the model of connecting to older Black grassroots artists, intellectuals, nationalists, and leftists in New York that he met through his different jobs as well as through Umbra, On Guard for Freedom, the Harlem Writers Guild, attending political and cultural events, hanging out in Stanley's Bar (a rendezvous for many of the Black artists and intellectuals of the Lower Eastside in the early 1960s), and simply wandering the streets of Harlem and the Lower Eastside. These encounters gave him an increased sense of the importance of grassroots artistic and intellectual ancestry to the creation of a new activist Black art and arts institutions in his hometown.[33] This sort of networking allowed him to get beyond a feeling of New Orleans's (and the South's) backward provincialism that had dogged him since his childhood and had motivated him to leave the region. Dent gradually discovered a personal feeling of local rootedness. Perhaps paradoxically, he came to see that connection to the local as significant to national and even international political, intellectual, and artistic networks. Like Amiri Baraka after he returned to Newark and met Amina Baraka, Dent came to believe that what he had taken for provincialism was a vital sort of Blackness that was intensely felt and simultaneously particular and multiple. He searched out the older New Orleans counterparts of New York's Black "shadow world," such as the jazz guitarist, banjo player, and composer Danny Barker, the poet, printer, and historian Marcus B. Christian (whom Dent had known as a child), and the poet Octave Lilly. As discussed in the previous chapter, Christian and Lilly had been involved in activist art and politics since the Popular Front era of the 1930s and the Federal Writers' Project's DHU group based at Dillard University.[34] One of Dent's great personal gifts was his success in convincing his New Orleans peers in the FST workshops (and later southern Black Arts groups) of the importance of such living repositories of African American artistic memory and experience as Barker, Christian, and Lilly. A complementary gift was his ability to woo these older artists from their former antagonistic stance toward the new generation into an appreciation of the work of the young Black Arts cadre.[35]

Dent's take on New Orleans and its Black cultural and political traditions can be seen most clearly in his 1976 self-published collection of poems, *Magnolia Street*. *Magnolia Street* consists of poems that he wrote in the early 1970s as he tried to come to terms with his complicated feelings about his return to his hometown. The book's front cover shows a photograph of the corner at the intersection of Magnolia and Felicity Streets in the old Black New Orleans Central City neighborhood. The picture is largely taken up by a grocery store. Tellingly, though, a telephone pole displays a poster for a show with B. B. King, Fats Domino, and Allen Toussaint, bringing together different strains of popular Black music, from Memphis to New Orleans. The back cover features a Larry Songy photograph of a New Orleans second line. A collection of Songy's jazz funeral portraits as well as line drawings of local stores and buildings by Gilbert Fletcher are interspersed through the text. Immediately not only is a multimedia and multi-generic Black sense of place established but also a Black New Orleans cultural lineage.

Of course, one of the complications of New Orleans is that white framings and interpretations of African American artists and culture and their ancestry are at the heart of the city's image in the United States, especially as retailed by the tourist industry. Dent not only repositions these artists and their work but also foregrounds a historic underground Black understanding of Black music, art, and politics, one that was always there but now is distilled and proclaimed openly, as he does in "Secret Messages," a poem dedicated to Danny Barker:

> tripping past raindrops with the ancient slick-haired
> Jelly Roll piano player
> to listen to some "modern musicians"
> at Lu & Charlie's
> & the old piano player saying
> "they can play a little bit can't they"
> teasing our god of fallen masks
> Check it out . . . [36]

One indication of the local impact of *Magnolia Street,* and Dent's connections to the sort of Black network that he describes in the book, is a letter from the son of the musician, composer, and founder of the proto–Black Arts New Orleans record label AFO Records Harold Battiste Jr., saying how much Battiste enjoyed *Magnolia Street* and ordering ten copies.[37]

Dent became increasingly important to both the administration and artistic activities of the FST. One of Dent's great assets was his range of contacts outside of New Orleans and the South. He was able to gain new support for FST from such ideologically diverse individuals and institutions as Langston Hughes, the NAACP Legal Counsel, Esther Jackson and *Freedomways,* Amiri Baraka, Toni Cade Bambara, Hoyt Fuller, Alice Walker, and Joe Goncalves (editor of the *Journal of Black Poetry*).[38] Perhaps his most difficult task was serving as chairman of the theater's board during the stormy period in 1966 when the FST more expressly moved from being an integrated civil rights institution to a more self-consciously Black theater with a strong nationalist bent. As in SNCC, CORE, and other civil rights groups, this move saw the departure of Richard Schechner and other important white FST workers, such as Murry Levy and Jamie Cromwell (both young white radicals with Old Left connections, particularly Cromwell whose father, John Cromwell, an actor and director, had been blacklisted in Hollywood during the McCarthy era) and financial supporters. This move was not accomplished without considerable conflict and tension.

Even though he was relatively new to the theater, Dent had much practice in the mechanics of organizing and maintaining a writers' workshop thanks to his leadership of Umbra and his participation in the Harlem Writers Guild. So, as he developed his own skills as a playwright, Dent brought a new stability to the FST's workshops. Dent ran the writers' workshop of the FST that coexisted with a playwrights' workshop headed by Robert "Big Daddy" Costley, a native of Buffalo who worked as a news director at a local Black radio station.[39] These workshops were not only practical clinics in the nuts and bolts of the writing of plays and poetry. They were de facto courses in African American literature. They gave the students some models and sense of literary ancestry as well as what was going on in contemporary avant-garde and politically radical Black literary circles—something that Dent was also well suited to do. Thus, these workshops can be seen as some of the earliest forerunners of Black Studies in the Deep South. While the curriculum of many Black elementary and secondary schools in the South during the Jim Crow era already featured work by Black authors, the workshops added new militant Black writing to the mix that would have been missing in the schools.

The professional touring portion of the FST suspended operations in 1967 due to the loss of funding and staffing issues. This period saw the exit of many key personnel, including Moses, Roscoe Orman, and Denise Nicholas, to the theater, film, and television in New York and Los Angeles.[40] O'Neal was himself absent at this time due to a stint in alternative service as a conscientious objector to the draft and the war in Vietnam. Nevertheless, the workshops continued to function, taking on a greater and semiautonomous existence. Since many of the same people belonged to both FST workshops, a decision was made to merge the two. This enlarged workshop started presenting poetry and short plays of its members who, again, were almost entirely local people. The combined workshops began to publish the journal *Nkombo* in 1968 and provided the core of what became BLKARTSOUTH, a performance-oriented, community-based poetry and theater collective that, as the name suggests, saw itself as both a regional organization and part of a burgeoning national movement.[41]

Out of the Gumbo: New Orleans and the Creation of a Regional Black Arts Infrastructure

A key event in the evolution of the Black Arts movement in the South from a loose network of activists to a much more coherent formation is the separation of the writers and theater workshops of the FST from the theater and the creation of BLKARTSOUTH from those workshops in New Orleans. This stimulated the growth of like groups from Texas to Florida affiliated with BLKARTSOUTH, particularly as the new group itself began to tour the region under the names the Black Mind Jockeys (poetry) and Freedom Hair Players (theater). BLKARTSOUTH left FST in 1968 largely over the longtime question of whether the primary focus of the group should be building an indigenous New Orleans (and southern) theater and literary organization geared toward developing local artists, local audiences, and a local body of dramatic work, or whether the company would continue to be oriented toward a professional standard rooted in the theater world of New York City.[42] This argument would continue between FST and BLKARTSOUTH, perhaps reaching is apogee in 1970 when Dent actually called for the dissolution of the FST in a letter to its board:

> The central issue in this conflict, which through the course of our existence appeared in many manifestations, was a disagreement or fundamental indecision over whether the FST should be basically New York oriented theater, with its main ideas, structural controls, finances and personnel emanating from there, or whether it would be a New Orleans southern oriented theater, with a commitment to New Orleans to build a theater meaning, as a consequence, that the controlling ideas and personnel of the theater would come from New Orleans.[43]

To be clear, one of the objectives of almost all the principals of the FST, regardless of their particular take on the questions of amateur vs. professional, the process of development vs. a more finished product, local vs. national, and so on, was to develop a southern Black theater and Black repertoire. And all the participants in the FST writing and theater workshops were committed to developing their crafts and presenting the best work they could. Still, few of the professional touring group came to the FST from the community—though some of those FST transplants, like O'Neal, remained active in the New Orleans African American arts community for decades after the founding (and demise) of the FST.

Again, the BLKARTSOUTH ensemble was far different from the professional touring unit of the FST in that it was made up almost entirely of local New Orleans people. Local here refers to people who were already living in New Orleans prior to their involvement in the FST workshops and BLKARTSOUTH. Some, like Nayo Watkins, came from elsewhere (Pittsburgh in Watkins's case) and had arrived in New Orleans for a variety of reasons, but not to pursue careers in the arts or as full-time political activists in New Orleans (or anywhere else). Others who had grown up in New Orleans, like Tom Dent and Kalamu ya Salaam, left town for longer or shorter periods of time to seek larger cultural horizons (as Dent did in New York) and were exposed to a variety of radical Black political and cultural organizations and ideas, but had returned home for the long haul. Some native-born New Orleanians, like Chakula Cha Jua, never left for any significant amount of time—except perhaps, like Cha Jua, for military service.

BLKARTSOUTH was dedicated to presenting the original work of its members. Its emphasis was more on the process of encouraging and developing New Orleans (and then regional) Black writers and a new nationalist Black cultural infrastructure in the city and, eventually, the South generally than on the presentation. Again, as with the FST professional group, there was an emphasis on the crafts of writing poetry and drama and on the mechanics of performance. But instead of the notion of exposing Black audiences to relatively polished productions of what was seen as the best of contemporary Black and white radical/avant-garde performance by trained theater workers, part of the excitement of the workshops/BLKARTSOUTH performances was a sense of growth of a genuinely popular theater rooted in the grassroots in which new artists and audiences evolved simultaneously.[44]

As Margo Crawford notes, even in the name BLKARTSOUTH, Tom Dent (who coined it) not only attempted to give the group a sense of regional identity but also posed a sense of New Orleans and southern Black multiplicity that he saw as at least partially in opposition to attempts, largely in the North and West, to set prematurely unitary and even stultifying political and cultural ideas of "blackness" and "Black Arts."[45] That is not to say that Dent's recognition of Black multiplicity and a resistance to the imposition of too rigid and too early standards of Black culture, Black identity, and Black politics led him to adopt sentimental white notions of New Orleans multiculturalism that Dent felt divided the Black community there. Dent expressed envy of Black communities elsewhere in the Deep South, especially nearby Mississippi, where culturally and even in phenotype, blackness was far less complicated and prone to confusion than in New Orleans.

As noted previously, there was always a certain feeling of improvisation and contingency in FST performances, especially as the theater interacted with rural or small-town Black audiences on tours in the countryside. Beyond or building on the popular Black penchant for active audience participation, the founders of FST advocated breaking down the "fourth wall" so that the audience was as much a part of the production as the actors, at least in theory:

> During a performance of Martin Duberman's *In White America*, O'Neal opened by telling the audience, "You are the actors." This statement

> expressed the FST's most idealistic goal: to create a democratic theater form akin to the discursive political practices of SNCC. But neither FST artists nor their audiences knew exactly how to achieve this goal. They were interested, more than anything, in creating theatre forms that promoted audience discussion and involvement in the making of the meanings of each production they staged.[46]

BLKARTSOUTH elevated this notion of building something truly new and truly—if sometimes complexly—Black that was of and by as well as for the community to a much higher level. In this, the art of contemporary jazz musicians of New Orleans showed Dent and the other BLKARTSOUTH activists the way. These musicians included the pianist Ellis Marsalis Jr. (whose career ranged from hard bop to soul jazz to the avant-garde to Dixieland) and his now nationally famous family (including Branford and Wynton Marsalis); drummer Ed Blackwell (who found national recognition during his time playing with one of the icons of free jazz, Ornette Coleman); avant-garde clarinetist Alvin Batiste; and banjo player and guitarist Danny Barker (a historically minded musician whose long career, playing, and writing also encompassed virtually the entire gamut of New Orleans jazz, from the early styles through swing, bebop, and post-bop). For Dent, this contemporary scene also contained the modern iterations of the Black New Orleans brass band and second line traditions—themselves engaged with soul/R&B music and various post-bop jazz idioms.[47] At the same time, while concerned with craft, few of the members of BLKARTSOUTH had much ambition to pursue professional literary or theatrical careers as such—which, in essence, meant leaving the South for New York or Los Angeles at the time.[48] (Tom Dent had already done this and returned.) This contrasts with the FST proper in which, as O'Neal (who was one of the proponents of recruiting professional Black actors from New York and Los Angeles even though he himself remained in New Orleans) later noted, there was a constant loss of personnel to New York and Hollywood as actors and directors left to pursue career ambitions in theater, film, and television.[49] The members of the workshops, in large part due to their local ties (and, to be truthful, in most cases, a lack of theater industry connections), were much less susceptible to these sorts of career temptations. Even those who continued to pursue theater and performance more or less full-time, did so in a way that was largely outside the orbit of commercial theater as it is normally understood. For example, BLKARTSOUTH and FST workshop veteran Nayo Watkins long made a living writing and directing local history plays for southern Black communities that were deeply meaningful for those communities, but of little interest to those outside those areas.[50] Some survived working as educators in various sorts of institutions, particularly the New Orleans public schools. Still others eked out livings through various sorts of day jobs. In other words, few of these writers thought of literary or artistic posterity in the sense of the normal metrics of artistic success despite their concern with questions of technique.

Nkombo was similarly devoted to the work of writers rooted in southern Black communities. It first appeared in 1968 as *Echoes from the Gumbo*—soon changing into *Nkombo,* a Kongo word for "runaway slave" that some have suggested was the antecedent for *ngombo,* a shortened Bantu word for the native African plant okra, which was a basic ingredient for gumbo. Whatever the precise etymological derivation of "gumbo," *Nkombo* was not only a more clearly African term for the famous stew that combined a wide variety of ingredients with different cultural origins and associations while remaining quintessentially Black and Louisianan, but also connected Black food culture to popular resistance to slavery and national oppression. New Orleans was and is famous for its indigenous food culture that even most white observers would admit was heavily influenced by Black cooks and Black foodways with roots in Africa. BLKARTSOUTH's engagement with Black foodways as a linked set of metaphors connected African roots with African American struggle. It rejected the notion of a multicultural New Orleans in which an element of blackness is admitted (for the most part) while subsuming (or digesting) it in a white southern New Orleans context in which a certain sort of tolerance is proclaimed while the oppression and continued subjugation of Black people remains firmly in place. In that sense, the BLKARTSOUTH emphasis was on the metaphor of Black foodways as a system, a complex of Black practices that is its own thing. Or if blackness in New Orleans in the South was seen by Dent, Salaam, and other New Orleans Black Arts activists as complex, multicultural in some respects even as it bangs up against Kawaidaist and other attempts to apply a more unitary sense of blackness, it is a Black multiculturalism that is perhaps kin to Crawford's notion of a "Black Post-Blackness."

The first issue of *Out of the Gumbo/Nkombo* features a statement by Tom Dent declaring the mission of the journal (and the FST workshop to which it was still attached): "ECHOES FROM THE GUMBO is a product of the Free Southern Theater writing-acting community workshop which meets weekly in New Orleans. This workshop was created as part of our program because we know for Black theater to have viability in our communities we must have a working tie to those communities—something more than mere performances of plays now and then (no matter how relevant the material). The community must have a stake in the life of the theater. This is the real meaning of a community theater."[51]

Here Dent sets up a reciprocal relationship between the FST, the workshop, and the Black community. For the theater to be viable, he claims, it needs to have a real stake in the community. However, it is also essential that the community have an interest in the life of the theater. There is a bit of ambiguity here about whether Dent is speaking particularly of the FST or is repurposing the timeworn phrase "the life of the theater" in general or both. That is to say that the FST needs the active engagement to remain viable while the community needs theater and art in general (and its own theater in particular) to fulfill a range of political, spiritual, aesthetic, and emotional needs, with liberation and self-determination in all these senses being at the top of the list. The instrument through which Dent sees the FST and the community coming together on a basis greater than the "now and then" performance is the workshop. He argues, contra many in the regular performing unit of the group, that the heart of the FST is the workshops, not the more finished performances of the formally trained touring group of professional actors and theater workers. In this, Dent and the artists who would form the core of the early BLKARTSOUTH are already valuing process over product, transformation (or the possibility of transformation) over a certain sort of fixed ending or stasis. As with Amiri Baraka, who was one northern Black Arts figure they frequently reference in their more theoretical or critical prose, Dent and Salaam in particular see Black music as a sort of improvisational process of blackness that, as jazz reed player and flutist Eric Dolphy once said, disappears as soon as it is played.[52] Crawford also notes that this resembles Baraka's notion that in many respects Blackness is a sound or sonic experience, which is to say that it has a material existence, but is constantly in motion and not fixed, except on recordings that even at their best never capture the excitement or profundity of the live performance.[53]

BLKARTSOUTH, Black Arts in the South, and the Southern (Re)Turn of Black Power and Black Arts

Many of the national organizations of Black Power and Black Arts increasingly turned their attention to the South by the end of the 1960s, resulting in the migration of Black artists and activists to the region to join their counterparts who were already there. Of course, as we have seen, this was not a new phenomenon. In the first place, many Black activists, artists, and intellectuals from the North (and from Africa and its diaspora) had come South to attend HBCUs, where they joined the civil rights movement and the Black student movement that coalesced into SNCC in the early 1960s. Others moved South later to work in SNCC and CORE field operations on the frontlines of the rural and small-town Black Belt. Some writers and artists, such as Askia Touré and Jayne Cortez, headed to the region expressly to work in urban SNCC projects. Again, as discussed previously in this chapter, the FST was significantly a product of that migration (or counter-migration, if you will) South. However, as the Black liberation movement became increasingly "Black," so to speak, and Black Arts and Black Power became increasingly national, both in concept and in practice, the South took on an even greater significance as it became a focus of such groups that arose outside the region as the Kawaidaists (and the various strands of nationalism that would intertwine in CAP), RAM, and the RNA, with great impact on the Black political and cultural infrastructure of the South.

Black artists journeyed to the South from the North and the West, some to live there permanently and others for longer or shorter sojourns. As with Tom Dent, A. B. Spellman (another participant in the Black bohemia of New York's Lower East Side in the 1950s and early 1960s), and Ebon Dooley (who had a literary apprenticeship in Chicago with OBAC), some were southerners who had sought out what they had seen as the wider, less provincial cultural vistas and opportunities of the major cities of the North and West, especially though not exclusively New York. Others were basically Northerners (though often with some family links to the South), such as Touré (who spent his early childhood in North Carolina and Georgia, but grew up in Ohio), David Henderson (a native Harlemite), and Lorenzo Thomas (born in Panama but basically a New Yorker from Queens). Some of these migrants, such as Touré and Henderson, would stay only for a time before moving on again elsewhere. Others, like Dent, Dooley, and Thomas, would remain in the South for the rest of their lives. All of them made important contributions to the creation of new Black Arts institutions, often with institution-building skills and experience gained up North, as well as in the connection of those institutions to Black organizations, institutions, and audiences outside of the South. As will be discussed in the next chapter, many of these migrants (or re-migrants) went to Atlanta, the nerve center of the civil rights movement and major hub of Black institutions of higher education. Others, however, traveled to New Orleans and other cities and towns that became part of the BLKARTSOUTH network from Houston to Miami. This network stretched along the Gulf Coast and inland to cities and campuses near the frontline communities that were the focus of SNCC projects in the Black Belt of Mississippi and Alabama.

As we have seen, Tom Dent in his work with FST and BLKARTSOUTH as it grew out of the FST workshops was an early and prototypical example of the Black Arts southern migration, which, in his case, was a return to his hometown of New Orleans. One can find in this a sort of "return of the native" story that was not uncommon in Black Power and Black Arts as artists and activists from Black communities in what might be seen as provincial cities return home after a time in the metropolis (most often New York but not infrequently Chicago or Los Angeles). No doubt the most well-known version of this, then and now, is Amiri Baraka's return to Newark, New Jersey. But Dent's homecoming to New Orleans happened at almost the same time as Baraka's to Newark. Perhaps surprisingly to some given the touristic veneer of New Orleans that Newark almost entirely lacked, as far as the economy went with regard to Black people, both cities were not unlike as important ports with a sharply declining industrial infrastructure and an emerging Black majority. As Catherine Michna observes about New Orleans in the mid-1960s, "The transformations in New Orleans's social and spatial landscapes mirrored those occurring in cities around the nation. This period of swift transformation from industrialized to de-industrialized urban cores was accompanied by shifts in the production of race- and place-based identities throughout urban and suburban regions in the US."[54] That is to say that in the minds of many white people and in the mainstream media, New Orleans, outside of the tourist areas of the French Quarter and the Garden District, like Newark became a sign of the "urban crisis" attributed to the character and actions of Black people as opposed to the racialized crisis of what William Junius Wilson memorably termed "when work disappears." This sort of reading of New Orleans, even before Hurricane Katrina, can be seen in the frequent admonitions in tour guides of the era (and later) about where never to go and streets never to cross (Armstrong Park, Rampart Street, and so on), admonitions that were almost entirely based in racial fear.

Dent's departure from New York back to New Orleans was an early expression, too, of what might be thought of as an Umbra migration in which members of the proto–Black Arts avant-garde poetry workshop and performance group with its own journal *Umbra* based on New York's Lower East Side departed New York for one reason or another. Ishmael Reed and, ultimately, David Henderson went to Northern California; Calvin Hernton left for London. But a larger number, including Dent, Touré, Thomas, and, for a time, Henderson, traveled South. Ironically, one of the few Umbra poets who stayed in New York, Steve Cannon, was a New Orleans native like Dent. These migrations had a number of consequences for the southern Black Arts movement. They brought (or brought back) to the region writers and artists who had gained valuable practical skills in organizing community workshops, reading, producing journals, and so on that were not tied to a campus. They also strengthened the ties of Black artists in the community and in the academy in the South to audiences and institutions outside the South and sometimes outside the United States. They reinforced a sense of experimentation and a search for new forms that already existed in the South to some degree but now gained a more organized expression with significant influence on the forming of a new Black avant-garde poetry. And, as Margo Crawford notes, they furthered a literary participation of the southern Black Arts movement in what might be thought of as a Black "Global South," strengthening a longstanding connection already in the consciousness of Black New Orleans through its status as a port from the slave era to the present, as seen culturally in everything from continued practice of syncretic African religions to the New Orleans variant of R&B that combined influences of (and exerted influence on) music from throughout the Caribbean and South America.[55]

By 1969, BLKARTSOUTH began performing outside New Orleans. In part, BLKARTSOUTH was able to organize these performances through the contacts forged by Dent and the FST throughout the region, drawing on Dent's wide range of acquaintances, the links made through the civil rights movement (particularly SNCC and CORE), and previous tours of the original FST traveling group. The involvement of many of the members of BLKARTSOUTH in Black Power organizations, particularly ALSC, was also key in extending the group's potential audience throughout the South. Some of the strongest chapters of ALSC were in the South, particularly in Texas, Louisiana, and North Carolina. At one point nearly half the executive committee of the ALSC was based in the South, including the chairperson Dawolu Gene Locke in Houston. As will be taken up at more length in Chapter 5, much of the impetus for such important Black Power groups as the Student Organization for Black Unity (SOBU) and the Youth Organization of Black Unity (YOBU) as well as the popularization of African Liberation Day came from below the Mason-Dixon line, especially through the efforts of Owusu Saudukai (Howard Fuller) and Nelson Johnson in North

Carolina. Again, the sheer concentration of African Americans in the South, especially students at HBCUs, made the region a fertile ground for such organizations and initiatives, significantly transforming the political climate at older educational/political institutions and leading to the creation of new ones, such as Malcolm X University in North Carolina and the Kawaidaist Ahidiana Collective (which did grassroots political work and ran a community school) in New Orleans. As was true of other Black Arts groups elsewhere, not only did the growth of Black Power, and institutions and programs funded by public War on Poverty money, bring the BLKARTSOUTH activists contacts in cities and campuses where they previously had none, it also allowed them to combine political organizing and artistic performance, often in the same venue and at the same event.[56]

BLKARTSOUTH's tours, as well as the orientation and openness of its journal *Nkombo* toward southern Black artists outside New Orleans (particularly along the Gulf Coast and upriver as far as Memphis—in other words, in fairly easy reach of the touring group), inspired African American artists across the region to set up groups in much the same spirit. Some of these artists had previously pursued their crafts in relative isolation or in small and informal groups. Others, particularly actors and playwrights, had been part of college arts programs, both at historically Black schools and at schools that had only recently begun to admit African American students. A number of these theater workers became involved in the local mainstream and experimental theaters of their hometowns as the breakdown of Jim Crow allowed them to audition successfully for these theaters.

However, in other ways Jim Crow lived on. As Memphis actor, director, and playwright Levi Frazier Jr. recalls, the range of roles available to Black actors was exceedingly small, restricted primarily to roles as servants, leading to considerable dissatisfaction among Black theater workers with the status quo.[57] At the same time, news about Black Arts initiatives elsewhere, sometimes brought by the migrant veterans of such northern Black Arts and Black Power and proto–Black Arts/Black Power groups as Umbra, On Guard for Freedom, the Harlem Writers Guild, and OBAC, circulated among these artists on southern Black campuses and in the community, producing tremendous interest and some early efforts to undertake similar initiatives locally, but with a southern focus that southern African American activists, artists, and intellectuals felt had been missing in the new Black theater to that point. As Frazier also remembered, he had read quite a few recent plays by African American authors, such as James Baldwin's *The Amen Corner* (1954), as a young person, but even as a child he wanted to write and stage plays about his native Memphis rather than simply try to read himself into Chicago's South Side or Harlem.[58] As a result, the poetry-performance tours of BLKARTSOUTH—in which the group would write, stage, and act or present almost all its sophisticated, well-rehearsed, socially engaged, *and* local material, and in which *all* the actors would be Black—came as a sort of revelation of what was possible.[59] This inspiration was not only by example but through the direct mentoring of emerging southern Black Arts groups by Salaam, Dent, and other BLKARTSOUTH members.

By this point a number of the leading members of FST-BLKARTSOUTH, especially Kalamu ya Salaam, had increasingly subscribed to the neo-Africanist cultural nationalism of Maulana Karenga's Kawaidaism, making New Orleans a stronghold of Karenga's Kawaida movement in the South. To a large extent, this interest in Karenga's philosophy as a guide to daily life (including political action) and as a powerful vision of an alternative liberated African-centered culture circulated in FST-BLKARTSOUTH through Amiri Baraka's public association with Karenga and Kawaida. This association was significantly inspired by Baraka's desire to build a stable radical Black cultural organization in Newark that avoided the personal and ideological chaos that destroyed BARTS in New York and Black Arts West and the Black House in the Bay Area. In other words, it was Baraka's heroic stature as well as their own desire for institutional stability and discipline that initially drew the interest of Salaam and others to Kawaidaism. Still, Karenga's ability to elaborate and project his vision through his speeches and writings and through the US Organization had much to do with his impact on the Black Arts and Black Power activists of New Orleans—though Salaam, like Baraka, never shared Karenga's rejection of the blues and other forms of Black popular music and, unlike Baraka during his high Kawaidaist period, was not inclined to fully accept the masculinist notion of Black women as "complementary, not equal" and submissive.[60] Karenga's neo-African ideology also helped connect BLKARTSOUTH and its emerging network to Haki Madhubuti, another Kawaidaist who was one of the central figures of Black Arts in Chicago. (Madhubuti, too, early on challenged or significantly ignored Karenga's position on gender.) This link to Chicago facilitated access to the Chicago-based Black Arts/Black Power journal *Negro Digest/Black World* through which BLKARTSOUTH, and later the SBCA, would have its most significant source of dissemination of news about its activities to the larger movement outside the South.[61]

Of course, what made Kawaidaism so useful to many of the BLKARTSOUTH activists was, paradoxically, not only its easily teachable and practical principles for building and maintaining a cohesive organization but also its flexibility. Again, unlike many more centralist Black Power and Black Arts formations, Marxist, nationalist, and Left-nationalist, there was no chairman, no general secretary, no pope, no central committee, no control commission of the Kawaidaist movement. Karenga exerted no direct organizational authority outside of Southern California (where his group US was, in fact, a hierarchal organization). So if a local Kawaidaist in the South wanted to reject important aspects of Karenga's pronouncements on Black popular music and other forms of black popular culture, on Black history, and on gender, they could do so without serious repercussions. That is not to say that Karenga's positions on these things had no influence, but it was possible to take aspects of Kawaidaism that one found practically useful and to participate in national Kawaidaist networks while diverging significantly from Karenga, especially in the area of culture. Some in BLKARTSOUTH, notably Tom Dent (who adopted the pen-name of "Kush" rather than the Swahili names more typical of the Kawaidaists), were really not Kawaidaists in any deep way, though they had some attraction to the neo-Africanist bent of Karenga and US.

A prime example of how this Kawaida-influenced BLKARTSOUTH stimulated the growth of a Black Arts network in the region can be found in Houston, traditionally the center of African American culture and politics in Texas with a deep and long-standing connection to the Black communities of Louisiana and Los Angeles. Black Arts flourished more in Houston than elsewhere in the state, though there were also Black Arts theaters, arts centers, galleries, and workshops elsewhere, including San Antonio, Fort Worth, Austin, and Dallas.

Houston's prominence was not only due to its history and demographics, but also because a nucleus of young political and cultural activists, catalyzed by the touring group of FST-BLKARTSOUTH, formed SUDAN/Southwest in the mid-1960s. In short order, this group became the seed of a dynamic, community-oriented African American arts scene that exists to this day as displayed in initiatives and institutions like Project Row Houses. While few of these writers and artists, until recently, became much known outside the South, SUDAN/Southwest and the Black Arts Center that grew out of SUDAN became the western anchor of a Black Arts circuit that stretched east through New Orleans to Miami.

Of course, there were important local sources of Black Arts. As noted in the previous chapter, painter John Biggers and the Texas Southern University art department that he chaired not only encouraged students to engage with the local Black communities but also helped find places for them to develop their art under the aegis of antipoverty programs like Model Cities. However Black community activists and artists in Houston beyond the TSU campus also became increasingly excited by the news they received about the new militant Black political and arts groups and institutions from California to New York that had received national attention, from San Francisco's Black House and Los Angeles's Studio Watts to Harlem's BARTS and many points in between, both in the so-called mainstream media as well as in the African American press. Early Black Arts groups, particularly from New Orleans, visited Houston, stimulating interest in the new Black politics and the new Black art. For example, early on the FST performed Douglas Turner Ward's *Happy Ending, Second Line Funeral For Uncle Tom* (a sort of New Orleans-focused revue of poetry and folklore), and the absurdist *The Lesson* by Eugene Ionesco in a Fifth Ward park in the summer of 1967.[62] This combination of poetry, Black drama, and international avant-garde theater was typical of FST through much of its early career.

However, it was the BLKARTSOUTH touring group that developed out of the FST's workshops that had the deepest impact on the emergence of Black Arts in Houston. The new currents of Black Power and Black Arts prompted several activists/artists (including Rashaan Cornell Linson, Muntu Thomas Meloncon, Harvey King, Sidney Wilson, and Bill Milligan) to meet in a Fourth Ward parking lot in 1968, a meeting where they discussed the need for a political/cultural group that aimed at organizing and radicalizing young Black Houstonians. Shortly thereafter, they initiated the Progressive Youth Movement in the Fourth Ward. Initially, the organization floundered in trying to find a viable program and coherent ideology that could provide the structure to reach the community in a sustained way. The primary arena in which these activists attempted to serve and transform the community was through antipoverty efforts. One such effort was through the HOPE project of Rev. Earl E. Allen, which had opened a youth center in the Pearl Harbor section of the Fifth Ward in 1968. A number of the Progressive Youth movement core became staffers at the center. These staff members invited the FST-BLKARTSOUTH touring group to perform in Houston in the Fall of 1969.[63]

When Salaam met with the artists and activists of the Progressive Youth Movement after the performances at the HOPE youth center, he not only presented them with the practical experience of creating and maintaining radical Black community-based arts workshops and performing groups he gained through the work of the FST and BLKARTSOUTH, but also shared a coherent and easily taught Kawaidaist ideological vision that could anchor such politicized arts groups. The resulting SUDAN/Southwest collective, poetry and dance performing groups with allied workshops along the lines of FST-BLKARTSOUTH, used Karenga's seven principles to guide both the daily and long-term practice of the collective. Despite the utility of these Kawaidaist principles for giving the group some organizational stability, like BLKARTSOUTH the art promoted by SUDAN/Southwest and its offshoots varied considerably aesthetically and ideologically from Karenga's views in important ways, and was much more engaged with popular Black music (especially the blues) than such an adoption of Kawaidaism might suggest.[64]

Linson, the initial director of SUDAN/Southwest, founded the Black Arts Center that became the mooring for Black Arts activity in Houston in the 1970s, serving as a performance space and school with classes in writing, drama, dance, music, and the visual arts largely supported by various sorts of public and private antipoverty program money under the auspices of Project HOPE. In this, SUDAN and the Black Arts Center resembled Studio Watts in Los Angeles, the Affro-Arts Theatre in Chicago, the New School of Afro-American Thought in Washington, D.C., Dopkwe House in Memphis, the Black Artists Group in St. Louis, and BARTS in New York though with more direct interaction with non–African American cultural institutions than in Los Angeles, Chicago, or New York.[65] Despite the cultural nationalist orientation of the SUDAN group and the leadership of the Black Arts Center, its activities took place within a multicultural context that featured much interaction between African American, white, and to a lesser extent, Chicana/o artists and institutions. In that sense of what we might think of as a radical Black-led multiculturalism, the Black Arts Center was much like the multinational, multiracial Black Arts Poco-Che group in the Mission District of San Francisco, a circle that included at times Ntozake Shange and Umbra Poets veteran David Henderson, Filipina-American Jessica Hagedorn, Chicano Juan Felipe Herrera, and Nuyorican Victor Hernandez Cruz.

So by the end of the 1960s, what one saw in the South—again, particularly along the Gulf Coast and up the Mississippi River—was the emergence of a Black Arts network of activists and institutions growing out of BLKARTSOUTH and *Nkombo*. This network was devoted not only to the building of Black cultural institutions but also to communication and cooperation between those institutions as well as with national Black journals, newspapers, cultural organizations, and political groups in a way that really did not happen in any other region.

CHAPTER THREE

From Campus to Community

The Early Black Arts Movement in Atlanta

Black Arts and Black Power activists in Atlanta did not build the same sort of regional network as did BLKARTSOUTH in New Orleans in the late 1960s and early 1970s. Neither did they move in the BLKARTSOUTH circles to a great degree—though they were certainly familiar with the work of FST, BLKARTSOUTH, and *Nkombo*. Nevertheless, it was during this moment that Atlanta built on its identity as the administrative node of the civil rights movement to become a national center of Black Arts and Black Power. This in turn began to put the South at the center of community-based Black "high" culture as well as popular culture.

The period from 1969 to 1972 saw the rise of new sorts of national Black Power/Black Arts organizations. Obviously, there had been radical Black political and cultural organizations and movements with a national presence, such as RAM, the RNA, the League of Revolutionary Black Workers, the BPP, and the complex of groups and institutions in the Kawaida movement. But these were primarily groups and movements guided by particular ideologies, be it Third World Marxism (BPP and the League of Revolutionary Black Workers), a Black separatist nationalism that revived the CPUSA's "Black Belt Thesis" (RNA), or Maulana Karenga's neo-African Kawaidaism—though, admittedly, RAM was something of a mixed bag of Left and nationalist ideologies. These groups, by and large, saw themselves (and were seen, both positively and negatively) as vanguard, cadre organizations that significantly operated through other mass organizations, such as the more militant chapters of the NAACP (Philadelphia, for example), SNCC, SDS, ACT!, and the Coordinating Council of Community Organizations (which led the boycott of the Chicago public schools by hundreds of thousands of Black students in 1963 and 1964).

The new organizations that appeared at the turn of the decade, such as the Student Organization for Black Unity (SOBU—later the Youth Organization for Black Unity or YOBU) in 1969, CAP in 1970, and the ALSC in 1972, contained strong Marxist and Kawaidaist elements in varying combinations. They were seen as Black nationalist unity organizations that, due to the increasing openness of the African American community to various forms of Black radicalism, were able to engage more mainstream Black politicians and institutions to an extent not seen since the Popular Front, if then. At the same time, they were not generally public-facing mass organizations through which smaller, vanguard radical parties or groups worked as RAM did in a host of organizations or the BPP did in the National Committees to Combat Fascism. The leaders of CAP and SOBU did not, for the most part, belong to cadre organizations operating within the larger groups at the groups' inception—though a number of these leaders would join such groups later in the 1970s. These unity Black Power organizations proved to be key in the greatly increased election of Black officials to office, both North and South.

Black southerners (and northerners who moved South) took on vital roles in the creation of key new national Black Power organizations that would be at the heart of Black Power in the early 1970s—the division and disintegration of which have often been taken as markers of the end of Black Power later in the decade. Quite a few, such as CAP, ALSC, and SOBU/YOBU held their founding meetings in the South, largely because of the demographics of the South (which still featured the largest number of African Americans of any region in the United States) and the sheer number of Black college students due to the overwhelming concentration of HBCUs there—even if the administrations of those schools often kept Black Power and Black Arts at a distance for ideological and for practical reasons. As will be discussed at more length in the following chapter, SOBU/YOBU in particular was a product of radical students at HBCUs in North Carolina who sought to maintain the character and mission of these schools as Black institutions. From the beginning, SOBU/YOBU, led by Black Marxists such as Nelson Johnson and Roderick Bush, had a marked Left as well as nationalist bent with the Marxist elements becoming more pronounced in a Maoist mode by the mid-1970s.[1] Concurrently and not coincidentally, SOBU/YOBU, like most Black Power/Black Arts organizations with a strong presence on campuses, also steadily reoriented themselves toward working-class Black communities, as signaled by SOBU's change to YOBU so as to include working-class Black youth who had never gone to college.

Electoral Politics and the Southern Turn of Black Power and Black Arts

One important decision that many of these organizations took, especially CAP at its founding convention in Atlanta in 1970, was to make the election of Black officials a primary goal as a step toward Black political power and self-determination. In his opening "Coordinator's Statement" at the Political Liberation Workshop of the CAP meeting, Amiri Baraka declared:

> Formally a party must be set up, in areas everywhere there are large concentrations of Black people, that can do the following.
> 1. Work on Voter Registration
> a. To create and increase power of the ballot within the community.
> b. Seize the incentive of campaigns as a means of mobilizing Africans.[2]

There were a number of important cities in the North, such as Detroit, Gary, Cleveland, and Baraka's own Newark where the election of Black mayors, city councilpeople, congresspeople, and so on, was a viable prospect (and in some cases already a reality). However, again, demographics and the mass re-enfranchisement of southern Black voters through the struggles of SNCC, CORE, and other militant civil rights organizations dictated that the greatest potential for successful Black electoral work was in the South. There was simply no other part of the country in which the absolute number and concentration of African Americans held more promise for Black success in the ballot booth. Julian Bond with SNCC had already demonstrated the viability of such campaigns with his successful run for the Georgia House of Representatives in 1965. Ten other Black candidates also won election to the Georgia legislature that year.

Electoral victories, it was seen (and to some considerable degree realized), would give Black people the administration of political apparatuses with significant control over material resources not before available to Black Power and Black Arts groups—or only available through institutions and agencies hitherto not directly administered by Black people. Also, such campaigns allowed CAP and other radical Black Power organizations the opportunity to reach and speak with a mass Black constituency in a way that few other types of political activity did. People were more open to political appeals during election campaigns, and various sorts of mass media were more willing to cover such appeals. This strategy, then, was to build Black political and cultural solidarity (and Black pride) through these campaigns as well as to gain political control of or a direct seat at the table of those institutions and agencies that managed or influenced the distribution of public funds and other resources and materials, cutting out the need for a white middleman or interlocutor. And if one had to deal with non-Black allies (or even enemies) of various backgrounds and political stripes, one would do so from a position of institutional strength rather than of supplication—or even of demand without institutional power.

These electoral campaigns were necessarily an alliance of a wide range of Black political, cultural, and social organizations, many of which were liberal at best and others not easily characterized on any political scale, such as many Black churches that could be liberal and even radical in some ways and profoundly conservative in others. Still, despite the participation of people from a broad spectrum of political beliefs and organizational affiliations, Black Power and Black Arts activists provided much of the energy, grassroots organizational skills, staffs, and street workers. Almost inevitably the arts and culture, including Black music and the burgeoning Black cultural infrastructure, were central features of these campaigns. This, of course, was not simply a southern phenomenon. For example, Stevie Wonder, James Brown, and Isaac Hayes came to Newark in support of Kenneth Gibson's successful mayoral campaign in 1970 and were photographed with Gibson; Wonder walked with Gibson as part of a Black voter registration drive there. Still, a cultural appeal, using music, performance, and other cultural resources, was a notably important and successful part of these southern campaigns.

Tom Dent noted that the increased numbers of Black officeholders, whose campaign organizations were significantly populated and even led by Black Power and Black Arts activists, opened new financial resources to radical Black arts initiatives. He also remarked that artists worked to create new institutions that shored up the popular base of those politicians and reinforced the community work that made it possible for them to be elected:

> Between 1970 and 1974, almost every substantial Black community in the South had a theatre crop up. These theatres attempted to add a cultural dimension to other community organizations and to community activities, generally revolving around the ideology of Black Pride. Theatre is an artistic activity that brings together artists from different genres- writers, actors, musicians, visual artists-and that in performance can provide an audience with a unified experience in a particular space. In that space other valuable things can happen which heighten community awareness: exhibits of visual art, photographs, book and newspaper sales, and, in the case of the Free Southern Theater, group discussions that often had not so much to do with the performance itself but current community issues which in some way the performance might have spurred. It was that coming together, the

> ensemble quality of theatre, the interaction of performers with audience, that made community theatre a very fine medium for carrying forth cultural questions and ideas.[3]

In that way, to build Black art (and Black Arts) was to build Black power (and Black Power) and vice versa.

So, one planned consequence of electoral success as a result of these efforts energized by the new Black Power/Black Arts organizational prioritization of the ballot, such as Maynard Jackson's election as mayor of Atlanta in 1973, is that it succeeded in giving local Black cultural activists access to public arts and educational funding to an unprecedented extent. This sort of access was true in many southern cities and communities where Black people were able to capture high political office, but was notably true in Atlanta because of Jackson's particular interest in the arts (in part, due to the presence of professional musicians and performers in his family) and his desire to be known as the "culture mayor." Also, unlike many other northern and southern cities with Black majorities or near-majorities and successful Black campaigns for mayor and other important offices in the 1970s, such as Gary, Newark, Cleveland, Detroit, New Orleans, and Birmingham, Atlanta's basic economy was healthy and growing, allowing it more resources to support the arts in ways less possible in cities where providing even basic services was a financial challenge.

Thus, what one could characterize as a dialectic of the national and the local arose in which the South became an organizational focus of national Black political and cultural radicalism to an extent not seen since the apogee of direct action civil rights with the result of energizing regional networks of local community-based Black Arts institutions, often closely related to CAP, YOBU/SOBU, and ALSC and their organizing efforts. Of course, what made the growth of these regional arts networks possible was earlier work that southern Black political and cultural activists had done, particularly in the FST and its tours and through the circuits of such civil rights groups as SNCC, CORE, and COFO as they evolved toward Black Power. In this, the Black Power/Black Arts South is perhaps the epitome of what the New Orleans poet, playwright, activist, and historian of Black Arts Kalamu ya Salaam calls the "local/national/local" or L/N/L. That is to say, local initiatives coalesce into a national movement that, in turn, inspires more local initiatives. One of the clearest early illustrations of this L/N/L model during the civil rights/Black Power/Black Arts era can be found in the South through the history of the southern Black student movement, the creation of SNCC with its national significance, and the establishment of locally based SNCC projects that in turn engendered new local groups.[4] Still, this dialectic of local and national with respect to Black Arts projects and institutions was most dynamic in the South in the 1970s, eventually transforming the geography of African American art (and U.S. art generally) so that such southern cities as Atlanta, Houston, and Nashville emerged as major centers of Black expressive culture alongside popular music, which had long been associated with the South.

The City Too Busy to Wait: The Emergence of Atlanta as a Black Arts Capital

Atlanta today is not only a sort of mecca for Black professionals seeking economic opportunity and advancement. It is simultaneously a major center of the arts in the United States, a hub of music, theater, dance, literature, and the visual arts with a plethora of galleries, museums, performance spaces, and so on—a simultaneity that is obviously linked. However, in the early 1960s it was still a city with a very provincial profile in the arts with a cultural infrastructure almost entirely segregated. Relatively few spaces for Black cultural offerings beyond popular music and Black vaudeville existed outside of the campuses of the HBCUs of Atlanta University Center.[5] While some community members did attend arts events at AUC, a profound divide between town (especially the working-class Vine City neighborhood adjoining the campuses) and gown remained—and to some considerable extent remains today.

One of the most significant arts stories of the late 1960s and early 1970s in the South was the expansion of Black Arts projects and institutions off campus and into the working-class Black communities of Atlanta in a conscious attempt to bridge the Black town-gown divide, accompanying as well as stimulating the growth of Black political and cultural power in Atlanta and Fulton County with the result of transforming Atlanta into the arts hub that it is today. As a result of the transformation, there remains a plethora of Black cultural institutions, such as Hammonds House, the Auburn Avenue Library, and the Fulton County Southwest Arts Center. The latter, strictly speaking, is not a Black institution, but it is in a Black community, is basically run and programmed by Black people, and was created through the efforts of Black activists and politicians, even though its offerings could be described as multicultural with a very strong Black component. African

Americans have key roles in the running and programming of major mainstream Atlanta arts institutions to a degree unmatched in longer-established arts hubs outside of the South, notably New York and Los Angeles—including the High Museum of Art, the highest-profile art museum in Atlanta and, really, the southeast. In the area of popular culture, the city came to be a national center of R&B and hip-hop, not only producing such artists as Outkast, Young Jeezy, Future, and the Migos and significantly shaping such hip-hop genres as crunk and trap but also becoming a recording center for the music on such local labels as LaFace and So Def.[6] Tyler Perry's Tyler Perry Studios and its subsidiary 34th Street Films have made Atlanta a Black Hollywood. It is notable that the first film produced by 34th Street Films, Tyler's vehicle for producing noncomedic movies, was *For Colored Girls*, the 2010 adaptation of Ntozake Shange's *for colored girls who have considered suicide/when the rainbow is enuf*, a landmark of the late Black Arts era.

Unlike the case with Houston because of John Biggers's presence at Texas Southern University, the African American arts community that centered on the campuses of AUC was lower-keyed during the 1950s than it had been during the 1930s and 1940s but still a substantial presence. Many of the leading cultural figures of the 1930s and 1940s had moved elsewhere, in part because of new opportunities and in part because of the intensity of the McCarthy era in the South. The sort of politicized art and outreach efforts aimed at the Black working class along the lines of Hale Woodruff (who joined the art faculty of New York University in 1948) and the "Outhouse School" were little seen.

Still, AUC remained the heart of high culture for the Black community in Atlanta with the Summer Theater founded by Anna Cooke and the annual exhibition of visual art that Woodruff established still occurring as yearly events. Of course, other sorts of popular art thrived in working-class Black Atlanta neighborhoods, especially R&B/soul music—jazz remained far less popular. Carlton Molette, who came to Morehouse College as a student from Kansas City, Missouri, recalls that drama teacher Baldwin Burroughs inspired in his students an interest in the process of theater, including the achievement of a high level of competency and the importance of doing things right. Molette got directly involved in the theater through a freshman roommate who was an actor. Since each role required an understudy, Molette found himself drawn into acting and directing and, especially, technical design. Molette left Morehouse to pursue a graduate degree in scenic design at the University of Missouri-Kansas City and the University of Iowa, finding jobs in community theater and theater departments at Tuskegee, Howard, and Florida A&M before he returned to Atlanta and the Spelman theater department in 1969.[7]

Molette came back at a crucial juncture of Black Arts and Black Power in the South. Atlanta was a fundamental site of the radicalization of the civil rights movement and the emergence of Black Power as a social formation. The city saw an intense, if relatively short, period of direct action civil rights efforts in the early 1960s, particularly as the Black student movement emerged after the first 1960 sit-in in Greensboro, North Carolina. Many students from the schools of AUC joined the sit-ins, pickets, and other forms of direct struggle against what Winston Grady-Willis has called the "petty apartheid" of Atlanta.[8] Among the local political consequences of these activities were the launchings of the electoral careers of both SNCC activist Julian Bond and segregationist Lester Maddox, whose notoriety skyrocketed when he handed out ax handles and baseball bats to his customers to ward off potential sit-ins at his fried chicken restaurant.

With SNCC and the SCLC headquartered there for much of the 1960s, Atlanta became the most important administrative center of the movement even as the frontlines of civil rights moved to the "Black Belt" of rural Mississippi, Alabama, and Georgia. It was from Atlanta that SNCC announced its opposition to the Vietnam War at the beginning of 1966—an opposition that Stokely Carmichael (Kwame Ture) and SNCC would tie closely to Black Power and pan-Africanism/Black internationalism. While many SNCC organizers had opposed the war and even spoken against it on occasion, and though SNCC (like SDS) had refused to genuflect before the anti-Communism that the domestic Cold War pressed on the civil rights movement, this was the first public antiwar statement by the organization. It was largely on the basis of this statement that the Georgia state legislature refused to seat SNCC leader Julian Bond, the son of the distinguished Black educator Horace Mann Bond and a Morehouse graduate who had won a seat in the Georgia House of Representatives the previous November. It took another victory in a special election, demonstrations, and a U.S. Supreme Court decision for Bond to assume his seat, beginning a career in the Georgia House and Senate that lasted twenty years. A year later, after keeping his misgivings mostly private, Martin Luther King Jr. (a Morehouse graduate and resident of Vine City) also spoke out forcefully against the war in a series of speeches, including a powerful sermon at Ebenezer Baptist Church in Atlanta on April 30, 1967, where SNCC leaders Ture and Cleveland Sellers were in the audience at the invitation of King.[9]

While SNCC's primary focus was on the rural and small-town frontlines, it turned its attention to organizing in urban working-class Black communities where the majority of Black people lived in both the North and the South by the mid-1960s. In 1966, it began an urban organizing effort in Vine City, the Black working-class community adjoining AUC that was the epicenter of town-gown conflicts in Black Atlanta. The project, known as the Atlanta Project (or sometimes the Vine City Project), took shape and grew through the challenges and opportunities provided by Julian Bond's successful election campaign as well as by the 1966 uprisings in the Vine City and Summerhill neighborhoods in response to police violence. These uprisings inspired King's famous statement in an interview with television journalist Mike Wallace, "And I contend that the cry of 'Black power' is, at bottom, a reaction to the reluctance of white power to make the kind of changes necessary to make justice a reality for the Negro. I think that we've got to see that a riot is the language of the unheard."[10] A number of the staff members of the Atlanta Project, including Gwendolyn Robinson, William Ware, Michael Stewart, Donald Stone, and Askia Touré (then Rolland Snellings), were influenced by various sorts of Black nationalism, especially the variations espoused by Malcolm X before and after his split with the Nation of Islam. They were increasingly concerned with issues of Black self-determination and self-reliance as the proper focus of SNCC and other militant civil rights organizations. Several of the project's members, including Stone, Stewart, and Touré (a poet and later one of the architects of BARTS in New York City), were members of or closely aligned with RAM, a class-conscious revolutionary nationalist cadre organization with headquarters in Cleveland and Philadelphia.[11] In addition to their day-to-day work in Vine City, the Atlanta Project also issued a series of position papers on, among other issues, Black consciousness, the need for organizing in poor Black neighborhoods in the urban South as well as in rural areas, community-based freedom schools, and housing.

The Atlanta Project paper on Black consciousness and self-determination argued for both a nationalist (as members of what was essentially a Black nation) and an internationalist (in solidarity with Black people in the diaspora and on the continent of Africa) sensibility on the part of African Americans and for the Black freedom struggle to be led and staffed by African Americans:

> The necessity of dealing with the question of identity is of prime importance in our own struggle. The systematic destruction of our

> links to Africa, the cultural cut-off of Blacks in this country from Blacks in Africa are not situations that conscious Black people in this country are willing to accept. Nor are conscious Black people in this country willing to accept an educational system that teaches all aspects of western civilization and dismisses our Afro-American contribution with one week of inadequate information (Negro History Week) and deals with Africa not at all. Black people are not willing to align themselves with a western culture that daily emasculates our beauty, our pride and our manhood. It follows that white people being part of western civilization in a way that Black people could never be, are totally inadequate to deal with Black identity which is key to our struggle for self-determination.[12]

The paper suggested that white civil rights workers should devote themselves to fighting racism among white people and gaining white support for Black empowerment rather than working in Black communities, as had been largely the case in the South to that point. And, in fact, one could see such initiatives of SDS and its Economic Research and Action Project (ERAP) efforts in northern urban centers contemporary with and in many respects cousins of the Atlanta Project as answers to this call. While some of the ERAP projects, such as the one in Newark, were in basically African American neighborhoods, others, such as those in Chicago and Cleveland, were in predominantly poor, white communities of Appalachian migrants and their children. However, it is worth noting that while SDS did undertake community organizing among southern white transplants to the North, it did not do so in working-class white communities in the South with the partial exception of the border city of Baltimore.

The position paper on Black consciousness, and the nationalist stance of the project staff, produced tremendous debate within SNCC and antagonism on the part of the group's leadership because of the disruption and confusion that leadership perceived arising from the paper. Still, it anticipated the Black Power slogan famously raised by Ture and Mukasa (Willie) Ricks that same year as well as influencing SNCC's formal decision to become a more strictly Black organization at the end of 1966.[13]

The Atlanta Project paper's impact on Black Arts in the South, especially Atlanta, was significant because it rendered its critique of the present role of white SNCC workers and of white civil rights supporters largely in cultural terms, seeing white SNCC workers as unable to truly understand African American culture in the South on one hand and inhibiting the growth of a new liberated Black culture on the other:

> Too long have we allowed white people to interpret the importance and meaning of the cultural aspects of our society. We have allowed them to tell us what was good about our Afro-American music, art and literature. How many Black critics do we have on the "jazz" scene? How can a white person who is not a part of the Black psyche (except in the oppressor's role) interpret the meaning of the Blues to us who are manifestations of the songs themselves?[14]

Thus, though it has not generally been read that way, one might see this Atlanta Project paper as among the earliest and most influential calls for a Black Aesthetic. It was also an appeal for the creation of new Black cultural institutions based in and for grassroots African American communities in the city of Atlanta as well as elsewhere, institutions that would present and instruct in the evaluation and creation of Black art to everyday people rather than simply a campus audience. It was also, no doubt, a deliberate echo of Malcolm X's appeal for the creation of such an institution in Harlem, one that the founders of BARTS saw themselves as answering, expanded to Black communities across the nation but especially in the urban South.

In 1967, the poet and music critic A. B. Spellman (who had interviewed Malcolm X) arrived in Atlanta from New York, where he had worked closely with his longtime friend and former classmate at Howard University Amiri Baraka and other early Black Arts activists. He found a community of increasingly radicalized and increasingly nationalist activists, many of whom had either just arrived from or were about to head out to the frontlines of civil rights struggles in the South where they faced an intense threat of physical violence and even death. To a considerable degree, it was the violent intransigence of segregationists, both in and out of local government, and the failure of the federal government to effectively curb that violence, that fueled that nationalist-inflected radicalization and its articulation. It was that violent repression, embodied by Kwame Ture's description of his twenty-seventh arrest during a speech at a protest in Greenwood, Mississippi over the shooting of James Meredith by a sniper, that occasioned Ture's famous call for "Black Power."

One result of the increased radicalization of the movement in the mid- to late 1960s, and indeed the politics of the African American community generally (particularly the intelligentsia) during that period, was that the Black colleges and universities of Atlanta were willing to appoint radical political and cultural activists as faculty members to a greater degree than had been the case since at least the 1930s and 1940s. As noted earlier, HBCUs had long been a haven for various sorts of radical artists and scholars. But now such faculty were hired with the knowledge that they would not mute their activism. Vincent Harding, for example, joined the Spelman faculty as chair of the History and Sociology Department in 1965 after several years in the civil rights movement. In that capacity, Harding would be key to the emergence of the Institute of the Black World (IBW) with important consequences for Black Power, Black Arts, and Black Studies. Sociologist Abdul Alkalimat (Gerald McWhorter), one of the founders of the germinal Black Arts group OBAC in Chicago, cowrote the IBW proposal with Harding and joined him at Spelman in a few years, teaching there in 1968 and 1969 before moving to Fisk University in Nashville. And academics already in place at the HBCUs of Atlanta and elsewhere moved toward Black Arts and Black Power. One such faculty member was Stephen Henderson, who chaired the English Department at Morehouse. Henderson became one of the most influential Black Arts literary critics, particularly after the publication of his *Understanding the New Black Poetry* (1973), which seriously attempted to provide a rigorous system for identifying and evaluating Blackness in African American poetry. It should be noted, though, that the experience of activist faculty of the HBCUs of AUC in the 1960s was uneven and that there were limits to faculty activism, especially if faculty sided with students in direct political challenges to college administrations. A couple of more notable examples of Black and white faculty members being punished for exceeding those bounds were the firing of Howard Zinn from the Spelman faculty for his support of student protests against the college code of conduct in 1963 and the expulsion of A. B. Spellman from the Morehouse faculty and Abdul Alkalimat from his position at Spelman for their defense of a 1969 student takeover of a board of trustees meeting in which the students essentially held the board members hostage over the issue of Black Studies.[15]

While the African American arts community of Atlanta was comparatively limited in the mid-1960s and centered on the Black university community, the city saw a small but significant in-migration of African American artists, drawn by the city's identity as an administrative nexus of the civil rights movement as well as a center of Black higher education. A number worked as artists-in-residence at one of the Black campuses.[16] Many, like A. B. Spellman, Ebon Dooley, and, later, Toni Cade Bambara, had some experience with Black Arts and proto–Black Arts organizations elsewhere.

Black artists, intellectuals, and civil rights activists became intertwined to a high degree. For example, falling in love with and marrying the SNCC national office manager Karen Edmonds, Spellman, a native southerner from North Carolina, left New York and settled in Atlanta. Stephen Henderson subsequently hired him to be a poet-in-residence at Morehouse College. Musician and music scholar Bernice Johnson Reagon came into SNCC during its campaign in her hometown of Albany, Georgia, where she became a SNCC field secretary as well as an initiator of the group's Freedom Singers. Moving to Atlanta, she founded the Harambee Singers in 1968. The Harambee Singers appeared at many Black political and cultural events in the city and region over the next few years, including the 1969 founding of Malcolm X Liberation University in Durham, North Carolina. Skunder Boghossian, a Pan-African, surrealist- and jazz-influenced painter, and the leading contemporary visual artist of Ethiopia was hired as an artist-in-residence at AU in 1969. Boghossian had received international recognition before his time in Atlanta. (The Museum of Modern Art in New York bought some his work in 1965. He was the first modern Ethiopian artist represented in the museum's collection.) Despite this international profile, Boghossian committed himself to build local Black institutions beyond the campus. He stayed at AU for three years before beginning a decades-long tenure at Howard University. Kofi (Herman) Bailey (who also went by Kofi X) was also a Pan-African visual artist. He hailed from Los Angeles where he was close to SNCC circles and much influenced by the painter Charles White. Prior to his arrival in Atlanta, Bailey had been part of the Left-nationalist expatriate community in Ghana until Kwame Nkrumah's overthrow in 1966 forced his departure. Bailey mentored many young Black visual artists in Atlanta. Much like Gaston Neal in Washington, D.C., Bailey presented a politicized bohemian persona with a pronounced predilection for alcohol and drugs. He worked closely with SNCC, IBW, the Poor People's Campaign, SCLC, and other local and national Black liberation groups. Numerous movement posters, pamphlets, flyers, and broadsides in Atlanta featured his illustrations, making his art an almost ubiquitous feature on the streets of Black neighborhoods there.[17] Like many leading Black Atlanta artists, he worked for a time at AUC, serving as an artist-in residence at Spelman in 1967. The poet Ebon Dooley, a native of Tennessee and veteran of OBAC in Chicago, moved to Atlanta in 1969 to run the Timbuktu Market of New Africa, a Left-nationalist, Black-owned bookstore (one of the very few in the South at the time) associated with the People's College group that Alkalimat led. Timbuktu was located near Vine City and AUC. Dooley and Spellman in particular would be crucial to the institutionalization of Black Arts in Atlanta.[18]

As the community of local and transplanted Black artists grew in Atlanta, these artists initiated grassroots-oriented cultural projects that attempted to reach beyond the campus into the larger Black community—and beyond the city. These efforts were generally independent of the schools of AUC, but often depended heavily on the academic community for staff, financial support, and audience—much as would happen in the Cardozo-Shaw-Columbia Heights area of Northwest Washington, D.C. Among the first of these initiatives was the Atlanta Center for Black Art. The Center for Black Art provided arts instruction aimed at working-class Black people outside the campuses as well as putting on performances of poetry, theater, music, and other genres and media. It was staffed by the emerging network of artist-activists, including Spellman, Dooley, Boghossian, Joe Jennings (a jazz musician and longtime faculty member at Clark, Spelman, and Morehouse colleges), and Cynthia Washington (another veteran of NAG at Howard University and former SNCC staffer). The center suffered from a lack of funding, limiting its impact on grassroots Black neighborhoods. Still, it helped prepare the ground for the NAC, which flourished under the Maynard Jackson administration, and which will be discussed at more length in chapter 5. Basically, the Black Arts Center gathered together artists and oriented them toward the training of new artists outside of the sort of programs offered by the HBCUs, which had previously done most of the training and credentialing of Black artists and teachers of art in the South. It also brought local Black artists as well as significant artists from outside the region to the attention of the public, hosting one of the first major solo shows of painter and graphic artist Elizabeth Catlett in the United States in 1972. Catlett, whose career in the United States suffered during the McCarthy era, also had shows at the Howard University Art Museum and the Studio Museum in Harlem that year, representing the earliest important solo installations of her work in museums outside of Mexico.

Much like Tom Dent and the BLKARTSOUTH circle in New Orleans, A. B. Spellman also saw a need for a journal to serve the southern Black artists, especially the growing Black Arts community in Atlanta. He tried to answer that need with the journal *Rhythm* in 1970, intending to give local artists a means of reaching an audience outside of Fulton County since they were mostly ignored by the national Black Arts/Black Power journals based in New York, Chicago, and the San Francisco Bay Area: "*Rhythm* is based in the southern u.s. and will focus on southern readers, writers and realities. However, we will publish any and all materials made to us which clarify in a relevant way the future, present, and past of African peoples."[19]

In point of fact, the writers from the Deep South who published in the journal were almost all based in Atlanta. (Quite a few writers from the Midwest and the Northeast also had work in *Rhythm*.) None of the BLKARTSOUTH network in New Orleans, Houston, Miami, and elsewhere appeared in the pages of *Rhythm*. Of course, few, if any, of the leading Black Arts activists of Atlanta showed up in *Nkombo*. This raises the question of why there was not more interaction between Black Arts in Atlanta and the areas in which BLKARTSOUTH operated, particularly New Orleans and the Gulf Coast from Houston to Miami. It was not as if the activists of Atlanta were not aware of those in New Orleans and vice versa. After all, the FST had performed in Atlanta. In fact, the Center for Black Art hosted the FST in a 1972 staging of, among other plays, Carlton and Barbara Molette's *Rosalee Prichett*.[20] As a Morehouse College graduate with many movement connections (not to mention through his father as president of Dillard University), Tom Dent undoubtedly had personal contacts to the scene in Atlanta too—though these links bore more fruit in the middle 1970s than in the 1960s and early 1970s. Certainly, with Atlanta's position as the headquarters for SNCC and the nerve center for the civil rights movement, the early FST founders all had some considerable knowledge and contacts there from their COFO/SNCC days in Mississippi, even if New Orleans was located in what was basically CORE territory. And many of the Atlanta activists who had been in SNCC had their own experiences in Mississippi, Alabama, Florida, and other states in which BLKARTSOUTH operated. Some of the BLKARTSOUTH activists, such as Kalamu ya Salaam, have suggested that this was due to the more academic orientation of the movement in Atlanta, but the disjuncture between Atlanta and New Orleans, especially in the early days of the Black Arts era, remains something of an open question.[21] Still, the idea of *Rhythm* being of, by, and for the Black South did clear the way for later collaborations and communications between the activists of Atlanta and New Orleans. There was a considerable interchange from early on between Atlanta and Washington, D.C., also an important civil rights administrative center and hub of Black higher education where important southern Black Arts and Black Power activists from Atlanta later moved, including Spellman, Reagon, Judy Richardson, Charlie Cobb, and Joyce Ladner.

Like the Center for Black Art, with which it was affiliated, *Rhythm* was independent of the Atlanta HBCUs, though many of its staff, contributors, and audience members were associated with the AUC schools as faculty members, students, or alumni. A number, like Stone and Reagon had been SNCC organizers in Georgia and elsewhere in the Deep South. Its staff and contributors included Amiri Baraka, the Washington, D.C. poet Gaston Neal, the Indianapolis poet, essayist, and editor Mari Evans, musician Marion Brown (born in Atlanta, but at that time living in New Haven, Connecticut), and Atlanta-based Pearl Cleage, Michael Lomax, Kwame Ture, Reagon, Bailey, Dooley, Stone, and Spellman.[22] The general ideology of the journal was a mixture of Left nationalism and cultural nationalism, encompassing both the Kawaidaist strand of nationalism that would dominate the 1970 founding convention of the CAP in Atlanta and Ture's more Marxist-oriented version of Pan-Africanist nationalism: "*Rhythm* is committed to Revolutionary Pan-African Nationalism, which we broadly define as the recognition that people of African origin did not cease to be Africans because they were enslaved; that we are citizens of Africa, responsible to work with other African people, wherever they are, to build liberated zones which ultimately can merge in the new Africa of the 21st century. *Rhythm* sees African people as having no moral or legal responsibility to the west except to oversee its destruction."[23] This fusion of Kawaidaism, Nkrumahist and Tanzanian African socialism, and Marxism prefigured similar hybrids in the South, particularly along the Atlantic seaboard and in Nashville. As will be noted below, Dooley, Cleage, and Lomax contributed in different ways to the growth of African American arts organizations in Atlanta and elsewhere during the twenty years that followed the founding of *Rhythm*.

Spellman, Alkalimat, and Henderson played significant parts in the genesis of one of the most important of the early independent Black Power/Black Arts institutions of Atlanta, IBW. IBW, the first Black think tank, from the beginning saw the promotion of African American culture and art as one of its primary tasks. Like other early independent Black Power/Black Arts institutions in Atlanta, IBW had strong connections, though not formal affiliation, with the schools of AUC. IBW was initially conceived in discussions between historian and activist Vincent Harding at Spelman and Henderson at Morehouse. As early as 1967 they began to talk about a research center inspired by W. E. B. Du Bois's early twentieth-century vision of an institute "which would develop a hundred-year study of the Black Experience" as well as help undergird the incipient Black Studies movement that was emerging from such schools as San Francisco State College (now University), Cornell University, Merritt College, and Wayne State University and root Black Studies on the campuses of HBCUs across the South with the intention of transforming them into truly Black universities.[24]

The murder of Martin Luther King Jr. galvanized Harding and Henderson beyond speculative discussion and provided an opening for the realization of IBW as they joined with other Atlanta artists, scholars, and activists, including Spellman. Initially, they imagined that the institute would be affiliated with the AUC schools. However, Atlanta University was cool to the idea because it feared that the public sponsorship of such a project would alienate donors who would see the institute as too radical. So when Coretta Scott King asked Harding to head a Martin Luther King Jr. "documentation center" to commemorate Dr. King and his work and to document the civil rights movement that emerged in the wake of *Brown v. Board of Education* in 1954, Harding suggested that an Institute for Advanced Afro-American Studies be included as part of the memorial center. Coretta Scott King agreed with Harding's suggestion.

Spellman wrote a letter in early 1969 that invited artists, educators, and activists to come to Atlanta that March to discuss IBW and consider serving on its advisory board. Harding, Henderson, and Spellman were then joined by sociologist Alkalimat, political scientist William Strickland, journalist Lerone Bennett, historian Sterling Stuckey, scholar of Black education Chester Davis, and sociologist Joyce Ladner as senior research fellows of the institute, now named the Institute of the Black World. Like Harding and Spellman, most of these scholars had histories as political and cultural activists. Strickland had been a leader of the National Student Movement, intended as a sort of northern analogue to SNCC but focusing on urban Black neighborhoods. Joyce Ladner had been active in SNCC itself. Alkalimat, as previously noted, had been one of the founders of OBAC in Chicago. Stuckey, also from Chicago after his childhood in Memphis, had been an active member of CORE and initiator of the Amistad Society, a left-leaning community group dedicated to the study of Black history and culture with close ties to the SNCC Freedom Schools. IBW began running seminars in 1969: Henderson on Black poetry, Davis on Black children and public education, Harding on Black biography, Strickland on Black radical politics of the twentieth century, and Ladner on the Black family and social policy. IBW issued its first "Black Paper," Bennett's *The Challenge of Blackness*, in 1970.[25]

As can be seen from the above list of seminars, the study and promotion of African American art and culture, particularly literature, were among IBW's early priorities. Vince Harding later recalled in a conversation with his daughter Rachel Harding, "We were trying to put forward the idea that Black scholarship and Black activism were not meant to be separated; that they should have some connection and relationship to each other and that all of that should be permeated by the arts as well. Steve Henderson sounded like you sometimes, Rachel; he never let us forget how absolutely crucial it was to keep the artists coming in, being there, being present. I remember one of the first artists was Marion Brown, the saxophonist, and also the visual artist, Kofi Bailey."[26]

As Harding also remarks, this emphasis on art reflects the prominent role of artists and literary scholars, such as Henderson and Spellman, in creating the institute—though Spellman was forced to leave Atlanta not long after the founding of IBW due to his support of the Morehouse student action holding the board of trustees hostage in 1969. Of course, both Henderson and Spellman were famously engaged with other artistic genres and media than literature—in fact, Spellman was probably better known nationally as a critic and historian of jazz, especially for his *Four Lives in the Bebop Business* (1966), than as a poet. And many of the IBW founders who were not formally artists or critics were deeply immersed in the arts. Stuckey, a historian who wrote on such varied artists as Paul Robeson and Herman Melville, was the son of one of Chicago's leading Black poets, Elma Stuckey. Once again, Alkalimat conceived OBAC with the journalist Hoyt Fuller (editor of *Negro Digest,* later *Black World,* the most important Black journal of the Black Power/Black Arts era) and the poet Conrad Kent Rivers.

The seriousness of IBW's concern with art and culture can be seen in the second point of its "Statement of Purpose and Program": "The encouragement of those creative artists who are searching for the meaning of a Black aesthetic, who are now trying to define and build the basic ground on which Black creativity may flow in the arts. Encounters among these artists on the one hand, and scholars, activists, and students on the other, must be constant in both formal and informal settings."[27] Here IBW takes up the widespread Black Arts imperative, one that had early on been articulated by the Atlanta Project of SNCC, to develop not only a distinct and liberated African American art created, disseminated, and judged by Black people but also Black aesthetic principles or criteria through which that art might be made, evaluated, and taught. At the same time, it is worth noting that IBW did not attempt to actually codify a "Black Aesthetic," only to foster a discussion. IBW also brought in nationally known out-of-town artists, both older and younger, such as the poet, educator, and novelist Margaret Walker, choreographer and folklorist Katherine Dunham, poet and publisher Haki Madhubuti, and musician Marion Brown, and supported local artists such as Kofi Bailey and Ebon Dooley.[28] Like the seminar leaders, these artists sought to provide an internationalist overview of the arc of Black art and culture in Africa and its diaspora. The formal opening of IBW featured a particularly stellar assemblage of older and younger, local and nationally known black artists, including Walker, Dunham, Dooley, the Harambee Singers, Haki Madhubuti, Val Gray Ward, Ojeda Penn, and the Black Image Theatre Group.[29]

Once more, it is typical of the earlier Black Power/Black Arts institutions in Atlanta that IBW was independent of the AUC schools, in part because Atlanta University, Morehouse, and Spelman did not want to be publicly identified with Black Arts, Black Power, and Black Studies, even as those schools employed many of the key figures of the institute and as its students, faculty, and graduates provided a support community that made IBW possible. In turn, IBW not only had an important national impact, particularly on Black Studies, but also locally as a fulcrum of the evolving and intertwining Black political and artistic community. Even during the later years of IBW when it focused much more on education and the social sciences and far less on directly promoting black artistic production, its staff continued to interact with local artists and such national artistic and intellectual institutions as *Black World*, Third World Press (which printed a number of IBW's "Black Papers"), the *Black Collegian*, and *Black Books Bulletin*.[30] Michael Lomax recalled,

> And we're in the middle of the Black Arts Movement and, you know, neighborhood art centers are developing and cool artists are there and, you know, you're—there's a black bookstore and you're reading black poetry and the IBW is, you know, Institute of the Black World [Atlanta, Georgia] is having, you know, Mrs. Du Bois do—I remember, I remember one evening, this was the, you know, a classic evening, an IBW event. Shirley Graham Du Bois is there and Coretta Scott King, in African garb, recites poetry. I mean, it's just, there's things that you wouldn't believe.[31]

These independent Black Arts and Black Power organizations continued to intersect with and rely on the AUC community in vital respects. A dynamic, if somewhat shifting Black theater community began to develop at AUC, particularly through the work of Carlton Molette, Barbara Molette, and Baldwin Burroughs with the Spelman drama program, the Morehouse-Spelman Players, and the AU Summer Theater. The dramatic programs and institutions of AUC provided a training ground for theater workers who went on to national careers as actors and directors much as they always had. However, many of these graduates increasingly engaged with new Black Arts theaters and dramatic works that interfaced with local community institutions, as well as with the larger Black Arts and Black Power movements. Some of these AUC graduates went on to start local companies and others often remained tied to the Atlanta Black theater community even after they attained national recognition. The Black Image Theatre was started in the late 1960s by what was essentially a group of alumni of the AUC schools. One of the founders, director and actress Andrea Frye, became a mainstay of African American theatre in Atlanta, often returning even after she no longer permanently lived in the city as her national career blossomed. The film star Samuel L. Jackson, a former Morehouse drama major who participated in the student actions of 1969, and his partner the native Atlantan and Spelman alumna LaTanya Richardson (who was nominated for a Tony Award in 2014 for her portrayal of Lena Younger in a revival of *A Raisin in the Sun*) began their professional careers in Atlanta at the Black Image Theatre. The poet, playwright, novelist, and columnist Pearl Cleage was a Spelman graduate in 1971 and later a Spelman faculty member whose career as a playwright was significantly nurtured at AUC and took off in the 1980s. Like Frye she has remained a pillar of the Atlanta theater community. The actor Bill Nunn, another longtime Atlanta theater mainstay, was also Molette's student at Morehouse in the 1970s and later an artist-in-residence at Spelman. Nunn played many film character roles, including that of Radio Raheem in Spike Lee's *Do the Right Thing*—Lee, too, was another Morehouse student in the 1970s.

Beyond the training of Black actors, playwrights, directors, and theatrical technicians, Burroughs and the Molettes did much to promote a historical and internationalist sense of Black theatrical practice and a Black repertoire. Burroughs made sure that the Spelman-Morehouse Players staged works by African and diasporic (outside of the United States) playwrights as well as by African American dramatists, including such local artists as the Molettes and Pearl Cleage. The Molettes, besides teaching, directing, and coauthoring plays, labored to uncover the history of the African American theater. Carlton Molette researched and compiled a bibliography of hundreds of plays written by African American authors over two centuries, dispelling the notion that Black drama in the United States was a relatively new and underdeveloped tradition. One practical contribution of Molette's archival work is that it greatly increased the number and historical sweep of works by Black playwrights accessible to African American theaters. Barbara Molette not only did this sort of scholarly archeology, but she was one of the chief chroniclers of the contemporary Black theater scene in Atlanta for African American journals outside of the city, notably *Black World*.[32]

At the same time that the theater programs and institutions at AUC mentored Black theater workers who would go on to have a large national impact as well as eventually anchoring local institutions outside the campus, they seem to have been little engaged with the regional community-based manifestations of the Black Arts movement in the South beyond Atlanta. The Burroughs, the Molettes, and the theater workers on and off the Black campuses of Atlanta knew about such groups as BLKARTSOUTH, but nevertheless were only marginally involved with them for the most part until the rise of the Southern Black Cultural Alliance. Perhaps not surprisingly, the programs at AUC were much more connected to their counterparts at other historically Black schools, particularly through the National Association of Dramatic and Speech Arts (an organization of theater workers, scholars, and educators primarily on historically Black campuses founded by Sheppard Randolph Edmonds in 1936 in the face of Jim Crow discrimination and exclusion) and its journal *Encore* (edited for a time by Carlton Molette), than to community theaters and Black Arts organizations in other parts of the South. The one exception was the formal FST touring group and John O'Neal in New Orleans. The FST frequently came to Atlanta.[33] The Molettes regularly sought the expertise of O'Neal in the area of fundraising, and O'Neal often consulted the Molettes about technical matters.[34]

However, what these younger radical artists, intellectuals, and activists did do in their efforts to reach beyond AUC, if not always the South beyond the Atlanta metropolitan area, was to engage with new Black electoral politics efforts, particularly those of Maynard Jackson in his mayoral candidacy as part of the imperative toward Black self-empowerment. This engagement was significantly in response to the call of CAP's 1970 founding convention in Atlanta, prioritizing the election of Black officials, even if CAP was not organizationally able to establish firm roots in the city. Such electoral success in turn led to the establishment of the NAC and, ultimately the Hammonds House Museum, the Auburn Avenue Research Library, and the Fulton County Arts Council's cultural centers, leading to an institutionalization and public support of grass roots and often radical Black art to a degree not seen anywhere else in the United States.

Kawaidaism had less direct impact along the Atlantic seaboard than the Gulf Coast of the South. While cultural nationalism certainly influenced the nationalist-Marxist hybrids found from Washington, D.C., to Georgia, and Marxist nationalists like Abdul Alkalimat publicly maintained a respect for Kawaidaism, there were relatively few important clearly Kawaidaist groups in the manner of the Ahidiana Collective in New Orleans. Nevertheless, as will be discussed at more length in Chapter 5, the 1970 founding convention of the then Kawaidaist CAP confirmed the city as a center of the new Black politics and culture.[35]

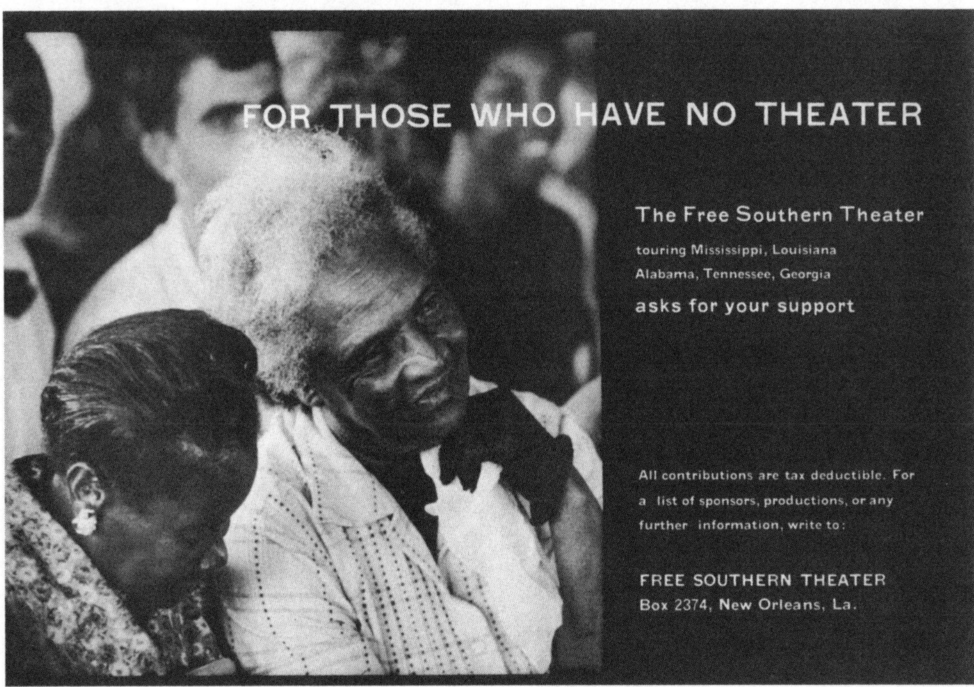

Free Southern Theater Poster (Tom Dent Papers, courtesy of the Amistad Research Center, New Orleans, Louisiana).

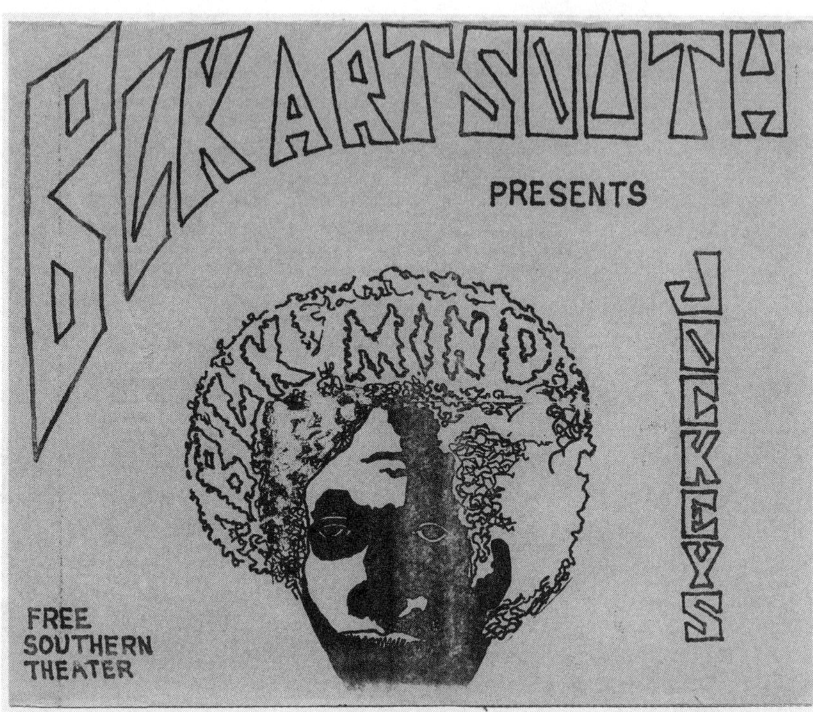

SUBSCRIBE NOW | **BLKARTSOUTH** | **SUBSCRIBE NOW**

FREE SOUTHERN THEATER
1716 N. MIRO
NEW ORLEANS, LA. 70119

___ NKÕMBÕ a journal of blk poetry $4 per yr

___ BLUES MERCHANT by val ferdinand $1 each

___ IMPATIENT REBEL by renaldo fernandez $1 each

___ DARK WATERS by quo vadis gex $1 each

___ I WANT ME A HOME by nayo ola $1 each

___ VISIONS FROM THE GHETTO by raymond washington $1 each

NAME ____________________

ADDRESS ____________________ (ZIP CODE)

MAKE ALL CHECKS PAYABLE TO FREE SOUTHERN THEATER

BLKARTSOUTH/Black Mind Jockeys Insert in *Nkombo* (Tom Dent Papers, courtesy of the Amistad Research Center, New Orleans, Louisiana).

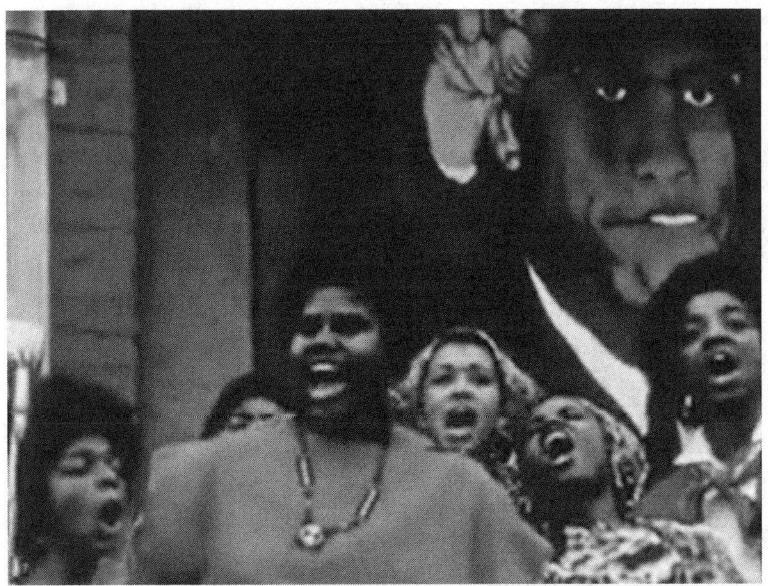

Bernice Reagon and the Harambee Singers at the Opening Celebration of Malcolm X Liberation University, Durham, North Carolina, 1969 (St. Clair Bourne, *Malcolm X Liberation University*, *Black Journal* segment, 1969, courtesy of WNET).

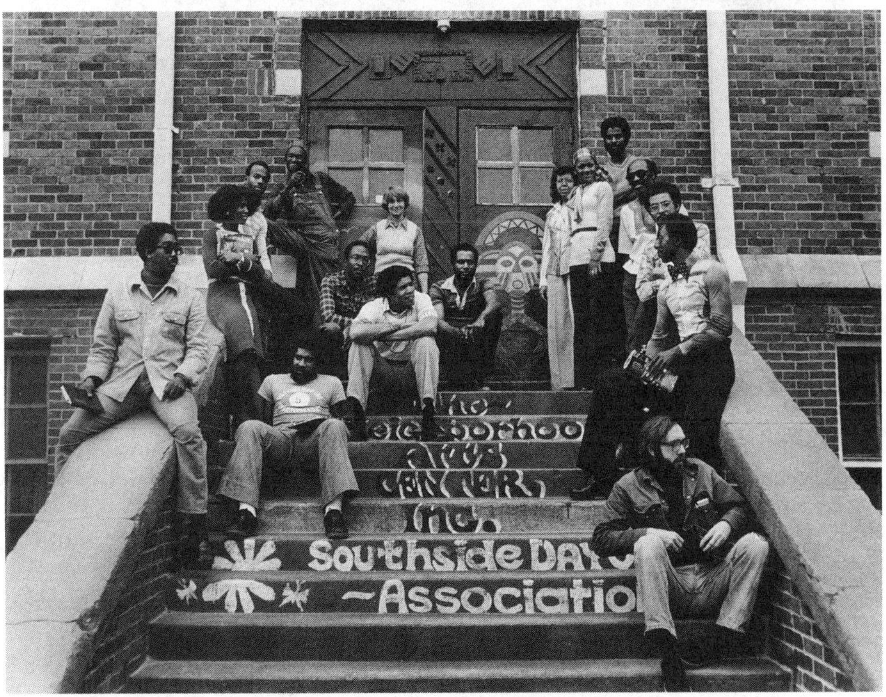

"NAC Staff Photo 1977": Neighborhood Arts Center, Atlanta. Photograph by Jim Alexander (Jim Alexander Collection, courtesy of the Auburn Avenue Research Center, Atlanta, Georgia).

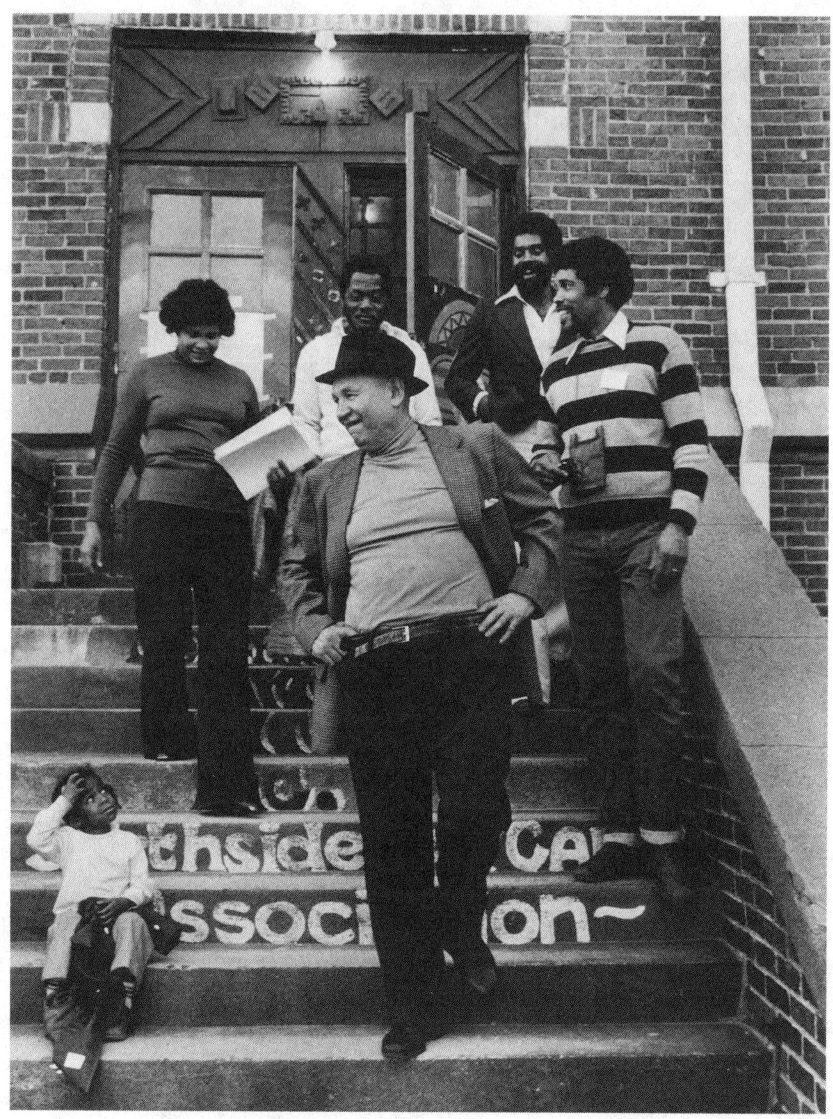

“Romare and Nanette at the NAC 1978”: Romare and Nanette Bearden Visit the Neighborhood Art Center, Atlanta. Photograph by Jim Alexander (Jim Alexander Collection, courtesy of the Auburn Avenue Research Center, Atlanta, Georgia).

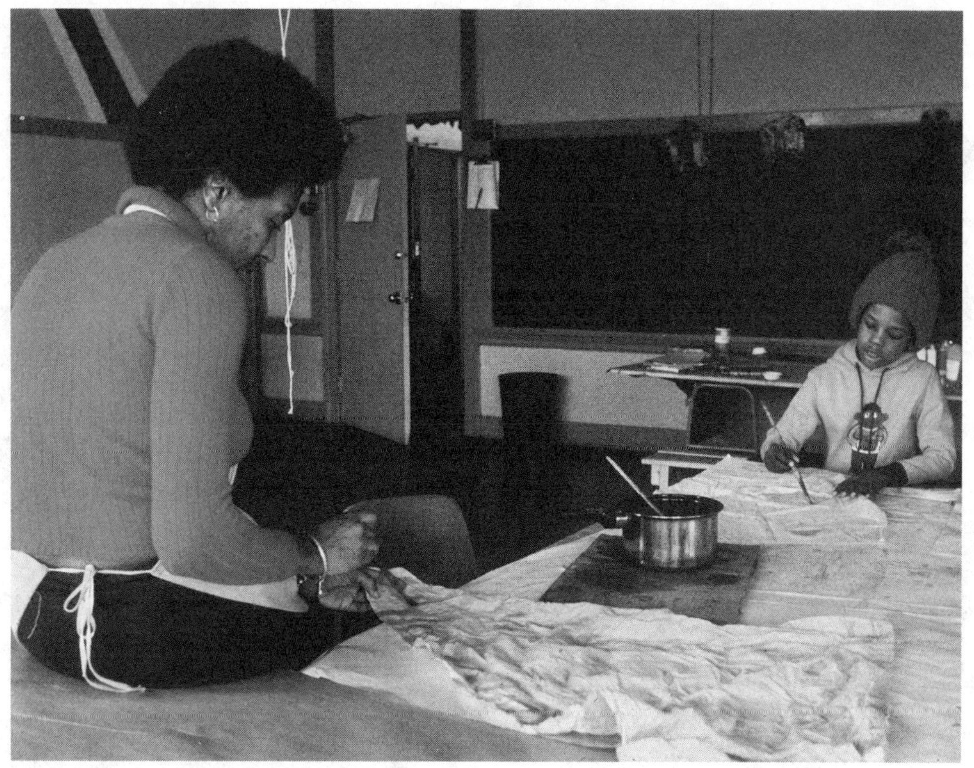

“Tina Teaching 1979”: Neighborhood Arts Center. Photograph by Jim Alexander (Jim Alexander Collection, courtesy of the Auburn Avenue Research Center, Atlanta, Georgia).

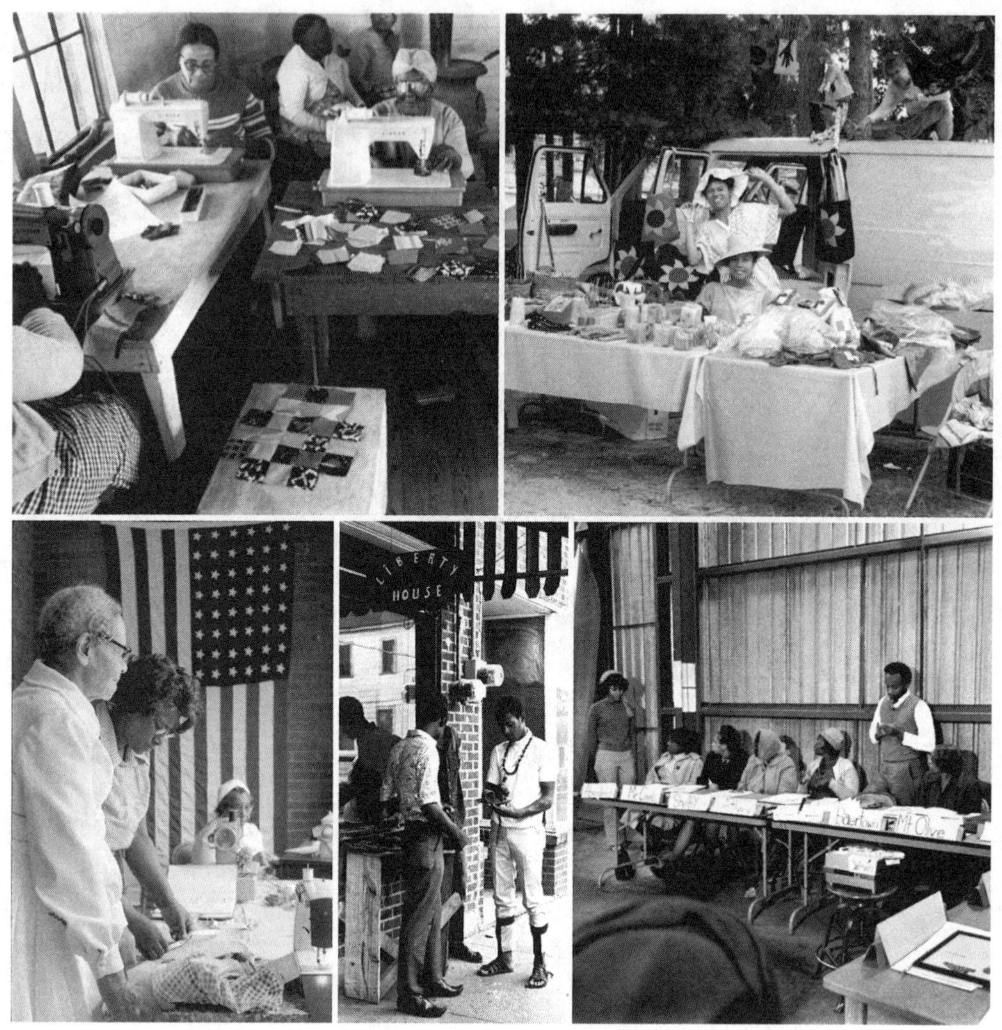

The Liberty House Craft Cooperative, Jackson, Mississippi.
Photographs by Doris Derby (courtesy of Doris Derby).

CHAPTER FOUR

Black Arts, Black Studies, Black University

Washington, D.C., Nashville, and North Carolina

Historically Black colleges and universities (HBCUs) are spread throughout the South and the border states, with a handful in Pennsylvania and Ohio. By the 1960s, their students and recent graduates provided much of the rank-and-file and grassroots leadership of everyday civil rights activism in the South. While the presence of HBCUs might be considered a defining, if underconsidered, characteristic of the entire region, these institutions took on a special importance in certain cities and states, notably Nashville, Washington, D.C., Atlanta, and North Carolina, because of their intellectual reputation and sheer size and number. In these places, Black Power and Black Arts first took root on the campuses and in the intertwined civil rights community of activists and organizations.

In Washington, D.C., Nashville, and Durham, Raleigh, Winston-Salem, and Greensboro, North Carolina, these early Black Arts and Black Power initiatives were closely tied to the rise of Black Studies and visions of the Black university serving the African American community, ultimately forming an important part of the infrastructure of a liberated Black nation. These efforts in the Upper South were in close communication not only with each other but also with their counterparts in Atlanta. While Atlanta's trajectory was ultimately somewhat different even than Washington, D.C., because of the opportunities for the institutionalization of Black Arts presented by the administration of Maynard Jackson, Black Arts and Black Power in all these cities were distinguished by powerful currents of Marxism combined with cultural nationalism to a degree not seen elsewhere.

It needs to be recalled that the professoriate outside of the HBCUs (and, with respect to gender, of predominantly white women's colleges) was overwhelmingly white and male at the beginning of the Black Arts and Black Power era in the mid-1960s. Frankly, this remained true into the 1980s and is still true even now at the level of full professor and the higher ranks of administration of a great many predominantly white institutions of higher education.[1] But in the 1960s, the whiteness and the maleness of the faculty of non-HBCUs (and non-women's colleges) was profound. The whiteness of the student bodies of most non-HBCUs, even urban public institutions in cities with large Black populations, was striking until the end of the decade. At my own campus of the University of Massachusetts Amherst, for example, there were more Africans studying in an agricultural program designed to aid African farmers than there were African Americans until the end of the 1960s and the founding of the W. E. B. Du Bois Department of Afro-American Studies. Many of the early members of the Du Bois department had significant ties to the HBCUs of Washington, D.C., Atlanta, and Nashville. The core of the new department was a group of Black graduate students who had been directed there by Sterling Brown to study with Sidney Kaplan, a pioneer of the interdisciplinary study of art, literature, and history, with an emphasis on African American art, literature, and history.

Black Studies initially emerged out of Black activists and educators in K-12 education, fighting first for community control of public schools in their communities. Practically, given the intertwined segregation of residential housing and educational systems in U.S. cities, this meant Black control of majority African American schools, including the idea of a relevant Black curriculum. As attempts at community control of schools were frustrated in New York and other U.S. cities, the notion of Black-run independent schools became increasingly popular among Black Studies advocates.[2] A similar dynamic appeared in the subsequent Black Studies movement in higher education. As in the closely linked Black Power and Black Arts movements, the ideologies and practical approaches (or praxis, if you will) of the leaders and rank and file of the Black Studies movement varied—and sometimes clashed sharply. However, for the vast majority of its advocates Black Studies was not simply about the inclusion of African American history, art, culture, thought, and so on, in the curriculum of U.S. colleges and universities or the integration of significant numbers of Black students and professors into the student bodies and the faculties of non-HBCUs—though certainly many in the movement supported those changes. Rather, it was about the establishment of Black institutions.

While there was overt and covert opposition to African American inclusion in the student body, faculty, and curriculum among more than a few white higher education administrators and faculty, generally most white faculty members and administrators would at least publicly support that inclusion to one extent or another by the 1960s. Of course, to this day, a certain "common sense" remains among some white educators that, say, devoting more space or even equal or near-equal space to Melvin Tolson as compared to Ezra Pound in an anthology of American" poetry is so obviously wrong that it needs no real argument. What was far more controversial (including among Black administrators and some faculty at HBCUs) was the notion of Black Studies as the beachhead of the "Black university"—that is, a Black institution, whether new and freestanding, new and located in a larger non-Black school, or a transformed HBCU, devoted to the self-determination of the Black community and producing a Black intelligentsia of that community and serving that community.[3]

In many of the early Black Studies units in non-HBCUs, their founders saw Black Studies departments as essentially Black colleges or universities operating more or less autonomously within the shell of the larger institution—or at least that was their objective. That is to say that the wide-ranging interdisciplinary character of Black Studies was not only a recognition of the value of interdisciplinary "area studies" work. Such interdisciplinarity was also a result of the belief that Black Studies departments should provide everything that Black students needed to get an education that would enable them to return to Black neighborhoods upon graduation and be of use to those communities in their efforts toward liberation and collective self-determination and self-development.[4] However, many of those departments and programs encountered much resistance to the idea of a Black university aimed at Black students housed within a larger institution. Consequently, the idea of freestanding, independent Black universities not answerable to white administrators (and white faculty members who traditionally were much involved with administration through practices of faculty governance) and white-controlled funding, be it controlled by boards of trustees or state legislatures (or in the case of Washington, D.C., the U.S. Congress) gained much traction within the Black Studies movement.

The HBCUs were somewhere in between, being freestanding institutions with largely Black student bodies, African American administrators for the most part, and very substantial numbers of Black faculty, including supporters of Black Arts, Black Power, and Black Studies—though often dependent on funding from white donors and/or money adjudicated by white politicians. The administrations and faculties of the HBCUs were almost always supportive of the general thrust of civil rights efforts, if sometimes cautiously, but often far more dubious about Black Power, Black Arts, and Black Studies for both ideological and practical reasons, including fears about loss of funding or accreditation. While the HBCUs were Black-run institutions largely for Black people with substantial personnel, resources, and physical plants and thus seemed far more likely as sites for the new "Black university," Black Studies at the HBCUs was driven by Black students and student activism (with the support of some faculty and community members) much like it was at many predominantly white institutions of higher education. The more academically elite HBCUs, such as Howard University and the AUC schools, experienced intense student activism, including sit-ins in main administrative buildings and offices, trying to establish Black Studies on those campuses.[5]

Of course, administrators recognized that these efforts to create Black Studies departments were not simply attempts to introduce a new sort of area studies and new courses to the curriculum but also a foothold for the project of transforming the entire university—a much more radical and, as far as most administrators were concerned, threatening matter. While students and some radical faculty were, with considerable struggle and significant community support, able to establish Black Studies on the campuses of many HBCUs, these Black Studies departments and programs were generally quite circumscribed and contained so as to frustrate the larger Black Studies goal of institutionally changing the HBCUs into Black universities. As a result, what one found, especially in the South and border states where HBCUs were overwhelmingly located, was the growth of radical Black educational think tanks, advocacy groups, and schools (K-12 and beyond), such as IBW in Atlanta, People's College in Nashville and Atlanta, and Malcolm X Liberation University, first in Durham and then in Greensboro, North Carolina. In all these cases, these groups and institutions were independent of the HBCUs, but nevertheless significantly dependent on HBCU students, faculty, and in some cases (such as People's College) physical plant.

The growth of Black Studies in its various iterations had a profound impact on Black Arts in the South, because of the Black Studies focus on Black art and culture. Interestingly, when one reads documents from the early days of Black Studies departments and programs and from such major Black Arts conferences as the March 1968 "Toward a Black University" (TABU) conference at Howard University (which will be discussed later in this chapter), the subjects and the disciplinary frames of those articles, statements, and so on, tend to be from the more social science side of the general field of education. Even though they often mention culture as an important aspect of Black Studies, very few of these pieces go into the arts in any depth.

However, in many early Black Studies departments and programs, including Black Studies at San Francisco State and Afro-American Studies at the University of Massachusetts Amherst, it was the artists who put those departments and programs on the map, not the young (for the most part) academics who accompanied them. At San Francisco State, Sonia Sanchez and Amiri Baraka were already far better known than the more conventionally credentialed scholars in the department. Similarly at the University of Massachusetts Amherst, as John Bracey notes, it was the artists—Max Roach, Shirley Graham Du Bois, Archie Shepp, Nelson Stevens, Paul Carter Harrison, Diane Ramos, Dorrance Hill, among others—who really distinguished the department early on, not the young activist-scholars like himself who had yet to make their academic reputations.[6] This was even more true in the South as a region where HBCUs were willing to hire and retain nationally known and up-and-coming radical Black artists, such as Sterling Brown, John O. Killens, Toni Cade Bambara, Margaret Walker, Jeff Donaldson, John Biggers, Haki Madhubuti, Audre Lorde, Tom Dent, and A. B. Spellman. These artists—and humanities professors who focused on Black art and culture—were key in presenting a face of Black Studies and in popularizing and clearing a space for Black Studies in HBCUs and other institutions that drew support and resources from the faculty and student bodies of Black schools.

Black Cosmopolis: Washington, D.C., as a Southern and International Territory

Washington, D.C., is in some ways more of a border zone between North and South than the so-called border states of Maryland and Kentucky. In many respects it was a southern Jim Crow city until at least the 1950s. Though much of the formal trappings of Jim Crow had been abolished by the early 1960s, the memory and legacies of Jim Crow and slavery were very much alive in the city—not the least among the many more recent Black residents who had come to Washington from the South, primarily from the Carolinas, Georgia, and Virginia. At the same time, the federal government, though filled with discriminatory practices, hired large numbers of African Americans. Though Black workers tended to be stuck in lower grades without the mobility of their white government counterparts, federal employment nevertheless provided one of the big draws for southern Black migrants. There was a certain sense, too, that as the national capital it was, as intended by its political founders, outside region. In addition, Washington obviously had an international character, not only among the political class but also within the Black community, especially its important higher education sector. Given the persistence of Jim Crow in Maryland well into the 1960s, Washington was in some senses south of the South as well as north of it. It was a node where North and South, domestic and international met.[7]

Washington had long been a center of Black art and literature. Like Atlanta, home of an elite, perhaps *the* elite, HBCU, Howard University, it was a hub of Black higher education with distinguished Black artists and writers such as Owen Dodson and Sterling Brown on its faculty in the 1960s. At Howard, Sterling Brown played much the same mentoring role as John Killens at Fisk—though with his own distinct style and over a much longer period of time. One of his students from the early 1960s, Ekwueme Michael Thelwell, recalls Brown's formal classes as extremely competent, but more or less standard literature courses of the day—though not entirely so since it was not unheard of for someone like pianist Willie "the Lion" Smith to show up. However, Brown's unofficial seminars and discussion sessions (often with bourbon) on African American culture, history, music, literature, and politics nurtured and inspired many writers before, during, and after the Black Arts era, including Amiri Baraka, A. B. Spellman, and Toni Morrison as well as Thelwell. Brown mentored in this manner the largely avant-garde literary grouping that published the journal *Dasein*, including Percy Johnston, Oswald Govan, Walter De Legall, and Leroy Stone, as well as the political activists in the Nonviolent Action Group (NAG), including Thelwell, Kwame Ture, Cleveland Sellers, Ed Brown, Rap Brown, Charlie Cobb, and Courtland Cox, who would later play key roles in the leadership of SNCC and the emergence of Black Power.[8] While members of the *Dasein* group rarely participated directly in the political activities of NAG and SNCC—and while the NAG activists considered the *Dasein* circle to be bohemians a little too concerned with their images as artists—the active existence of both groups linked in part through Brown (and to a lesser extent Owen Dodson) contributed to a sense of a dynamic political and cultural environment on campus. At the same time, the fact that NAG and *Dasein* were never recognized as official groups by the Howard administration highlights some of the contradictions of political and cultural life on historically Black campuses in the early 1960s.[9] Later, after his move from Atlanta to Washington, D.C., Stephen Henderson would play a similar role of cultural and intellectual community-building at Howard, particularly after he was appointed director of Howard's Institute for the Arts and the Humanities in 1972, where he would work with Brown, John O. Killens, and Haki Madhubuti. Among the students whom Henderson would profoundly touch was the poet and educator E. Ethelbert Miller, who has long been at the center of Black poetry and African American Studies in Washington.[10]

The demographics of the student body at Howard in the 1960s, which included many Black students from Africa and the Caribbean, interacted with the growth of African and third-world embassies as former colonies won their independence to give Washington a Black internationalist character unmatched by any U.S. city with the possible exception of New York City. While Black students from outside the United States attended many HBCUs, Black international students at Howard made up over a third of the student body.[11] Radical anticolonial thought from across the Black world, including all the regions of the United States, circulated among interested students of Howard in a firsthand way unusual even among HBCUs, much less historically white campuses. Thus, with Washington at the northern edge of the South and an important center of the civil rights movement, not the least because of the presence of Howard and NAG/SNCC there, it had a unique identity as a significantly southern Black city, a city in which a comparatively large intelligentsia played an active role in the broader Black community, and a Black internationalist city. Not surprisingly, then, Black Arts in Washington, D.C., as in Atlanta and Nashville, was very closely tied to Black Studies and Black educational institutions and programs, such as Howard, the New School of Afro-American Thought, Black Studies at Federal City College, and the Center for Black Education as well as to institutions in other nexuses of Black higher education, such as IBW in Atlanta.

Washington was the site of rapid, if somewhat contradictory, demographic changes in the 1950s and 1960s. The Black community of the city grew quickly as new areas of government employment opened up to African Americans, drawing migrants from other areas, especially the South. And, as in many other cities, white residents fled to the suburbs of Maryland and northern Virginia. By the early 1960s, Washington became the first major U.S. city with a Black majority population. At the same time, vast urban renewal projects in southwest Washington displaced tens of thousands of largely poor Black inhabitants, many of whom moved to such southeast Washington neighborhoods as Anacostia and Congress Heights (previously a virtually all-white working-class neighborhood), disrupting the social fabric of Black Washington.[12] In other words, as in many U.S. cities, one found in D.C.'s Black neighborhoods a mixture of optimism and frustration, of striving and desperation, of growth, disruption, and displacement.

One peculiar aspect of Washington was that as the Black community expanded, and with it potential Black political power in the city, D.C. remained a political stepchild of the federal government, largely disenfranchised without even a local government until 1973. As the Black proportion of the population swelled to 71 percent by 1970, this disenfranchisement and the local struggle for political representation increasingly took on a racial character in which local political control became increasingly identified with Black Power.

Gaston Neal and the School of Afro-American Thought

The vast majority of Black migrants to Washington came from the South. Still, because of its identity as a Black educational and intellectual center, its international (and internationalist) Black community even before the new 1964 immigration laws that made it much easier for non-Europeans to immigrate to the United States, its Black majority status, and its role as a hub of the civil rights movement, D.C. attracted Black activists, artists, and intellectuals from across the United States and from across Africa and the rest of its diaspora. As noted earlier, Howard was the home of the avant-garde Black writers group Dasein as well as the NAG, which became part of the larger Black student movement and provided much of the national leadership of SNCC. The nearby Black northwest D.C. communities of Cardozo, Shaw, and Columbia Heights remained long-standing centers of Black music, theater, and dance, especially in the U Street, 14th Street, and 7th Street areas.

A major moment for Black Arts in Washington was the October 1965 opening of the New School of Afro-American Thought in the 14th Street corridor that ran from Cardozo in the south to Columbia Heights in the north. The 14th Street area contained a very large percentage of D.C.'s civil rights and incipient Black Power and Black Arts institutions and organizational offices, including SNCC, CORE, and, later, Pride Incorporated (a culturally oriented jobs and social service program founded by former SNCC national chair and future Washington mayor Marion Barry in 1967), and Drum and Spear Bookstore. This concentration of Black political and cultural groups and institutions led to 14th Street's moniker, Liberation Street.

In many respects, the creation of the New School mirrored that of BARTS in Harlem earlier in the same year. The key figure in the establishment of the New School was the poet Gaston Neal. A native of Pittsburgh's Hill District, Neal apprenticed in the Beat/bohemian arts scene of D.C. after a peripatetic life across the United States following his discharge from the army in the 1950s. Like his friend Amiri Baraka, whom he met at a reading of Baraka, Allen Ginsberg, and the younger white New Jersey Beat poet Ray Bremser in Washington, Neal moved away from an interracial bohemian milieu to building arts institutions in Black communities.[13] Also, like Baraka and BARTS in New York, Neal (who worked at an antipoverty agency, the United Planning Organization) was able to leverage War on Poverty money to fund an arts initiative, the Cardozo Area Arts Committee. Though it had some white members, the committee was basically a Black Arts organization in its orientation toward the Cardozo/Shaw neighborhood and bringing radical Black art to the community as well as in training young Black artists. The committee's signature event was the Three Days of Soul festival in 1965, featuring jazz, R&B, gospel, and rock-and-roll music, Black dance, and other sorts of performance contextualized as an expression of Black pride and nationhood. Neal declared, "We think that Three Days of Soul will deal a death-blow to the psychology of self-hatred that contributes so much to the poverty syndrome of this city's poor black population."[14]

The festival included "new jazz" reed player and composer Marion Brown and his Quintet, the Kenny Fisher Quartet, Marc Primus's Afro-American Folkloric Troupe (a radical proto-Black Arts theater group from the San Francisco Bay Area), and a host of local Black R&B, gospel, blues, jazz, and dance groups and artists, of whom Shirley Horn was probably the best known nationally.[15] The festival reached a large community audience as well as the attention of the locally based Black press. The *Baltimore Afro-American* (the leading Black paper of the region, but with a national reach) ran an editorial praising the festival for its efforts to instill pride in Black culture.[16]

Baba Lumumba (Donald Freeman), a Howard student from Oakland, California, and activist in RAM who worked with Neal and the Cardozo Area Arts Committee, suggested to Neal that a school/cultural center be formed to institutionalize the work the festival did.[17] RAM was a semi-underground revolutionary nationalist cadre group that saw its primary mission as building institutions and mass organizations to promote radical Black self-determination in the spirit of Malcolm X and Robert F. Williams, the former Monroe, North Carolina, NAACP leader who advocated Black armed self-defense and served for a time as the honorary chairman of RAM while he was in exile in Cuba and China. Baba Lumumba was particularly close to the West Coast RAM organization, including his brother Mamadou Lumumba (Kenneth Freeman), which in 1964 started *SoulBook*, one of the early national Black Power/Black Arts journals. The two primary leaders of RAM were Muhammad Ahmad (Max Stanford) in Philadelphia and Donald Freeman (no relation to the D.C. and Oakland Freemans) in Cleveland. RAM was a radical political organization that saw art and culture as a primary arena of Black liberation, containing among its most active members the writers Askia Touré (Rolland Snellings) and Larry Neal (no relation to

Gaston Neal). Ahmad, himself a painter, made a suggestion to Baraka in 1965 very similar to that of Lumumba to Neal, saying that a fitting way to go forward after the assassination of Malcolm X was to begin a cultural center and school in Harlem. In short, the establishment of such institutions was a RAM goal.[18]

The result in D.C. was the establishment of the New School, with Neal as the director and Lumumba essentially overseeing the more strictly political programming—though, again, the arts and culture were seen by both Neal and Lumumba as a central area of the school's political work. Neal (along with Cardozo Area Arts Committee cochairman Elijah Smith) sent out a letter announcing the new institution and inviting participation in the grand opening of the New School. The letter emphasized the importance of culture and education, and the unity of the Black working class and the intelligentsia, in the movement for African American liberation and self-determination in much the same spirit as Neal's comments about the Three Days of Soul festival: "This is not a petty middle class project. But instead includes sincere black people from both the ghetto and the middle class who have joined together to break the psychological ropes that have for 400 years bound the black man's mind . . . soul . . . belief in his own mysticism and self."[19]

The New School's grand opening itself was one of the major events of the Black Arts era in D.C., featuring jazz, R&B, blues, gospel, theater, poetry, visual art, and dance by both local and visiting artists. Among those who performed were musicians Oscar Brown Jr., Sunny Murray, Jackie McLean, and Giuseppi Logan and poets Amiri Baraka, Sterling Brown, Owen Dodson, Larry Neal, K. W. (Willie) Kgositsile, A. B. Spellman, and Ronald Stone. Sterling Brown and Dodson, of course, were well-known writers whose careers matured in earlier moments of Black radicalism, basically the later Harlem Renaissance and the Black Left of the early 1930s in the case of Brown and the Popular Front in that of Dodson (though Brown was very active in the Popular Front era of the 1930s and 1940s too), and, as mentioned, both were Howard University faculty. Oscar Brown Jr., a radical and former Communist, was well-known as a witty songwriter and performer and the librettist of the *We Insist: Freedom Now Suite* (1960) on which he collaborated with Max Roach and Abbey Lincoln. Jackie McClean was a well-regarded alto saxophonist whose career began in the hard bop era, but who increasingly incorporated elements of free jazz in his work. K. W. Kgositsile was an exile and African National Congress activist from South Africa who came to the United States as a student, where he became active in Black Arts. After some decades in the United States and Tanzania, he returned to South Africa in the 1990s and became the country's first Poet Laureate in 2006.

As Neal noted, this event brought together the middle-class Black intelligentsia, many with connections to Howard, and the larger community, as well as younger and older artists of a wide variety of radical Black ideological and aesthetic positions from across the United States as well as (in Kgositsile's case) Africa. One might see this opening, with the different genres of Black music represented as both an anticipation and an embodiment of what Baraka termed a "unity music" of R&B and free jazz in his groundbreaking Black Arts essay, "The Changing Same" (1966)—though apparently the audience's reception of the different sorts of music varied.[20]

The New School continued to be an important locus of jazz performance in D.C. during its four years of existence, presenting nationally famous artists such as Sun Ra and his Arkestra and Joseph Jarman (later of the Art Ensemble of Chicago) as well local D.C. jazz musicians. While the New School focused particularly on various forms of avant-garde jazz, as in the grand opening it also featured concerts in other genres of Black music, especially gospel. In short, Neal and the other activists of the New School took their own version of Black unity music quite seriously.

Neal and the New School promoted a unity literature, too, emphasizing the arc of Black literature essentially as a continuum rather than a break between old and new, as can be seen by the generational and stylistic range of the poets who read at the New School's opening. Neal had a particular affection for Langston Hughes, who encouraged Neal as a young poet—as Hughes had done with other young Black artists for decades.[21] Following Hughes's death, the New School sponsored a program of Black poetry from the Harlem Renaissance to Black Arts in honor of Hughes and his work, featuring Sterling Brown, Carl Holman, Samuel Allen, James Butcher, and Neal.

The New School was also an early beachhead of Black Studies in D.C., antedating and influencing efforts to bring Black Studies to Howard as well as the Howard Toward a Black University (TABU) conference.[22] However, as was the case with BARTS, Black Arts West, and many other early Black Arts groups and institutions, the New School was plagued by financial difficulties, internal debates (particularly between Neal and Lumumba), and the personal issues of its leaders, especially Neal. During this period Neal struggled with drug addiction and had various legal problems stemming from his substance abuse as well as from his radicalism, resulting in erratic management of the New School. One issue between Lumumba and Neal was over the question of funding. Lumumba opposed taking money from federal or local government, feeling that the school should be supported by the Black community, avoiding the potential strings that would be attached to government funding. Neal was more open to the idea and did use antipoverty and foundation sources from time to time. In any case, the New School was unable to develop a reliable cash stream, whether from the community, government, or foundations. Those financial issues combined with internal debates and Neal's erratic leadership due to his personal problems led to the New School's decline and final closure in 1970.

However, the New School, like BARTS and the FST, though relatively short-lived, not only provided important educational and cultural offerings but served as a model, both in positive and cautionary ways, for future radical Black cultural, political, and educational projects in Washington, such as the Drum and Spear Bookstore (and Press) and the Center for Black Education. Participants in the New School's programs and events as well as in the Cardozo Area Arts Committee remained active in Black art, politics, and education in D.C. Lumumba continues as a widely respected radical Black nationalist political elder in the city to this day. Neal was one of the best known Black poets and cultural organizers in Washington until his death in 1999. He organized and hosted a "Black Expression" series of jazz concerts at the Corcoran Gallery in the late 1960s and early 1970s that included such younger jazz artists and accompanying poets as vocalist Leon Thomas, reed player Pharoah Sanders, bassist Jimmy Garrison, and Larry Neal.[23]

Tear Gas in the Air: Drum and Spear Bookstore and Press

Drum and Spear Bookstore and Drum and Spear Press were anchors of Black Power/Black Arts in the Liberation Street corridor of northwest Washington. Located on 14th Street in the southern portion of Columbia Heights, Drum and Spear grew out of the initiatives of increasingly nationalist civil rights workers, particularly from SNCC. Quite a few of these former SNCC activists started their lives in the civil rights movement at Howard and NAG, and retained ties to the university, members of its faculty, and fellow alumni in D.C. and beyond. From the very beginning, Drum and Spear had a close relationship, too, to the New School and Gaston Neal, especially in Drum and Spear's work in literature and the arts—though its founders are remembered primarily as political rather than cultural activists.

Both because of the Howard connection and because of the need to maintain an office in the U.S. capital for the purposes of lobbying politicians and other sorts of legislative action, SNCC had a strong presence in Washington, D.C. Consequently, there was much back and forth between D.C. and Atlanta, where SNCC's administrative headquarters was located, during its life as a viable organization from 1960 to 1968 or so. Not surprisingly, a significant number of former SNCC leaders (many of whom had gone to Howard) migrated to Washington from Atlanta and other SNCC centers in the Deep South as the organization began to unravel in 1967, plagued by internal debates and factional fighting. This group included the former Mississippi field secretary Charlie Cobb, program coordinator Courtland Cox, Judy Richardson, Ivanhoe Donaldson, and Curtis Muhammad (Hayes), who, like their SNCC comrade Kwame Ture (Stokely Carmichael) were increasingly drawn toward an idea of a Black or African socialism—though more in the cultural nationalist Pan-African vein of the Tanzanian Ujaama of Julius Nyerere than the Nkrumahist socialism of Ture.[24]

The seed for the Drum and Spear bookstore was planted when Charlie Cobb visited the Présence Africaine bookstore in Paris in 1967 with Courtland Cox en route to West Africa. Cobb became convinced that such a radical Black bookstore providing information to Black people about the Pan-African world was necessary for Washington, D.C., where he was able to bring the network of former SNCC workers there into the project.[25] Given that the Présence Africaine bookstore was to a large extent a product of what was significantly a cultural movement, Négritude, and strongly oriented toward Black international literature and art, it reinforced the notion that such literature and art were among the essential information that a Black bookstore needed to make available. The constituency for such a bookstore grew, and its purpose took on a greater urgency as it officially opened in June 1968 soon after Dr. Martin Luther King Jr.'s assassination and the uprisings that followed his murder, including a particularly fierce revolt in Washington with its epicenter in the Columbia Heights neighborhood. "There was still tear gas in the air," remembered Judy Richardson. "You felt it in your nose."[26]

Like other Black bookstores (and feminist and radical bookstores of the time generally), Drum and Spear quickly became a place for political meetings, discussion groups, classes, poetry readings, book parties, and so on—not surprising given the founders' experience in SNCC and the emerging Black Power movement. It was also intertwined with the New School to a considerable extent. Baba Lumumba joined the Drum and Spear board of directors. Gaston Neal was a mainstay in the bookstore's poetry events, which the organizers saw as a crucial part of their mission. Perhaps because Charlie Cobb was a published poet, and because of the common sense that art and culture were essential parts of changing the consciousness of Black people into a revolutionary one, poetry and poetry readings were at the heart of the activities of Drum and Spear. Both Judy Richardson and Tony Gittens point out the importance of poetry to Drum and Spear's mission—and of Drum and Spear to the D.C. poetry scene:

> "Black poetry was central to Drum and Spear," Judy Richardson says as she also drops the names of a few poets of note who read their work at the store: "Gaston Neal, Charlie Cobb . . . Sonia Sanchez."
>
> Tony Gittens, former longtime Director of the DC Commission on the Arts and Humanities, and co-founder of the store, remembers the poetry well and cites one person in particular who harnessed the poetry energy in the store and presented it to the public.
>
> "The main poetry person was Gaston Neal," Gittens says. Gittens eventually became manager of the store when it became the largest Black bookstore in the country.[27]

Like the Présence Africaine bookstore that inspired it, it had a decidedly internationalist cast. As Courtland Cox noted:

> We decided to—you know, information was important, and we decided that, you know, a bookstore and a press would be good. Um, and so, we opened a bookstore on 14th and Fairmont Street, you know, dealing with African and African American history and also things that dealt with, you know, Palestine, dealt with Vietnam, dealt with issues of war and stuff like that.
>
> And, I mean, we, it was, you know, I mean, it was—it was a great political venture, but I'm not sure it was a great business venture, in the sense that we did a lot of stuff, but I don't think we ever made any serious money. But it was important because it—I mean, people remember it today. In fact, there is a plaque on that building, you know, that, you know, the bookstore was there. And Drum & Spear, you know, we were able to publish, you know, C.L.R.'s book and, you know, some other books that we did, um, Palestinian poetry and other things, a book of African names and so forth.[28]

Again, it says much about the politics of Drum and Spear Bookstore and the affiliated Drum and Spear Press, that poetry was part of the essential knowledge that the store and the press tried to impart to Black people. The run and number of titles of Drum and Spear Press was relatively small, certainly far less than some other Black Arts/Black Power publishers, notably Broadside Press in Detroit and Third World Press in Chicago. Nevertheless, Drum and Spear printed some extremely important titles. The most groundbreaking was undoubtedly the publication of *Enemy of the Sun: Poetry of Palestinian Resistance* (1970). It was the first English-language collection of Palestinian poetry published in the United States. It translated the work of the leading living Palestinian poets, including Mahmoud Darwish, Sameeh Al-Qassem, Fadwa Tuqan, and Tawfiq Zayyad, quite a few of whom felt a kinship to poets of the Black Arts movement. Many Black Power and Black Arts activists, too, saw a special relationship between Black people and Palestinians, seeing Palestinians not only as an oppressed people under the rule of a settler colony but also, in many cases, essentially an African people.[29] Drum and Spear also published Black children's books promoting a Left Afrocentric ethos that drew significantly on Tanzanian socialism and that was also akin to Maulana Karenga's Kawaida philosophy, though the Drum and Spear group was not institutionally close to Karenga and his US Organization.[30]

Drum and Spear's other major publication besides *Enemy of the Sun* was a 1969 reprint of C. L. R. James's 1938 *A History of Pan-African Revolt,* the first book issued by the press. James was teaching at Federal City College. Among his colleagues were activists in Black Arts and Black Power, notably the playwright and educator Jimmy Garrett (a founder of Black Studies at San Francisco State who was brought on as the chair of Black Studies at Federal City) and many of the Drum and Spear group (who were hired by their former SNCC comrade, Garrett). As Robin Kelley remarks in his introduction to a 2012 edition of *A History of Pan-African Revolt*:

> By this time, members of the collective had grown fairly close to C.L.R., who had moved to Washington a year after Drum and Spear Bookstore was founded. They had come to know James through Federal City College, some of them having been fellow faculty members there. His 16th Street apartment soon became a kind of meeting ground for these young activist/intellectuals to discuss Black liberation, community organizing, history, sociology, politics, and a whole host of issues. Indeed, James not only participated in discussions leading to the founding of Drum and Spear Press, but it was he who volunteered *A History of Negro Revolt* as its first title. The Drum and

Spear collective was happy to oblige, for they clearly respected James as an elder mentor for their generation. In the introduction to the new edition, Marvin Holloway of the Center for Black Education characterized James as a living revolutionary who had seen and experienced struggles that most young militants only read about. At a time "when Black people throughout the world are clamoring for self-knowledge," the sixty-eight-year-old C.L.R. "has become a great source of wisdom and counsel to youth in the Resistance Movement."[31]

Originally published as *A History of Negro Revolt* in the same year (1938) as James's better known *Black Jacobins*, *A History of Pan-African Revolt*, as the name suggests, took a Pan-African (and Marxist) view of the rebellion and resistance by Africans and African descendants in the diaspora against slavery, colonialism, Jim Crow, and other forms of racial, national, and class oppression, linking, among other things, slave revolts in the Americas (particularly in Haiti and the U.S.) to Black participation in the U.S. Civil War, the Garvey movement, independence movements in Africa and its diaspora. For the 1969 Drum and Spear edition, James added an epilogue in which he discusses U.S. Black Power, African independence and the development of new African states, and anticolonial and incipient Black Power movements in the Caribbean. He ends with, like the Drum and Spear group with whom he had much discussion, a particular enthusiasm for Tanzanian socialism, declaring that it was in African forms of socialism, not those of the Soviet Union or the Communist parties of Europe and North America, that one found the true spirit of Lenin and revolutionary socialism. In this, James not only affirms his basically Marxist, if decidedly anti-Stalinist, ideology (albeit with a deep suspicion of "vanguard" parties despite his admiration of Julius Nyerere and his Tanzanian African National Union party) echoing in important respects the Third World Marxist stance of many Black radicals, including most of the Drum and Spear group.[32]

As Kelley observes, one of the things that made *A History of Pan-African Revolt* (and *Black Jacobins*) particularly copacetic with the project of the Drum and Spear Bookstore and Drum and Spear Press, and distinguished it from the work of Communist historian Herbert Aptheker on slave rebellions in the United States following the initial publication of James's book, was its attention to the cultural dimensions of Black revolt against slavery, colonialism, and white supremacy: "What is unique is James's claim that revolutionary mass movements take forms that are often cultural and religious rather than explicitly political. He forces the reader to re-examine these seemingly odd movements with new eyes, to take the beliefs and superstitions of Africans and African descendants seriously."[33] In this way, one can—and indeed many Black U.S. radicals did, especially those connected to the emergent Black Studies movement and such institutions as the IBW in Atlanta, and the Center for Black Education in Washington, D.C.—see James's histories of Black revolt in Africa and the diaspora as ancestors of Black Power/Black Arts and the almost universal emphasis in Black Power/Black Arts on the importance of the cultural in revolutionary Black politics. *A History of Pan-African Revolt* and *Black Jacobins* also long antedated and anticipated the cultural turn in the academic discipline of history that was especially associated with leftist (generally past or present Communist) scholars, such as Eric Hobsbawm, E. P. Thompson, and Christopher Hill.

Federal City College, Drum and Spear, and the Center for Black Education

The Black Studies movement in higher education developed initially in non-HBCU urban campuses, such as San Francisco State College and Wayne State University. Subsequently, the movement spread to a wide range of public and private higher education institutions, often through rallies, lobbying, sit-ins, and other forms of direct action by Black students and their allies demanding the establishment of Black Studies programs and departments. These programs and departments generally faced hostile administrations and, frequently, faculties, especially since many in Black Studies felt that existing standards of credentialing, programmatic goals, and evaluation did not serve them and their aims well. While student activism and community pressure were able to force the creation of Black Studies on predominantly white campuses, there was often a constant battle against attempts to circumscribe those academic units and deny them the ability to determine their own standards and goals. Consequently, a debate as to the viability of building Black institutions within predominantly white or white-run institutions as opposed to creating freestanding Black universities run by revolutionary Black people for the Black community gained new strength.

Often early Black Studies units grew in spaces attached to experimental colleges, whether new independent institutions or attached to an existing college or university (as at San Francisco State and Wayne State), in response to new radical currents of thought and of pedagogy that gained currency among educators and significant segments of the general population in the United States during the 1960s. One might see the experimental colleges as earnest attempts to explore new ways of teaching and to serve new groups of students, especially Black, Latinx, and Asian American students entering non-HCBUs in large numbers for the first time, or as safety valves that siphoned off potentially rebellious students while attempting to allow the nonexperimental colleges and universities to run more or less as they had in a time of great student unrest—or as both simultaneously. One such experimental college was Federal City College, which was conceived during the Kennedy administration to serve the majority Black population of Washington, D.C., authorized by Congress in 1966, and opened for classes in 1968.

James (Jimmy) Garrett was hired to run the Black Studies program at Federal City. Garrett came from an activist family and had grown up in Texas and California. His father had been active in the Left-led SNYC. As a young man in Los Angeles, Garrett joined the Avalon branch of CORE (a militant African American–led branch rooted in the South Central Los Angeles African American community) and participated in the youth group of the CPUSA, the W. E. B. Du Bois Clubs. Later he moved toward a more nationalist, if still leftist stance.[34] He had been one of the founders of the Black Student Union and Black Studies at San Francisco State. He was instrumental in getting first Sonia Sanchez and then Amiri Baraka to come to San Francisco State to work in the new Black Studies program. Sanchez, particularly, was an anchor of the program in its early days. Garrett was also the author of the well-known, if misogynist, Black Arts play, *And We Own the Night: A Play of Blackness*, which debuted at a Black Panthers Party rally in 1967.[35] Garrett had been active in SNCC too, where he became familiar with most of the former SNCC members in the Drum and Spear collective. When he was brought on to develop Black Studies at Federal City, he hired Charlie Cobb, Courtland Cox, and Jean Wiley, all former SNCC field secretaries and part of the Drum and Spear circle.[36]

Almost immediately Garrett and the Black Studies group clashed with the Federal City administration and, even more intensely, the faculty over their vision of the mission and organization of Black Studies. At its heart, the proposal for Black Studies at Federal City, as at many other institutions, was not for a traditional academic program or department or even an interdisciplinary program along the lines of American Civilization at Harvard University or American Studies at Yale University or Amherst College, but for a community-oriented, activist, fundamentally nationalist department. As Charlie Cobb recalled:

> However, we clashed with the university over the idea of education, because we made the argument—and it's in writing. Maybe, I don't know—we wrote it up anyway. And our argument was, we said that to do Black Studies, in the sense of studying Richard Wright or James Baldwin or John Hope Franklin, or something like that, was inadequate. Yes, it's fine to know Langston Hughes. Yes, it's fine to know Zora Neale Hurston, etcetera, if you, you know, have important figures in literature, or historical research, or something like that. But what we really needed was black education. And the question of black education turned on the question or issue of what you were going to do with your education once you finished. And it didn't matter what you took if you wanted—you might want to be a doctor or an engineer or a teacher, or whatever it was you wanted to be, the question you had to confront as a college student was, "Upon graduation, how am I going to use my education for the black community?"[37]

Garrett said succinctly that Black Studies at Federal City sought to "Africanize" Black students.[38] One might also say that it sought to "Africanize" the curriculum, at least in the space of Black Studies. Black Studies was not simply about courses on Black literature, Black history, and so on, but about making every field taught, whether literature or chemistry relevant to the African American community and its needs and goals. Liberal and radical white faculty members at Federal City were generally in favor of the inclusion of Black faculty, texts, and history to a point. However, with a few exceptions, they opposed the idea of a total Black curriculum. The notion that "hard" sciences and even the social sciences and humanities were not basically objective, which is to say not race- and class-neutral, especially rankled. The faculty and ultimately the administration and board of trustees also objected to the Black Studies proposal that they only hire Black instructors and that their course be directed to Black students and refused to allow Black Studies to hire new instructors.[39]

Consequently, just a year after the founding of Black Studies, Garrett and most of the department's faculty left to form an independent Black community school, the Center for Black Education (CBE). Like Black Studies at Federal City, CBE was essentially an alliance of artists, activists, intellectuals, and teachers from the overlapping groups of the New School,

Drum and Spear, Federal City Black Studies, and others in what might be thought of as the SNCC/Black Power/Black Arts networks of Liberation Street and Black Washington. Because of the connections that were retained from SNCC, CORE, and other radicalized civil rights groups, CBE had markedly close ties to like-minded people in Nashville, Greensboro, and Atlanta, also loci of Black higher education in the South.

CBE and many in its networks had a strong Left-nationalist orientation, increasingly moving toward a Maoist/Third World Marxism that emphasized Mao, of course, but also the thinking of Amilcar Cabral and the PAIGC in Guinea-Bissau, Nyerere and TANU in Tanzania, Agostinho Neto and FRELIMO in Mozambique, and both the ANC and the more nationalist (and far less friendly to the South African Communist Party) Pan-African Congress (PAC) in South Africa. CBE leaders aligned the school with other Third World Left-Nationalist groups and institutions, such as People's College in Nashville and Atlanta and SOBU and Malcolm X Liberation University in North Carolina. As with these other groups, most of the documents from CBE that survive tend to be more in the vein of the sociological side of education than focused on art per se. However, culture and the cultural approach practiced by the New School and Drum and Spear were very much a part of CBE.

Probably the most influential event organized by CBE and the overlapping institutions of the New School, Drum and Spear, and the other radical Black cultural and political organizations and institutions of Washington, D.C., was the TABU conference in November 1968. This conference, though it has not attracted the detailed scholarly attention that it deserves, was a landmark in the establishment of Black Studies in higher education, providing inspiration, impetus, and various frameworks, especially the Black university models (inside and outside established campuses), for emerging Black Studies departments and schools across the country. Again, most of the surviving documents about the conference, especially those published in *Negro Digest* in March 1969, take up the educational debates about the possible and most promising institutional locations for Black Studies. Nevertheless, it was also a major cultural event with Black art presented as a major component of Black Studies.

The cultural highlight at TABU was a night of performance dedicated to the poet and longtime Howard professor Sterling Brown as a forerunner of (and living participant in) Black Studies and Black Arts. Much like the opening event for the New School, "Sterling Brown Night" (also entitled, "The Black Artist in Perspective") joined artists of different generations and different media and genres. This put together the different cultural and political eras that Brown's writing traversed, from the Harlem Renaissance to the Popular Front to civil rights to Black Power and Black Arts. The program that night included Brown himself as well as poets Amiri Baraka (his former student), Sonia Sanchez, Bobb Hamilton, Ted Joans, Haki Madhubuti, and Gaston Neal, musicians Abbey Lincoln, Max Roach, and Lloyd McNeil, actor and playwright Ossie Davis, and the African Heritage Dancers and Drummers.[40] The conference also featured a concert by local Washington jazz luminary Hilton Felton and his group. The program, in fact, had much the feel of a unity event organized at the New School by Gaston Neal, acknowledged as the chief younger figure of Black poetry in Washington, D.C.

A Better Way to Deal With Reality: Black Arts and Black Studies in Nashville

The second-largest city in Tennessee after Memphis, Nashville is not notably associated with African American cultural production in either the elite intellectual circles of U.S. high culture or in the world of popular culture—with the exception of the Fisk Jubilee Singers in the late nineteenth century and the wide circulation of spirituals arranged in light European art music format. In high culture, the city is still probably most commonly linked to the neo-Confederate Agrarians and Fugitives at Vanderbilt University of the 1930s who would go on to play a big part in the establishment of the conservative New Criticism in the 1940s as the reigning literary critical doctrine on most U.S. campuses for decades. And, in the popular sphere, Nashville is famously celebrated as the center of the country music industry and home of the Grand Ole Opry radio program, which broadcast from the downtown Ryman Auditorium during most of the Black Arts and Black Power era until its departure for the more suburban (then semirural) Pennington Bend section of Nashville in 1974.

However, Jefferson Street in north Nashville was a center of Black popular music rivaling any in the South, serving as an important way station in the careers of major stars from outside the region, notably Little Richard and Jimi Hendrix, as well as local talents such as Bobby Hebb (whose work crossed genres, including jazz, R&B, soul, and country) and blues singer Marion James. However, the lack of a record label that focused on local Black musicians the way, say, Motown did in Detroit or Stax did in Memphis, and the association of the city with the country music industry that overshadowed other popular music genres, limited the reputation of Nashville as a hub of Black music outside of the immediate region.

Nashville *was* recognized nationally as a major site of the Black freedom movement, particularly the Black Student movement of the 1960s that produced SNCC, and a longtime locus of Black intellectual thought due to the presence of major HBCUs, notably Fisk University, Tennessee A&I State College (becoming Tennessee State College in 1968), the American Baptist Theological Seminary, and Meharry Medical College, a concentration of Black institutions of higher education rivaled only by Atlanta. Not surprisingly then, as in Atlanta and Washington, D.C., the Black Power and Black Arts movements in Nashville were closely tied to the historically Black campuses of the city (and HBCUs elsewhere, particularly in Atlanta, Washington, and Greensboro). One might say that these movements focused inward in their attempts, as in other centers of Black higher education in the South, to transform the HBCUs, particularly Fisk, into "Black universities," while also attempting to reach outward into the community. The Nashville HBCUs, particularly Fisk (where Aaron Douglas taught) and Tennessee State (where Douglas's protégé Gregory Ridley was on the faculty through much of the Black Arts era) were, like Texas Southern in Houston, Dillard in New Orleans, the schools of AUC in Atlanta, and Hampton in Virginia, longtime centers of Black visual art and the training of Black artists.

One advantage that Nashville had in this regard was, like Howard University and the Black popular culture and movement culture scene of Cardozo/Shaw and unlike Atlanta (where AUC was relatively far from the old Black commercial and popular culture district of Auburn Avenue), its Black businesses and HBCUs centered on Jefferson Street in North Nashville. This area was the heart of jazz, blues, and R&B/soul music in Nashville through the 1960s, though urban renewal buffeted the neighborhood from the 1950s on and the construction of the I-40 interstate highway in 1968 severely damaged the commercial district. It was also the center of the Black Student movement and civil rights movement in Nashville as SCLC and SNCC moved between campus and community.

Nashville's Black institutions of higher education, like HBCUs elsewhere, had long hired leading Black and white intellectuals and artists, many of them with radical pasts (and sometimes presents), who would not have been hired at most predominantly white colleges and universities, particularly during the McCarthy era. To take Fisk again, its faculty and staff included such artists and intellectuals with activist and even leftist pasts as Aaron Douglas, James Weldon Johnson, Arna Bontemps, Robert Hayden, and John O. Killens. It also trained activist-intellectuals who went on to make large contributions in artistic, intellectual, and political spheres—of whom the most notable was undoubtedly W. E. B. Du Bois. In short, there were traditions of student activism, socially engaged art, and radical thought on the Black campuses of Nashville that flowered again during the civil rights era.

The most significant manifestation of this tradition during the civil rights period was the Nashville sit-in movement of 1960. James Lawson was the guiding spirit of this movement. Lawson was a pacifist minister long active in CORE, the Fellowship of Reconciliation, and the Projects Committee of the Nashville Christian Leadership Council, the local affiliate of the SCLC. The first principle of one of the Nashville Christian Leadership Council's early documents was "To discover ways of nonviolent resistance in love to all forms of racial, social, economic or political injustice."[41] As with NAG at Howard, a considerable section of the early leadership of SNCC and the Black student movement, including Diane Nash, James Bevel, Marion Barry, and John Lewis, came from this Nashville student group. The influence of Lawson and the power and organization of the Nashville student movement was perhaps even more decisive than the thinking of Martin Luther King Jr. in making nonviolence a primary tactic of the Black student movement that emerged in the early 1960s. The Nashville movement early on had a cultural bent in that one of its major successful campaigns was the Open Theater movement led by Bevel aimed at desegregating Nashville's theaters.

As in many other HBCUs, the administrations of the historically African American schools of Nashville were often politically cautious and even conservative, paternalistic, and hierarchical—and sometimes expelled students who went too far beyond the political boundaries set by the administration. For example, Ishmael Flory, then a graduate student in sociology, was expelled from Fisk in 1934 for leading a demonstration protesting the appearance of the Fisk University Singers at a segregated theater in Nashville. Flory went on to become a radical labor organizer, a leader of the CPUSA, and long a familiar figure of African American politics known by Black activists of all ideological stripes in Chicago.[42]

Neither was the Fisk administration or a lot of the faculty at the time much interested in openly supporting radical political or cultural initiatives, especially in the early Black Power/Black Arts era. John O. Killens described his experience as a writer-in-residence at Fisk from 1965 to 1968 as one in which he had to contend with not only conservative (often white) trustees and nervous (often Black) administrators, but also conservative and liberal faculty members who had very traditional, old-school notions about the tasks and deportment of the faculty and the student body. Killens complained that most faculty saw "Fisk as a finishing school to train Black boys and girls how to be nice little young white ladies and gentlemen in Black skins."[43] Killens recalled that when he organized the Black Writers Conferences at Fisk that brought to campus many of the most famous and most dynamic older and younger Black writers, theater workers, and scholars, the heads of the Fisk English, speech, and drama Departments did not attend.[44] Still, whatever the conservatism and/or reserve of the administration and faculty of Fisk, it did not stop them from hiring faculty, like Killens, with a radical past and current engagement with Black Power and Black Arts as critical supporters, if not actual members. This was especially true as the decade wore on and the constituency for Black Arts, Black Power, and eventually Black Studies grew within the broader African American community as well as in academia.

Killens's term as a writer-in-residence at Fisk University led to some large contributions to the development of Black Arts at a crucial moment. Important Black Arts writers, most famously Nikki Giovanni, passed through Killens's workshop. Like other older radical writers, Killens felt one of his main tasks to be reminding the young militants of their artistic and political ancestors, especially those associated with the Popular Front era, such as Paul Robeson, while bringing younger writers to the attention (and respect) of their elders.[45] When Killens returned to New York, the workshop continued under the direction of the poet and coeditor of a major Black Arts anthology (*Black Arts: An Anthology of Black Creations*, 1969) Donald Lee Graham (Le Graham and, later, Ahmed Legraham Alhamisi) until Graham's untimely death in 1971. It was under the direction of Graham, a member of the Black Marxist People's College collective, that more efforts were made for the workshop to reach off the campus into the broader Black community of Nashville, mirroring similar efforts in Atlanta and Washington, D.C., to extend cultural efforts rooted on historically Black campuses into working-class Black neighborhoods.

Fisk, of course, was the institutional home of other well-known Black writers and anthologists of Black literature, such as Robert Hayden and Arna Bontemps. Bontemps in particular in his work on anthologies of Black poetry with Langston Hughes was open to and promoted the new Black writing. But it was Killens who took the lead in organizing the Black Writers Conferences there in 1966, 1967, and 1968.[46] The first two of these conferences in particular were watershed events in the marking of the emergence of the Black Arts movement as the ascendant force in African American letters, even though few younger writers were present at the first conference in 1966. They were important in building Black Arts networks, connecting younger artists to older artists and even bringing younger artists together for the first time, particularly in 1967 and 1968. They also presented in material form a sort of passing of the torch from one generation of radical (or formerly radical) writers to another as the older writers, such as Killens and Gwendolyn Brooks acknowledged the leadership of the new militants and even fully associated themselves with Black Arts.

In the first Fisk conference, Killens drew on the Black Left networks of the 1930s, 1940, and 1950s (and beyond). Veterans of such organizations, journals, and institutions as the Harlem Writers Guild, the American Negro Theater, Committee for the Negro in the Arts, *Freedom, Harlem Quarterly, Freedomways, Liberator, People's Voice*, and the more leftwing elements of the American Society for African Culture (AMSAC), such as Ossie Davis, Saunders Redding, Bontemps, Hayden, Margaret Walker, Loften Mitchell, and Melvin Tolson, dominated and overwhelmingly populated the first conference. However, one might say that the new militant nationalist writing was a specter haunting the conference. The only younger writer of note to appear on the program of the conference was William Melvin Kelley. Killens claimed Amiri Baraka (then still LeRoi Jones) was invited but did not attend. Kelley at that point was a promising Black postmodern (and post-Faulknerian) fiction writer whose published work already exhibited some of the bitter humor, fragmented narration, and concern with possibilities of Black consciousness and Black language (and white apprehension about that consciousness and language) that would characterize his later novels, such as *Dem* (1967) and *Dunford's Travels Everywhere* (1970). Kelley was not particularly associated with the emerging Black Arts movement, but he took it on himself to speak for it—and ask why the bulk of the younger artists were not there.

Perhaps even more telling, older participants constantly raised Baraka's name as a sort of synecdoche for the new militant Black writing, either with disapproval or as positive acknowledgment of the wave of the future. Some older writers took up the banner of the new militants, as did Walker in her reading of a poem to Malcolm X, and as did Melvin Tolson during his notorious debate with Robert Hayden in which he asserted, "I'm a black poet, an African-American poet, a Negro poet," in response to Hayden's claim that "he was a poet who happens to be Negro." It was also at this conference that a chance meeting between Walker, Dudley Randall (himself a bridge between the older and younger writers as a member of the generation who came of age in the 1930s and 1940s, but who would become the leading publisher of Black Arts poetry at Broadside Press), and Margaret Burroughs and an ensuing discussion about the many new tributary poems to Malcolm X that were being written, resulted in Broadside Press's first book project, *For Malcolm*.[47]

Young nationalist artists, particularly Baraka and playwright Ron Milner, dominated the 1967 Fisk conference in person.[48] Older writers, including Killens, Gwendolyn Brooks, Margaret Danner, and John Henrik Clarke, actively took part in the conference. However, these literary elders were or became, for the most part, some of the most fervent Black Arts supporters among the older generation; Hayden pointedly did not attend. A number of those older artists not previously identified with the new cultural and political militancy, most famously Brooks, publicly embraced Black Power and Black Arts at the conference. In fact, these conversions, particularly that of Brooks, gave the conference much of its charge as an event marking a new day in African American letters. In some ways, the conference was a reverse of the previous year where Kelley had stood in for the new nationalist writing as the older generation predominated. In 1968, the younger members of the audience took the lead, frequently charging the older participants with accommodationism or irrelevance even though, in fact, these elders supported the movement. Though these attacks might have been unfair, reflecting in the view of a *Negro Digest* correspondent the ignorance of the attackers as to the work of those they attacked, nonetheless they demonstrated a much changed atmosphere from the previous year when the Black Arts movement was present mostly through its noticeable and much remarked upon absence.

The 1968 conference was similarly shaped by the now completely ascendant Black Arts movement. Perhaps the most significant aspect of this conference was the introduction of Haki Madhubuti to a national audience outside the Midwest. Gwendolyn Brooks had recommended that Killens invite Madhubuti—though Killens must have had some previous knowledge of Madhubuti through their mutual participation at the Detroit Black Arts Conventions. Madhubuti's successful presentation at the convention not only increased his national visibility, perhaps contributing to his appointment as a writer-in-residence at Cornell University later that year, it also increased Chicago's reputation as a fulcrum of the new Black art and writing.[49]

After Killens left Fisk, Nashville was not the visible center of such national Black cultural events with major Black literary festivals and conferences moving elsewhere, including Howard University where Killens and

Madhubuti would help create a whole new series of conferences. However, if the Black Arts/Black Power era was one of, as the critic and poet Eugene Redmond called it, "festivals and funerals," then Fisk and Nashville were crucial in institutionalizing the festival/conference aspect of the movement. Fisk was not the first place such festivals and conferences had taken place and it certainly would not be the last. However, the three Fisk festivals organized by Killens had a national profile not seen before. They also made material the emergence and ascendancy of a major new cultural movement, the Black Arts movement, highlighting its connections and conflicts with earlier generations of engaged African American writers. African American literature (and U.S. culture) would never be the same. Finally, because of the work of artist-activist-organizers like Killens and Graham, especially as they reached off the campus into the community in a city with a significantly radicalized civil rights movement infrastructure, as in other cities like Atlanta, Washington, and New Orleans, they began to create the situation where the center of Black artistic gravity shifted to the South.

People's College in Nashville (with an affiliate in Atlanta) can be seen as another take on the concept of the "Black university" that allied it with CBE, Malcolm X Liberation University, and TABU but with a different twist. People's College appeared in 1970 as a sort of guerilla university in the sense that rather than trying to create a freestanding institution or transform an existing institution, it essentially commandeered the resources of the existing HBCUs of Nashville as well as using community spaces at local churches and the YMCA. It would find empty classrooms at these campuses for its classes. Eventually, the People's College collective was able to use class schedules to determine well in advance which classrooms would be already occupied so that it could have its own regular schedule.[50] Since most of the cadre of People's College, including Abdul Alkalimat (Gerald McWhorter) who was the leading figure of the institution and veteran of the Black Studies struggles at AUC, Lucius Outlaw, and Ron Bailey, worked at Nashville's HBCUs, they had salaries and access to materials that would have to be otherwise bought. In fact, they traced the ancestry of People's College to earlier efforts of HBCUs to establish community education, such as the founding of People's College at Atlanta University in the 1940s by John Hope. The difference was that instead of emphasizing hygiene, home economics, literacy, and so on, the new People's College emphasized political and cultural analysis. However, what the second People's College shared with its predecessor besides outreach to the community was the sense that learning needed to be applied rather than existing in some more abstract sphere.[51]

What made People's College possible was the confluence of a lively community of often radical scholars and artists on the faculty of Fisk, Tennessee State, and the other HBCUs in Nashville and a geographically diverse student body that drew members of the Black middle class and intelligentsia from across the United States and Africa and the rest of its diaspora. In addition to People's College, this confluence resulted in the 1969 founding of Radio Free Nashville (now WFSK), a campus station that featured cutting edge jazz, community news, and political commentary.[52]

The ideological perspective of People's College could be characterized as Third World Marxist or Black Maoist, much like the groups and institutions with which it had close relations: CBE, Malcolm X Liberation University, SOBU, and YOBU. However, that shorthand does not adequately comprehend the complexity of its ideology. For one thing, like many Black Third World Marxist groups and institutions, it was much more attached to Black nationalism than any predominantly white Maoist group. It was certainly more so than the Progressive Labor Party, the original Maoist group in the United States that came to see all forms of nationalism as inherently reactionary. While People's College's 1971 "Notes on Art and Liberation" cited Mao's *On Literature and Art* (a staple of Maoists of various stripes), it also cited James Boggs (who might be thought of as a Black post-Trotskyist whose early organizational affiliations had been with Max Shachtman's Worker's Party and C. L. R. James's Facing Reality group), Robert Allen, Frantz Fanon, and Harold Cruse. Though Fanon's *Wretched of the Earth* was certainly a favorite of many Maoist groups, Allen, James, and Cruse were far more eclectic choices, if not uncommon ones for many Third World/Black Marxists, such as the League of Revolutionary Black Workers. Cruse, who was influenced by Marxism, was no one's idea of an orthodox anything by the 1970s, even if he did popularize the idea of "revolutionary nationalism" in the 1960s. The core group of People's College, in fact, saw itself as most in tune ideologically with the League nationally.[53] However, it is worth noting that unlike the League and the Black Panther Party for Self-Defense on the West Coast, but like many in RAM and SOBU/YOBU, many of its members adopted Muslim, Swahili, African, or otherwise distinctly "Black" names (e.g., Abdul Alkalimat and Ebon Dooley). At the same time, it diverged from Maulana Karenga and many Kawaidaists in the insistence that a Black aesthetic should be drawn from actual African American popular culture, especially music. People's College emphasized the need for a traditional approach to art that was resolutely anticommercial, anticonsumerist, anticareerist, and committed to the notion of "functionality":

ART MUST NOT BE SOLD
IT MUST BE FREE.
ART MUST NOT BE PRIVATE
IT MUST BE PUBLIC.
ART MUST NOT BE STORED
IT MUST BE USED.
ART MUST NOT BECOME OUR REALITY
IT MUST HELP US FIND A BETTER WAY TO DEAL WITH REALITY.[54]

This notion of the function of art as being a way of people processing reality with the aim of changing society dovetailed with the basic People's College take on Marxism as something that was ultimately validated in the street, in the daily life of Black working people, not simply in the classroom.[55]

There are some obvious contradictions here for any artist who has to find a way to actually practice and make a living through their art. Interestingly, as is often the case in discussions of radical art and culture, nowhere does this mini-manifesto say that artists must be paid, must be able to make a living in some fashion. Nevertheless, it is a Black Marxist version of the common Black Arts notion that a career in the old commodity culture sense indexed by one's value on the commercial art exchange was not the yardstick by which art and the artist, particularly the Black artist, should be judged. Rather it was her or his contribution to the larger Black community/nation that was the measure of success. Of course, what functionality exactly meant was contested. Maulana Karenga, too, spoke of the need for Black art to be functional, which is to say promoting Black revolution and the creation of a new society.[56] However much the People's College core group might have disagreed with Karenga in the area of political economy, sociology, and so on, Alkalimat and the People's College cadre basically saw cultural nationalism as a necessary step toward building a Black nationalist and internationalist consciousness in the United States. Where they differed fundamentally with the Kawaidaists was in People's College's insistence on the importance of economic class.[57]

Possibly the most important contribution to Black Arts by People's College was the Timbuktu Bookstore and Market of New Africa on Jefferson Street. (It had a sister store in Atlanta run by the poet and Black Arts activist Ebon Dooley, who had been recruited to come to Atlanta from Chicago by his old OBAC comrade Alkalimat.) It was the nerve center and permanent public face of People's College to the Black communities of north Nashville and to the students of the nearby Black colleges. One can see Timbuktu, like many other Black bookstores of the era, as a Black Arts creation, a sort of freestanding performance that promoted revolution. It provided important works of literature, art, and criticism, as well as a space in which these works and Black art generally could be discussed. It also made manifest a radical Black culture and worldview. The People's College collective members themselves considered Timbuktu a part of the revolutionary Black Arts movement as a community information center working in tandem with community cultural centers like the Atlanta Center for Black Arts, community theater groups like Concept East in Detroit, and community schools like Malcolm X Liberation University in North Carolina.[58] Timbuktu and People's College in the South faded with Alkalimat's return to Chicago in the mid-1970s. People's College, mostly in the person of Alkalimat, continued in Chicago for several more years. Still, in conjunction with like-minded allies in North Carolina, Texas, Washington, D.C., and Georgia, particularly in SOBU, YOBU, CBE, and ALSC, People's College made the concept of the Black university much more of a reality, particularly in the center of Black higher education. It was important, too, in bringing a class-conscious perspective to Black Studies.[59] The Timbuktu Bookstores were also key in the establishment of a radical Black bookstore tradition in Nashville and Atlanta. This, in turn, directly and indirectly generated much Black cultural activity.

Nation Building: North Carolina

Black Art and Black Power in North Carolina were also closely tied to the state's many HBCUs, particularly in Greensboro, Durham, and Winston-Salem, sometimes through the work of students and faculty at HBCUs and sometimes through the work of recent HBCU graduates who received training in the arts on campus and returned to the community (or stayed in the community if they were from somewhere else) after leaving college. North Carolina contained two of the ten largest HBCUs in the United States, North Carolina A&T in Greensboro and North Carolina Central University in Durham. North Carolina Central (then North Carolina College) provided the bulk of the participants in the 1960 sit-ins in Durham. Another North Carolina HBCU, Shaw University in Raleigh, was the site of the meeting at which SNCC was born in the spring of 1960. As elsewhere, these were schools with drama programs, student theater groups, art departments, galleries, and so on that not only presented Black art to both campus and community audiences but also trained Black artists in their respective crafts. These artists in turn often performed and helped build cultural institutions in the Black neighborhoods that adjoined HBCUs as the Black Arts movement, with its imperative to serve the community, grew.

Much like the case of Black Studies at Federal City College in Washington, the development of Black Power and Black Arts in North Carolina also had much to do with the arrival of the first cohorts of Black students at non-HBCUs, such as Duke and the University of North Carolina, Chapel Hill. Early Black Studies efforts at these schools and the frustration of African American students and faculty with the limitations of trying to establish Black institutions in HBCUs led them into attempts to transform HBCUs into revolutionary Black schools or draw on HBCU student bodies and resources (and Black students from predominantly white schools) to build new freestanding institutions.

Durham's Hayti neighborhood was a long-standing focal point of Black business, education (home of the HBCU North Carolina Central University, established 1910), art, and culture in North Carolina, with roots in the immediate post–Civil War era as freedmen and freedwomen established the first institutions of the community. Obviously, the very name of the community suggested a sense of Black pride, militancy, and self-determination. Though buffeted by urban renewal in the 1950s like so many Black commercial and culture hubs in the urban South, Hayti continued to draw jazz, blues, and R&B artists from across the United States to its clubs and theaters and also promoted local artists, such as the blues musician Blind Boy Fuller. Further ravages of urban renewal and the construction of the Durham Highway through the heart of the neighborhood finally devastated its commercial district in 1969–1970. As with Jefferson Street in Nashville, as the main interface between community and campus in Black Durham and with its proximity to downtown, Hayti was the original epicenter of sit-ins and the Black Student movement in Durham in the 1960s.[60]

Antipoverty program money financed a short-lived but dynamic Black Arts site in the late 1960s and early 1970s, the Your Own Thing Theater. Your Own Thing took over the former Regal Theater in Hayti, a Black variety theater that had featured such jazz luminaries as the Count Basie Orchestra and Duke Ellington and his Orchestra. It combined music, theater, poetry, political meetings, and so on, much like the Affro Arts Theater in Chicago and The East in Brooklyn. Karen Rux, a North Carolina Central graduate who had worked in college theater and the new Black theater in New York, directed the theater and its associated group, the Ghetto Players, the members of which were primarily Black Durham high school students.[61]

During its relatively brief existence, the Your Own Thing Theater gained renown as a soul music hub, a reputation that Black Durhamites still recall.[62] Probably due to its identity as a Black Arts/Black Power hotspot, the theater was bombed in 1970, leading to the end of Your Own Thing—though no one was ever arrested for the attack.

Connected to Your Own Thing was the Black community radio station WAFR-FM, where Rux was the program director and oversaw a show featuring Black teenagers, *Black Seeds*. The station played community-oriented material, soul, and jazz.[63] The chief force behind the founding of WAFR was another North Carolina Central alumnus, Robert Spruill, who became the president of the station. Taking advantage of federal money for the creation of noncommercial radio stations, Spruill and others, again mostly NCCU alumni, were able to build WAFR with eventually 138 hours of programming a week and an audience of 75,000. In short, it was a community-based Black Power/Black Arts institution with a mass audience.[64]

A landmark Black Power/Black Arts moment in Raleigh-Durham was the establishment of Malcolm X Liberation University in 1969. Like elsewhere, the inauguration of the school in Durham was the convergence of campus and community in the attempt to create a Black university. As in Washington, D.C., civil rights activism, antipoverty program work, and HBCU and non-HBCU higher education institutions intersected at that moment in Raleigh-Durham, creating a dialectic of cooperation and conflict similar to the conditions that created the New School, Drum and Spear, and CBE.

Previously all-white Duke University in Durham admitted five Black undergraduates in 1963 under the threat of the loss of federal money. Duke hired its first Black professor in 1966. By 1969, there were just over 100 African American undergraduates at Duke, a small proportion of the university's 5,000 undergraduates, but one that was highly organized and politicized. The Afro-American Association (AAA) formed the primary vehicle of Black political activism at Duke, agitating for more Black students and faculty and a Black Studies department as well as supporting labor rights for African American cafeteria workers on campus.[65] In 1969, the AAA organized a Black Week celebration for Negro History Week. Black History Month was promoted by Black students and Black Studies advocates on college campuses and in the community, becoming widely observed by the mid-1970s. It featured speeches by comedian Dick Gregory and Mississippi civil rights leader Fannie Lou Hamer, a show by James Brown, a Black visual art exhibit, the dramatic performances of James Weldon Johnson's *God's Trombones* and Amiri Baraka's *The Baptism*, poetry readings, lectures on Black history, and a theater workshop led by Karen Rux, demonstrating an increasing interaction between Black Duke students and North Carolina Central graduates.[66]

Many of the AAA activists spent the summer of 1968 working in local antipoverty programs in Durham's Black communities where they met social worker Howard Fuller (Owusu Sadaukai), a Left nationalist in much the same vein as the cadre of People's College in Nashville and of CBE and Drum and Spear in Washington, D.C. Born in Louisiana, Fuller grew up in Milwaukee and earned a master of social work degree from Western Reserve University in Ohio before coming to Durham to join Operation Breakthrough, a federally funded antipoverty program, and the Foundation for Community Development, another antipoverty agency, working in Hayti and other nearby Black communities. (About 40 percent of Durham's population was Black in the late 1960s.) These agencies officially labored primarily to improve housing and neighborhood infrastructure—though Fuller and his colleagues increasingly saw political empowerment as their goal and various sorts of direct action tactics as their primary vehicle.[67]

Following the assassination of Martin Luther King Jr. in 1968, the Duke campus was roiled by protests of the AAA and its African American and white supporters, primarily around the struggles of Black cafeteria and other blue-collar workers at Duke (who went on strike that year for better wages and conditions and recognition of their union), the establishment of Black Studies, the recruitment of more Black students, and greater engagement with Durham's Black communities and their struggles. While the Duke administration made some token gestures, including the establishment of a committee to study the creation of more courses focusing on Black topics, Black students were almost entirely shut out of any real input into these decisions and processes. By turns frustrated by the administration and inspired by the upsurge of Black political and cultural activities on and off campus, the AAA took over the Allen Building, Duke's main administration building, shortly after Black Week in 1969. The AAA demanded that the Duke administration settle the issues of Black labor rights, community engagement, increasing the number of Black students, the establishment of Black Studies, and student involvement in decision making regarding issues affecting the Black students, faculty, and community. After the Black students ended the takeover, local and state police tear-gassed, violently clashed with, and arrested many in the crowd of a couple thousand Black and white supporters of the AAA who had gathered outside the Allen Building.[68]

This fracas galvanized Duke students and community members who had not been a part of the protests to support the AAA and its demands. At the same time, the incident led the Duke administration to more publicly resist student demands in some regards while negotiating more seriously in others. Howard Fuller was among the negotiators with the Duke administration. Again, many of the students already knew Fuller from their internship in the Foundation for Community Development the previous summer. One upshot was that there was an agreement to form yet another committee to study and implement the creation of Black Studies at Duke, which would make it the first southern university to have such a program or department. However, there was an impasse over the issue of African American student participation in the creation and shape of the new unit—and given the miniscule number of Black faculty members, Black faculty input was necessarily going to be small.[69]

Frustration with the Duke administration caused Black students to threaten to leave the university for a new Black institution, Malcolm X Liberation University. This institution was envisioned by Fuller as a part of the new Black university movement that was particularly strong in the Upper South. The initial location of the new school was an old warehouse building on Pettigrew Street between downtown Durham and the center of the old Hayti business district. While only a portion of those who had said they would drop out of Duke actually enrolled in Malcolm X Liberation University, the new institution's opening was a major cultural, political, and educational event in North Carolina. Part of the cultural impact of the opening events of the school involved clothing fashion. The crowds in the streets of Durham contained many men and women in self-created variations on traditional dress of a wide range of African cultures—an arresting sight in a small southern city.[70] Tanisha Ford notes that such adoption of "soul styles" was a key element of Black Arts and Black Power, "The international struggle for black liberation provided a space for black people to use clothing to not only adorn but also re-aestheticize the black body."[71] This prefigured similar spectacles on African Liberation Day, which was introduced on May 27, 1972, leading to the establishment of ALSC. While ALD was celebrated throughout the United States, it was particularly strong in the South since Fuller and other Malcolm X Liberation University and SOBU/YOBU activists had played important parts in the holiday's establishment. The Malcolm X Liberation University inaugural featured, too, a powerful performance by a women's a cappella group, the Harambee Singers, formed by

Bernice Johnson Reagon and other Black women in Atlanta in 1966 and a forerunner of the better known Sweet Honey in the Rock.

Malcolm X Liberation University remained on Pettigrew Street for only a year and then moved to another location in Hayti for a relatively short time before being forced to relocate again by the construction of the Durham Highway. It left Durham altogether and settled in Greensboro, where there was a greater number of Black college students at North Carolina A&T and nearby Bennett College as well as a by-then famous tradition of Black student activism. However, the school had persistent funding issues and closed in 1973—though Fuller and others connected with Malcolm X Liberation University and SOBU/YOBU remained active in North Carolina political and cultural life. (Fuller eventually returned to his native Milwaukee.) A number joined the Communist Workers Party, which was the target of the infamous Greensboro massacre by the Ku Klux Klan in 1979.[72]

North Carolina lacked an urban center with the status of Atlanta, New Orleans, Houston, Washington, or Miami. However, because of the sheer number of HBCUs, the interlocking political and cultural activity (which often combined Marxism and cultural nationalism) of Black students on HBCU and non-HBCU campuses, and the expansion of those activities into the community joining radical political and cultural initiatives already underway, North Carolina built an important tradition of intermingled radical campus and community organizing with a strong cultural aspect that would extend into the twenty-first century. This tradition can be seen in the National Black Theatre Festival, founded by Larry Leon Hamlin of the National Black Repertory Theatre in Winston-Salem in 1989 and continuing until the present, and the Moral Monday protests and the call for a "new fusion politics" led by William Barber II, the former NAACP leader and advocate for a new Poor People's Campaign.

CHAPTER FIVE

The Southern Black Cultural Alliance, the Neighborhood Arts Center, and the Institutionalization of Community-Based Black Arts in the South

In much of the United States, the period from 1973 to the late 1970s was one of conflict, decline and collapse for many Black Power and Black Arts institutions and organizations. Part of this decline occurred due to various sorts of ideological and organizational disputes between different sections of the Black Power and Black Arts movements. Such conflicts, of course, had previously riven and destroyed Black Arts institutions, such as BARTS in Harlem, the Black House in San Francisco, and Black Arts West also in the Bay Area. The conflict between the BPP after Eldridge Cleaver's rise to leadership and Maulana Karenga's US was particularly destructive. While the 1969 shootout between members of US and the Black Panthers that killed Panther leaders Alprentice "Bunchy" Carter and John Huggins on the UCLA campus can be seen as the most intense moment of this conflict, related disputes between the Panthers and artists associated by the BPP with cultural nationalists both inside and outside US did much to damage the Black Arts infrastructure of Los Angeles and the Bay Area and drove such artists as Ed Bullins, Amiri Baraka, Sonia Sanchez, and Marvin X to other regions for longer and shorter terms.

However, those earlier conflicts and losses can be seen as largely local (and often as personal conflicts between individuals that were cast in terms of political principle) primarily affecting individual neighborhoods, cities, or, perhaps regions. The later battles between "reformists," cultural nationalists, and Marxists of various stripes affected Black Arts and Black Power nationwide, contributing to a decline in the mass base for Black Power and Black Arts. These battles were heightened, and were often in part instigated, by the organized disruption of the FBI and police "Red Squads" repurposed from the general Cold War focus on the Communist Left to Black radicalism more generally. The result was the destruction or decline of such national institutions and organizations as *Black World*, CAP, ALSC, SOBU/YOBU, the *Journal of Black Poetry*, and *SoulBook* as well as many local groups and institutions.

The South saw some similar losses among Black Arts organizations, though, perhaps due more to the movement of artists into political and educational organizing and away from cultural work than to ideological infighting. BLKARTSOUTH and its associated journal *Nkombo* slowly came to an end as a number of key figures, notably Kalamu ya Salaam, withdrew from arts activities to devote their time to the building of independent nationalist educational institutions and community organizing. Certainly, art and culture were important elements of the curriculum at these schools. And former cultural activists, like Salaam, maintained friendly relationships with the surviving arts organizations and institutions that, in many cases, they had helped form. However, the new priorities of Salaam and others took a toll on BLKARTSOUTH and other existing Black Arts groups, resulting in a need for new initiatives and the renewal of older ones.

Still, Black Arts in the South negotiated this period with fewer losses than other regions, by and large. Many participants in the southern Black Arts and Black Power movements argue that the sort of factionalism that consumed many northern activists, such as the prominent debates between Amiri Baraka and Haki Madhubuti, in ALSC, CAP, and other organizations largely bypassed the South even if, as will be noted, those debates elsewhere did have a practical effect on Black Arts in the region.[1] There was a sense that the political environment of the South was so hostile to Black radicalism, and civil rights generally, that the sort of conflict that attended the movement elsewhere was a luxury that southern Black activists could not afford.[2] It also may be that Black Marxism in the South, particularly as seen in the Drum and Spear group, CBE, the early People's College, Malcolm X Liberation University, the Timbuktu bookstores, and YOBU/SOBU, was often so intertwined with cultural nationalist ideology, particularly with respect to Black art and culture, that the gap between Marxists and Kawaidaists seemed not as wide as it often was in the North and the West.

At the same time, while southern Black Arts activists may not have engaged in this infighting to the same degree as their peers in the North and the West, the factional disputes and the diminishment or outright collapse of national political and cultural institutions in which Black southern radicals had been extremely active, such as CAP, SOBU/YOBU, and ALSC, could not but have an impact on the South and the Black Arts and Black Power infrastructure there. As previously noted, much of the networking and communication between radical Black cultural activists in the South took place through the circuits of CAP, ALSC, YOBU/SOBU, and other radical

Black political organizations—just as theaters and other traveling arts collectives advanced national Black Power work on their tours.

Despite the impact of the fracturing of national Black Power organizations shared with other regions, two things happened in the South that did not occur elsewhere. First, as BLKARTSOUTH became moribund, southern Black Arts organizers who remained primarily dedicated to cultural work, particularly Tom Dent in New Orleans, set out to build a new regional network dedicated to fostering Black art throughout the South and to showcasing that art across the region and beyond. This resulted in the creation of the Southern Black Cultural Alliance (SBCA), by far the most successful regional Black Arts organization in the United States.

Second, with the election of Maynard Jackson as mayor of Atlanta in 1973, the first major southern city to elect a Black mayor since Reconstruction, Black Arts became institutionalized in the broader political structure to a degree not seen before. As will be discussed, this was largely a result of the confluence of previous Black Arts and Black Power initiatives in Atlanta, the concentration of major Black educational institutions in the city, Black Arts activists and supporters who played significant roles in Jackson's election campaign and early administration, Jackson's own desire to be known as the "culture mayor," and the relative economic health of Atlanta as compared to most larger cities where Black mayors were elected in more or less the same period, such as Detroit, Gary, Newark, and Cleveland. (Tom Bradley was elected as mayor of Los Angeles, also a city with a comparatively vibrant economy, in 1973. However, the social forces that propelled Bradley to office in a city where African Americans were about 11 percent of the population were far different and less tied to Black liberation struggles than in nearly all other large cities that elected Black mayors in this period.) This institutionalization and new levels of public support of African American art and arts initiatives in Atlanta facilitated by new levels of Black political power provided a model for similar efforts elsewhere and began the transformation of Atlanta, and the South generally, into the centers of Black visual arts, theater, literature, dance, and so on that they are today—of course, the South was already and had always been a center for the production and circulation of Black music.

New Orleans and the Rise of a Southern Black Arts Network

The performance tours of the FST and then BLKARTSOUTH after it emerged from the workshops of the FST, as well as the orientation and openness of

BLKARTSOUTH's journal *Nkombo* toward southern Black artists outside New Orleans, inspired African American artists across the region to set up new groups in much the same spirit. Some of these artists had previously pursued their crafts in relative isolation or in comparatively small and informal groups. Others, particularly actors and playwrights, had been part of college arts programs, particularly at historically Black schools, but also at schools that had only recently begun to admit African American students in any numbers. By nature the theater (and musical performance, for the most part) was a collective endeavor that involved networking. Some of these theater workers became involved in the local mainstream and experimental (and previously white) community theaters of their hometowns as the fraying of Jim Crow in the 1960s allowed them to audition successfully for these theaters.

Also, the rise of early Black Arts theaters in the South (and elsewhere) dedicated to serving and representing the history, culture, and current conditions of grassroots Black people inspired similar theaters by, for, and of poor southerners of varied backgrounds in the late 1960s and early 1970s, especially, but not exclusively, in Appalachia. While these multicultural theaters were often largely white, from the beginning they sought to include Black southerners and to actively build alliances with Black performance groups and arts institutions in the region. The most prominent institutional expression of this sort of alliance was the Regional Organization of Theaters South (ROOTS, eventually Alternate Roots), which was formed in 1976 at the Highlander Center (a direct descendant of the old Highlander School) in New Market, Tennessee.

However, Jim Crow lived on in other ways. As Black Memphis actor, director, and playwright Levi Frazier Jr. recalls, the range of roles available to Black actors (much less directors, stage designers, and other theater craftspeople) in the community theater of the 1960s South remained exceedingly small, leading to considerable dissatisfaction among Black theater workers with the status quo. When I told Frazier that leading Black Arts director Woodie King said something similar about Detroit in the late 1950s and early 1960s—that Black actors were only given "buddy roles" (that is, the "buddy" of the white lead) and never the lead—Frazier commented, "Buddy roles? Hell, we were only allowed to play butler roles."[3] At the same time, news about Black Arts initiatives elsewhere in the North, West, *and* South circulated among these artists on southern Black campuses (some of whom like Karen Rux at North Carolina Central University worked in northern and western Black theaters during the summer) and in the community, producing tremendous interest and some early efforts to undertake similar initiatives locally. As a result, the poetry and theatrical performance tours of BLKARTSOUTH—in which the group would write, stage, and act or present almost all its sophisticated, well-rehearsed socially engaged material to Black community audiences, and in which *all* the actors, the director, the technical workers, and so on, would be Black and primarily trained locally—came as a sort of revelation of what was possible in the South, both in terms of staging and of reaching an audience.[4]

By the 1970s, a profusion of community-based Black theaters, performance groups, art centers, and arts workshops had arisen across the Deep South. Like SUDAN/Southwest and the Black Arts Center, many of these groups and institutions were directly inspired or shaped by *Nkombo*, BLKARTSOUTH and its tours—as well as by the more high-profile national Black Arts and Black Power institutions outside the region, such as the New Lafayette Theater in New York; the ETA Theater, Kuumba Theater, OBAC, Third World Press, and the Institute for Positive Education in Chicago, Broadside Press in Detroit, and Spirit House in Newark, and by such publications as *Black World*, the *Journal of Black Poetry*, and *Black Theatre*. Like the FST, a number of those new southern groups had roots in campus theater and arts programs that under the influence of BLKARTSOUTH and the burgeoning national movement had migrated into the community. For example, the Dashiki Project Theatre opened in 1968 in a coffeehouse at St. Francis de Sales, a Black Catholic church in New Orleans's Central City, a hub of Black commerce and culture. It was the brainchild of Theodore Gilliam and other faculty members, graduates, and students of the Dillard University drama program. As with many other Black Arts initiatives in the late 1960s and early 1970s, it was made possible by antipoverty program funding. Dashiki held itself apart from FST/BLKARTSOUTH and the more distinctly nationalist direction that FST/BLKARTSOUTH took, and did not have the regional impact of BLKARTSOUTH. Other than its early development and an original production of Norbert Davidson's *El Hajj Malik: The Life and Times of Malcolm X* in 1968, Dashiki functioned more as repertory theater bringing Black (and some non-Black) drama from around the United States, including stagings of work by Ed Bullins, Ntozake Shange, and August Wilson, to Black (and mixed) audiences in New Orleans rather than as an incubator of local plays after the manner of BLKARTSOUTH. In that sense, Dashiki was like the early FST but without the more polemical side of FST. Nevertheless, it was the most consistently functioning Black theater in New Orleans from the late 1960s through the 1980s.[5]

Similarly, the M-Ensemble (now Florida's oldest surviving Black theater) was launched on the campus of the University of Miami in 1971 by Theodore Cooper (later the head of the drama department at Howard University) but soon migrated to Miami's Liberty City, yet another urban Black community in the South that had thrived commercially and culturally in the 1940s and 1950s, but which was much scarred by highway construction in the 1960s. Run for decades by Pat Williams and Shirley Richardson, M-Ensemble represented the southeastern United States at the Second World Black Festival of African Arts and Culture (FESTAC) in Lagos, Nigeria, in 1977. Another example of the FST-inspired move from campus to community can be seen in Memphis. There a group largely made up of graduate students in theater from the historically Black LeMoyne-Owen College and relatively recently integrated Memphis State University (now the University of Memphis) and Southwestern at Memphis (now Rhodes College) got together to create the Beale Street Repertory Theater in 1974, stimulated in part by a performance of John O'Neal's revived touring unit of the FST.[6]

In other cases, groups grew directly out of the community, again often with immediate connections to BLKARTSOUTH, as with BLKARTSOUTH veterans Chakula Cha Jua's Ethiopian Theater in New Orleans (which would stage the first production of Tom Dent's *Ritual Murder* in 1976) and the Theater of Afro-Arts founded in Miami in 1969 by Wendell Narcisse, a New Orleans native who became the president of the SBCA and joined Dent and Salaam as an editor of *Nkombo*.[7] Other groups within this southern African American arts network included the Black Arts Workshop in Little Rock, Arkansas, the Black Belt Cultural Center and the Children of Selma Theater in Selma, Alabama, the Urban Theater in Houston, and the Last Messengers in Greenville, Mississippi.

However, though BAM organizations and institutions proliferated in the South, Dent and other southern BAM activists remained frustrated by the degree to which they saw the northern-based "national" BAM journals and media replicating much the same sort of narrow focus on Black theater in a handful of northern and western cities (basically, Chicago, the San Francisco Bay Area, Los Angeles, and, especially, New York) as did the white cultural apparatus, both mainstream and bohemian:

> For me personally, SBCA came out of a great dissatisfaction with the situation in the early '70s, because I knew that what they were doing in New York was about on the same level with us, but we just didn't have any money. I knew that some of the productions of the Free Southern

> Theatre were better than what was being done in New York. But the Black cultural establishment, as it existed, particularly *Negro Digest/Black World*, which was very influential, was as New York, Northern-city-based in its appraisals as were the White critical journals. This came as a shock to me at first.
>
> No matter how many good short stories or poems we might publish in our literary magazine *Nkombo*, or might be published in other small, community literary magazines, that didn't mean as much as one book published by Macmillan, which the Black journals reviewed, and then these writers became known. As far as theater was concerned, anything New Lafayette or the Negro Ensemble Company did received an attention which dwarfed anything we did. That was just a reality, without taking anything away from Douglas Turner Ward or Bob MacBeth or the value of their work.[8]

The SBCA was Dent's answer to the lack of attention paid to southern Black artists and cultural institutions. Part of the impetus for the SBCA issued from Dent's desire to continue and extend the work of BLKARTSOUTH, particularly as the older group began to unravel around 1973 with its New Orleans members moving in different directions even as the network that BLKARTSOUTH built across the South remained large, in fact growing. Unlike the disintegration of many early Black Arts or proto–Black Arts collectives elsewhere at that time in the United States, there were few sharp conflicts or ruptures within BLKARTSOUTH that led to its decline. Rather its leading members found themselves emphasizing different priorities while remaining friends. Salaam, for example, became more focused on political and educational organizing through the Ahidiana Collective and his editorship of the *Black Collegian*. Of all the leading figures of BLKARTSOUTH still active in New Orleans, Dent remained most interested in the arts. He wanted to institutionalize the less formal connections with many of the new southern Black theaters and cultural groups forged by the FST and BLKARTSOUTH. A successful regional Black theater/performance conference brought many such groups to West Point, Mississippi (where Dent taught at the historically Black Mary Holmes College, commuting back and forth from New Orleans) in 1972. Dent used the conference as a jumping-off point for the SBCA.[9]

Dent envisioned the SBCA as an umbrella organization that would allow the development and exposure of Black theater, dance, poetry and other forms of expressive art throughout the South. He intended it to serve also as a medium or circuit of cultural transmission that would allow southern Black artists and community-based arts groups to reach audiences (and gain financial support) beyond the South. Of all the southern groups, only O'Neal's FST had been able to achieve such a regional and national visibility previously. And even the FST's financial situation was hand-to-mouth and its ability to reach outside the region a function of the time O'Neal and the theater spent performing and fundraising in New York rather than a result of the national Black journals and other media looking South. Such coverage as the FST and the SBCA were able to achieve occurred because southern Black activists, especially Dent and Salaam, wrote and sent in reports, not because those journals sent regular staff members and correspondents down South.[10]

Without new financial support from inside and beyond the region, Dent felt, the new Black cultural institutions of the South would not be able to grow—or even survive: "I felt we in the South, no matter how faithful we were to our community mission or how important the work we were doing was, would never get any recognition unless we did something to present ourselves more aggressively. Not that we wanted to be famous, but we had to have some recognition if we were going to survive in terms of funding, or whatever rewards you need to keep going. Otherwise we would very soon be back to the situation where young actors and writers in New Orleans felt they had not arrived until they left here."[11]

The SBCA was partially successful in its goal of gaining national attention for southern Black artists. *Black World* and *Black Theatre* did increasingly cover Black performance in the South—*Black World*'s annual theater roundup in the spring was (and is) a particularly good source for news about these productions. However, again, as Dent and Salaam pointed out, SBCA members, generally Dent or Salaam, nearly always had to cover these performances themselves because of the extreme difficulty in getting staff from these journals to come South.[12] (Barbara Molette played much the same role for *Black World* in Atlanta.) While it may have been difficult to attract reviewers to the South, members of northern and western Black theaters and arts institutions did attend the annual meetings of the SBCA, especially the performance festivals in the fall, giving southern playwrights an exposure that they would have otherwise lacked, and leading to the production of works by these playwrights across the country.[13] This participation of Black theaters from outside of the region also began to establish the South as a center (eventually, *the* center) for national Black cultural festivals and showcases of Black art, anticipating the National Black Theater Festival in Winston-Salem, North Carolina, Art Africa Miami and Prizm Art Fair in Miami, and the Atlanta Black Theatre Festival and the Black Arts Festival in Atlanta. In this way, the SBCA began to shift the cultural geography of Black art in the United States. Of course, New York and Los Angeles remained the chief nexuses of commercial theater, film, and television, but increasingly Black theater companies and other sorts of artists and arts institutions came South to be seen rather than simply the reverse with actors, directors, writers, and so on having to travel North or West to gain national visibility and careers.

Despite the only partial realization of its goal of gaining national recognition for southern Black artists, the SBCA was extremely successful in its goal of inspiring, promoting, and supporting the work of Black artists and arts institutions within the South. Its two most important activities were its annual business conference, which generally took place on Memorial Day weekend, and its annual performance festival, which usually occurred on Thanksgiving weekend. These meetings and festivals took place in cities and college campuses in Alabama, Arkansas, Florida, Georgia, Louisiana, Mississippi, North Carolina, Tennessee, and Texas. While difficult to verify, the SBCA's claim that "over eighty per-cent of all Black cultural organizations in the South have participated in at least one of the festivals, conferences, or business meetings of the S.B.C.A." suggests something of the group's reach—a reach unparalleled by any other regional Black Arts organization in the United States.[14] As Levi Frazier (who first attended an SBCA meeting in Tallahassee in 1976) remembered, these meetings and festivals were invaluable in opening doors and gaining exposure for southern Black artists' work outside their hometowns. They were also crucial in a very practical sense, allowing formal and informal discussions about how these grassroots groups dealt with common problems of funding, organization, audience, and artistic development, particularly as the national Black Arts and Black Power movements fractured and declined and pressures were brought to bear on groups to tone down their radical politics.[15]

This combination of artistic networking and hands-on discussion of common problems (as well as a much lower degree of ideological conflict between Marxists and cultural nationalists than in many other places in the United States) allowed the SBCA to survive until the early 1980s, far longer than most Black Arts and Black Power umbrella groups. The SBCA finally succumbed to many of the same forces that undermined radical arts initiatives elsewhere, including the depoliticization and bureaucratization of funding for radical Black community-based cultural groups (or perhaps it might be more accurate to say that the cultural bureaucracy increasingly emphasized the funding of depoliticized arts initiatives), the curtailing or complete elimination of federal initiatives, such as the Comprehensive Employment and Training Act (CETA)/Neighborhood Arts Program (enacted in 1973 and ended in 1982) that underwrote many arts groups and theaters, and the decline of the larger movements across the country.[16]

Nevertheless, even long after the end of SBCA, many veterans of the FST, BLKARTSOUTH, and SBCA, such as Levi Frazier in Memphis, Tom Dent in New Orleans, Wendell Narcisse in Miami, and Nayo Watkins in Durham, North Carolina, were able to draw on the SBCA network to create new African American arts institutions and projects supported by public resources after the model of Atlanta where new Black political power was significantly expressed through the support of such institutions and arts projects. Watkins, for example, coordinated the Alternate Roots Community/Artists Partnership Program that created ten major projects in Durham and surrounding counties during the early 1990s. While Watkins's projects engaged, drew in, and served a variety of communities, the African American communities of Durham were at the center, and Black artists from the area and the South more generally, including Atlanta Black Arts poet and cultural organizer Alice Lovelace, largely staffed the projects.[17]

The legacy of SBCA remained particularly pronounced on the Gulf Coast. Early Black Arts participants in Houston were joined by artists who had been active in the movement in other cities and regions, including poet and critic Lorenzo Thomas (a member of New York's Umbra Poets Workshop who moved to Houston in 1973 as a writer-in-residence at TSU, eventually becoming a professor at the University of Houston), visual artist Bert Long (a Fifth Ward native who returned to Houston in 1977 from California), and poet, editor, and publisher Ahmos Zu-Bolton (who came to Texas from his hometown of DeRidder, Louisiana). Thomas quickly became a leading figure at the Black Arts Center, where he taught writing classes, and in the Houston poetry scene generally. He brought his experience in Umbra to building new Black writers groups and journals and editing the Houston Black Arts journal *Roots* at TSU, as well as a commitment to the necessity of the establishment of Black cultural institutions outside of the mainstream arts milieu:

> The Black Arts movement—which effectively came to the South in the 1970s—had purposes and goals based on the concept that mainstream American culture is anti-black. Mainstream American culture is

> antagonistic and maybe even dangerous for black people. That was the rhetoric of the poetry of the era.
>
> Well, what then, do you propose? Then you propose the establishment of alternative cultural institutions. The Black Arts movement was not satisfied with the NAACP concept of, "We're going to work hard for the day when our work is no longer necessary." Its whole purpose was to propose alternative culture and, therefore, alternative cultural organizations to a mainstream that was considered to be antithetical to the lifestyle, lives, and goals of African-American people.[18]

Thomas, an old comrade of Dent's at Umbra, immediately became a point person of SBCA in Texas on his arrival in Houston where he often worked with Zu-Bolton building the local Black poetry scene.[19] He also became deeply involved in the organizing of Black music performances and events, notably the Juneteenth Blues Festival from the 1970s to the 1990s.[20]

Zu-Bolton edited *HooDoo Magazine* in DeRidder, Washington, D.C., Houston, and elsewhere and in Houston founded Energy BlackSouth and Black Box Publishers, which issued a series of poetry cassettes by Black writers. Zu-Bolton was the chief organizer of the HooDoo Poetry and Culture Festivals that took place in a variety of cities in the late 1970s, including Galveston in 1979 and Austin in 1980. The Texas HooDoo festivals included a significant number of Chicanas/Chicanos, epitomizing a sort of Texas Black Arts multicultural cross-fertilization that was relatively unusual for the South at that time. Zu-Bolton recalled that it was the 1979 HooDoo Festival in Galveston that put him, Lorenzo Thomas, Jerry Ward, and other southern Black artists in touch with Chicana/o writers like the San Antonio–based Evangelina Vigil-Piñón.[21] Because of geographical proximity during Zu-Bolton's Texas years, shared aesthetic sensibilities, and a penchant for institution-building, Zu-Bolton and Thomas quickly struck up a relationship that extended SBCA's reach in Texas. (Zu-Bolton would later bring *HooDoo* and Energy BlackSouth to Washington, D.C. where E. Ethelbert Miller joined the *HooDoo* staff. Zu-Bolton mentored Miller in the nuts and bolts of journal and small press publishing. Zu-Bolton and Miller brought out *Synergy: An Anthology of Washington D.C. Blackpoetry* under the Energy BlackSouth imprint in 1975).[22]

Through Thomas, Zu-Bolton, and the SUDAN writers and their links with the FST/BLKARTSOUTH/SBCA circles for which New Orleans was the hub, the Black Arts movement in Houston became part of a much larger network of Black southern theaters, performance groups, journals, presses, writers workshops, and so on. Houston artists, especially Thomas and Zu-Bolton, and groups, such as the Urban Theater, were active participants in annual business conferences and performance festivals of the SBCA. Much like the Black Arts Center, SBCA finally succumbed to the hostile funding climate and a general move to depoliticize public arts projects in the early 1980s. However, Black arts in Houston, as elsewhere, continued to undertake community-based arts projects, such as Sum Arts (which produced, among many other concerts, the annual Juneteenth Blues Festival) founded and run largely by Black musicians and poets, including Vivian Ayers and Lorenzo Thomas.

Atlanta and the Institutionalization of Black Arts

The founding of CAP at its first convention in Atlanta in 1970 in many respects confirmed the city as a center of the new Black politics and culture. The CAP convention had been organized largely by cultural nationalists influenced by Maulana Karenga and his US organization, most prominent among them Amiri Baraka. However, the convention drew a wide range of Black political and cultural activists, including many who were seen as basically centrists or reformists by many in Black Power and Black Arts. Among the well-known civil rights veterans who addressed the meeting were Ralph Abernathy, Julian Bond, and Whitney Young, all of whom reminded their listeners of the history of struggle for civil rights and Black liberation in Atlanta, particularly in the schools of AUC. The visible participation of Julian Bond and other former SNCC leaders might be unsurprising given the militant nature of SNCC, but the appearance of Young and various mainstream Black politicians marked the advent of a new sort of unity politics.

While it is hard to gauge the local impact of the founding of CAP in Atlanta, the emphasis that CAP placed on the election of Black officials unquestionably had a considerable consequence. The most visible campaigns for mayor of large cities by Black candidates to that point, such as Richard Hatcher's in Gary, Indiana, Carl Stokes's in Cleveland, and Kenneth Gibson's in Newark, New Jersey (which was in full swing at the time of the convention) took place in northern cities. Despite this, as CAP recognized, the demographics of the African American community in the United States dictated that the greatest opportunities were in the South (where more than half of the Black population was concentrated). Atlanta already had a modern tradition of successful Black electoral activity as seen in Julian Bond's campaigns for the state legislature and Maynard Jackson's 1968 run for the U.S. Senate against Herman Talmadge in which Jackson lost the election but carried the city of Atlanta.

It was in this climate of Black political self-reliance and electoral possibility that Jackson, who was president of the Atlanta city council, decided to challenge the white mayor Sam Masell in 1973, breaking with the tradition of consensus (and some would say cooptation) that had dominated local politics for decades. Gaining overwhelming support and a high turnout from the Black neighborhoods of Atlanta, Jackson won with more than 60 percent of the vote. From this moment on, Black politicians would exercise more power in Atlanta than in any other major city in the United States. (All the mayors of Atlanta elected from that point until the writing of this book at the end of the second decade of the twenty-first century were Black.)

Jackson, who wanted to be known as the "culture mayor," decided to make the promotion of the arts a centerpiece of his administration from the very start. Photographer Jim Alexander, a key chronicler of the Neighborhood Arts Center (NAC) and still at the center of Black art in Atlanta, notes, "Maynard was a true progressive with all the political and business skills needed to make plans work. Not afraid to be the boss. He would listen to people, but you had to bring for real—had to know what you are talking about and that your project was workable—and why it was worth doing. Always found him to be two or three thoughts ahead of the average person. Never above anybody. Dedicated to building cultural infrastructure."[23]

Jackson saw culture as an important calling card to the outside world for Atlanta as well as something that could potentially appeal to every major constituency in the city. In his inaugural address he promised increased municipal attention to and funding of the arts. His first act toward this end was the establishment of an Ad Hoc Advisory Committee for the Arts, which was charged with planning a Mayor's Day for the Arts, making recommendations for future financial support of the arts, and addressing the particular immediate concerns of Atlanta's arts communities.[24] Jackson's support of Black cultural and intellectual activities both helped make possible the growth of new institutions and supported the work of existing groups—for example, a grant from the city's Bureau of Cultural Affairs financed the printing of IBW's monthly report.[25] The new Black political power—and the attention of the Jackson administration to the arts—also facilitated grants and donations from the private sector, including local economic giants like Coca-Cola.

Michael Lomax was the key Jackson administration figure in carrying out the mayor's focus on the arts. A Morehouse graduate and a literature professor at Spelman, he joined the Jackson campaign as a speechwriter. Lomax, who was married to playwright, poet, fiction writer, and journalist Pearl Cleage at the time, had close ties to the African American arts community on and off the campus, having worked at the Atlanta Center for Black Art and *Rhythm*. Jackson appointed Lomax as the director of Cultural Affairs in 1975. In that capacity, Lomax tirelessly supported public backing of arts initiatives in Atlanta and was an important conduit for the private funding of African American arts institutions in the city. Shirley Franklin, later mayor of Atlanta, succeeded Lomax as the head of the city's Bureau of Cultural Affairs after Lomax's 1978 election to the Fulton County Commission, the powerful legislative body of the county that includes Atlanta and with a population at that time almost evenly divided between Black and white. Atlanta, then, was perhaps unique among U.S. cities in that what might be seen as the public arts infrastructure was a base for the launching of major political careers. It is hard to think of another U.S. city in which the arts became such a pathway.[26]

Directly and through Lomax, Black cultural activists, particularly poet Ebon Dooley, lobbied hard to make sure that the Black community got a significant share of the resources made available through Jackson's cultural focus instead of channeling those funds to more established "high" art institutions, such as the High Museum. Dooley organized a program of the public performance of jazz in parks and public housing projects through grants from the city and the Atlanta Musicians Union.[27] Dooley and other Black Arts activists also pushed for the establishment of the NAC, the most important locus of African American arts efforts in Atlanta from its inception in late 1974 until its demise in 1990, particularly from 1975 until 1985. As Candy Tate demonstrates in what is by far the best treatment to date, her dissertation "Our Art Itself Was Our Activism: Atlanta's Neighborhood Arts Center, 1975–1990," the NAC was the linchpin of the institutionalization of Black Arts in Atlanta. If it was Jackson and Black Arts activists in city hall that put African American art and the public support of that art at the center of the cultural world of Atlanta, it was the NAC that to a large degree established Black Arts and a Black Arts sensibility as a model for public art in Atlanta, moving the city from a relatively provincial backwater to a national center of the arts in the United States. And, there was no real separation between the Jackson administration and the NAC. Not only did you have people connected to the NAC, such as Pearl Cleage (who served a stint as the Jackson administration press secretary) and Michael Lomax, with key positions in the municipal government (and in the case of Lomax, *the* key position so far as the arts were concerned), Jackson himself took a hand in promoting the NAC. Jim Alexander (the most important documenter of the NAC) recalled that he met Jackson at the 1974 National Black Political Convention in Little Rock, where Jackson was a plenary speaker. The New Jersey–born and raised Alexander was living in New Haven, Connecticut at the time. When Alexander mentioned to Jackson that he wanted to leave New Haven, Jackson suggested that Alexander relocate to Atlanta where he could work at the NAC. Alexander did move to Atlanta around 1975, meeting up with Ebon Dooley whom he had known from political work. Through the interlocking network of civil rights and Black Power activists, the Jackson administration, and the NAC, Alexander got a job at the National Federation of Southern Cooperatives while volunteering at the NAC, where he ran workshops in photography and later served as photographer-in-residence.[28]

The NAC was housed in Black communities, first in an old school building in Mechanicsville, a working-class neighborhood in southwest Atlanta and later on Auburn Avenue, the traditional commercial and civic heart of Black Atlanta.[29] While the initial support of the NAC came from Jackson's Ad Hoc Advisory Committee on the Arts and a 1974 National Endowment for the Arts Expansion Program facilitated by Spellman (who was now working at the NEA), much of the funding of NAC staff salaries and internships was made possible through CETA, which had been enacted by the federal government in 1973.

The NAC ran classes in a wide range of arts and crafts. At different times it housed the most important off-campus Black theaters of the 1970s and 1980s, including Jomandi Productions (a theater that survived from 1977 into the 1990s) and the Just Us Theater as well as the Southern Collective of African American Writers (SCAW) founded by the poet Alice Lovelace, the fiction writer and editor Toni Cade Bambara, and Dooley in 1978. The NAC's artists-in-residence included at various times Dooley, Bambara, Alexander, jazz musician Ojeda Penn, and actors Samuel L. Jackson, LaTonya Richardson, and Bill Nunn—Spike Lee, too, participated in its programs. It also brought artists, such as writers Gwendolyn Brooks and Maya Angelou, painter Romare Bearden, and dancer Arthur Miller to Atlanta, often under the auspices of its Paul Robeson Lecture Series in which the lectures were generally paired with some sort of performance and/or workshop. The NAC's Jazzmobile project, like its counterpart in New York City, brought jazz to communities around Atlanta and reached thousands.[30] Beyond formal NAC programs and projects, artists and activists who had honed their skills in building arts events and institutions at the NAC organized large festivals, concerts, art exhibitions, and classes throughout Georgia, particularly in the greater Atlanta area. For example, a collective of artists and organizers, including Lovelace, Dooley, and other NAC stalwarts organized Arts for the People's Sake festival that involved more than three hundred artists in more than fifty performances all across Atlanta over three weeks in the early 1980s.[31] Similarly, the NAC and the Bureau of Cultural Affairs partnered in creating the Annual Atlanta Free Jazz festival, which featured such local musicians as Ojeda Penn and the Neighborhood Arts Ensemble and such national stars as Betty Carter, Max Roach, and the World Saxophone Quartet, as well as a lecture by A. B. Spellman.[32]

The Black Arts infrastructure and networks created by the NAC and people trained at the NAC were able to survive and even grow through their engagement with increasing Black political power beyond city hall even as some important institutions, including the NAC itself, declined and eventually closed, in part due to the ending of the CETA program by the Reagan administration in 1982. The NAC limped along for several years before shutting down in 1990. As Jim Alexander notes, the NAC's board was not very adept at fundraising and was not able to adequately compensate for the loss of federal money.[33] Promoting the arts as he rose, Michael Lomax continued to move up through the Atlanta political structure. In 1979, he was instrumental in passing legislation in the Fulton County Commission establishing the Fulton County Arts Council, which became a major source of arts funding in the Atlanta metropolitan area. The council also became a crucial conduit of radical Black influence on the arts in the city. In 1981, Lomax went on to be the first African American ever elected chair of the Fulton County Commission, a post he held until 1993.

In that position, Lomax undertook more arts initiatives. Undoubtedly, the largest was (and is) Atlanta's National Black Arts Festival (NBAF). Conceived by Lomax and others in 1987, the NBAF was inaugurated in 1988. It was significantly paid for by the Arts Council and other private and public money facilitated through the efforts of Lomax. The first ten-day festival featured a premiere of Philadelphia Black Arts playwright Charles Fuller's play *Sally*, performances by the Alvin Ailey Dance Company, a musical choreographed by George Faison (who gained fame for his work on the stage versions of *The Wiz* and *The Lion King*), workshops by choreographer Katherine Dunham, Maya Angelou, and directors Woodie King, Douglas Turner

Ward, and Lloyd Richards. There was also a reading of poetry from the 1960s and 1970s hosted by Ossie Davis and Ruby Dee. The executive director of the festival, Michelle Smith, optimistically hoped for an attendance of 250,000; the festival drew a half million.[34]

While 1988 is generally considered far beyond the end of the Black Arts era, the connection of many of the featured artists with the movement, the session of poetry from the 1960s and 1970s, and, obviously, the name of the festival itself attest to the desire of the event's founders to link the current moment to radical, politically engaged, and often mixed media work of the Black Arts era, asking the audience (and the artists) to revisit the earlier period.

Also in 1988, the Hammonds House gallery opened in the former home of the anesthesiologist and art collector Otis T. Hammonds. (Hammonds had been the president of the board of directors of the NAC.) Ed Spriggs (a poet, visual artist, essayist, Black Arts veteran, and a founder and the second director of New York's Studio Museum in Harlem who moved to Atlanta in 1980) led the efforts funded by Fulton County that eventually transformed the house into a major showcase of African American art from around the United States despite recurrent physical plant problems.[35]

Hoyt Fuller, *First World*, and the Contradictions of the New Black South

Another paradigmatic event that demonstrates the complex and uneven development of Atlanta as a dynamic center of Black political and cultural empowerment as well as the decline of Black Arts and Black Power nationally was the inception and relatively brief life there of the journal *First World*. *First World*'s birth was directed by former *Black World* editor Hoyt Fuller in 1977. With tens of thousands (and perhaps even more) readers, *Black World* (originally *Negro Digest*) had been the most widely circulated periodical of the Black Arts and Black Power movements, both chronicling and significantly shaping those movements. *Black World*'s parent company, Johnson Publications (best known as the publishers of *Jet* and *Ebony*) shut down the journal in 1976. The ostensible justification was an allegedly anti-Semitic article about Israel. Many observers and participants in the debate with publisher John Johnson suspected that the real issue was that Johnson no longer wanted to continue printing a magazine that did not make money due to its inability to sell much advertising, particularly when the Black Power and Black Arts movements increasingly splintered and declined as

Marxists, cultural nationalists, and liberals bitterly feuded with each other. Even though John Johnson had a certain respect for Fuller and his staff, the contradictions of a commercial journal with a radical Black editorial stance had always been considerable.

After *Black World*'s demise, there were a number of meetings in Chicago and New York to discuss the creation of a new journal to replace *Black World*. *First World* was designed to be that journal, with the important difference that it would not be owned by a company concerned primarily with the bottom line but would instead be the collective property of the political and cultural liberation movements.[36] Fuller chose to establish the new journal in Atlanta rather than in Chicago, New York, Detroit, Philadelphia, San Francisco, Oakland, or some other northern or western city better known (outside the South, at least) as an epicenter of Black Power and Black Arts.

Of course, after the founding CAP convention in 1970 and Maynard Jackson's election as mayor in 1973, Atlanta's profile in the Black liberation movement had risen considerably. With Jackson's election, and with his focus on culture and supporting new cultural institutions, Atlanta projected a considerable optimism and sense of possibility. Again, though much of the African American population of the city was poor, Atlanta also seemed more economically viable than, say, Detroit or Newark. It was also a city in which the debates between the different factions of the movement were less virulent than was the case in the Northeast and the Midwest. On a more personal level, Fuller, who was originally from College Point, a small city just south of Atlanta, had family ties to the region. He was also close to Richard Long, a literature professor and founder of the Center for African and African American Studies at Atlanta University—Long would eventually become the executor of Fuller's papers. Still, it was not merely sentiment that drew Fuller to Atlanta. Even though, like many HBCUs, the AUC schools had been comparatively slow in developing Black Studies programs, Long's Center for African and African American Studies and IBW, as well as the growing African American arts community and the sheer concentration of Black intellectuals, activists, and students affiliated with AUC and the interconnected civil rights network seemed to offer a promising support community for the journal.

While its layout was somewhat different, *First World* did in fact carry on in much the same manner as *Black World*. It featured articles about national and international political issues with a particular focus on Africa. It also showcased much cultural criticism as well as fiction and poetry. Its various departments contained reviews of books, films, plays and news about Black cultural institutions and events across the country. While it was not particularly oriented toward Atlanta and the South, it covered southern Black arts and political activities more consistently than other national African American journals besides *Callaloo* in its early days. *First World*'s editorial advisors included an impressive list of artists, scholars, and intellectuals associated with Black Power, Black Arts, and Black Studies—though such prominent Third World Marxists as Amiri Baraka, Kwame Ture, and Fuller's old OBAC comrades Abdul Alkalimat and Ebon Dooley are conspicuous by their absence. Whether that absence was by Fuller's design and by the choice of Baraka et al. is unclear (to me, at least)—though it suggests the sort of factional conflict that split CAP and ALSC.

One notable aspect of the journal is that it represented the first time where the Black Arts nexuses of Atlanta and New Orleans were really institutionally united. Longtime FST, BLKARTSOUTH, and Ahidiana Collective activist Kalamu ya Salaam was one of the journal's advisory editors. The second issue of the journal featured Tom Dent's detailed review of the SBCA's first performance festival in New Orleans in the fall of 1976. The Mississippi-based writer, educator, arts funding administrator, SBCA stalwart, and a founder of *Callaloo*, Jerry Ward, frequently contributed poems and essays to *First World*, particularly on the public arts funding scene in the Deep South. Salaam, too, contributed essays and interviews, including a very important interview with Toni Cade Bambara where she talked about, among other things, the conception of *The Salt Eaters*, including the change of its siting from a fictional place much like New Orleans to a place in Georgia that resembled Atlanta.

After a promising start in 1977, *First World* failed, publishing its last issue in 1980. Fuller's premature death in 1981 foreclosed hope that it might be revived. In part, *First World* suffered from the divisions that caused the movement as a whole to decline nationally, especially since much of the early impetus to initiate a journal to replace *Black World* took place outside Atlanta.[37] After all, *First World* was hardly the only important Black intellectual or cultural journal to disappear in that era. It never was able to create a reliable funding stream, something that could not have been generated from a single city the size of Atlanta (probably around 450,000 in the mid-1970s) even with Black control of city hall. Still, part of *First World*'s failure was not only due to the decline of Black Power and Black Arts nationally. It was owed to a lack of personnel and an inability to build a stable local support structure in Atlanta much beyond Hoyt Fuller and *First World* associate editor Carole Parks (the organizational heart of the journal who had followed Fuller from *Black World* and OBAC in Chicago) that replicated the sort of network rooted in the Black communities of Chicago crucial to the success of *Black World*. Fuller did give a keynote address at a writer's workshop held by SCAW at the NAC in 1978, suggesting that some sort of local connection had been made, but not deep enough.

Atlanta, the NAC, and the Inception of a Southern Black Arts Feminism

One thing that particularly distinguished Black Power and Black Arts in Atlanta was their open and generally supportive engagement with feminism and the women's movement. Of course, Black women, such as Alice Walker, Audre Lorde, and Florynce Kennedy, had made significant contributions to the development of mainstream feminist organizations and institutions, such as NOW and *Ms.*, across the United States from the very beginning as well as creating Black feminist groups, such as the Black Women's Liberation Committee of SNCC, the National Black Feminist Organization, and the Combahee River Collective. Still, Atlanta was unusual in the willingness of artists and activists to announce that they were both feminists as such (and not, say, "womanists") and Black nationalists and that they thought there were no contradictions in such a statement. Perhaps even more unusual was the willingness of nearly all of the segments of the broader Black Arts and Black Power communities in Atlanta, by and large, to accept such statements without serious criticism.

Undoubtedly, the key institution that made the contributions of Black feminist women to the civil rights, Black Power, and Black Arts movements in Atlanta so dynamic, especially early in those movements, was Spelman College, the premier historically Black women's college. The faculty of Spelman was not all Black or all female, and the arts programs of the college were shared with the other schools of AUC, particularly Morehouse College. However, its hiring of Black women artists to be part of the faculty, especially as artists-in-residence, both brought a series of vital female cultural activists to the city and did much to develop local male and female artists who would go on to play key roles in the development of the African American arts infrastructure of the city. As was the case with the growth of SNCC and the grassroots civil rights movement in the city, Spelman graduates like Pearl Cleage and Andrea Frye figured prominently in the development of the Black Arts base in Atlanta, an arts infrastructure that was practically nonexistent in the city outside of AUC before the late 1960s.[38] In tandem with the cultural initiatives of Maynard Jackson's administration (and the surge of Black elected officials generally), Black women artists were able to exert a powerful influence on the creation and institutionalization of this infrastructure. In part because of the institutional position of such Black Power/Black Arts feminists as Cleage and Bambara, the contradictions and conflicts, real and perceived, between Black nationalism and feminism seem to have been less pronounced than in many other cities in the United States.

The growth of Atlanta as a center of Black Arts/Black Power feminism took a quantum leap with the arrival of Bambara in 1974 as writer-in-residence at Spelman, a job that was arranged through the intercession of Michael Lomax after a promised position at Clark College fell through. By the time she reached Atlanta, Bambara had already edited the groundbreaking Black feminist anthology *The Black Woman* (1970) and published a collection of short stories, *Gorilla, My Love* (1972) that put a woman-centered cultural continuum between North and South at the center of the new Black art and politics. Almost as soon as she arrived, she looked for a base off-campus to do community political and cultural work. She found that base in the NAC. There and at Spelman Bambara inspired and mentored other writers, such as Lovelace and Cleage, through her generosity to developing artists and her commitment to the highest degree of craft even as she remained resolutely a political artist dedicated to grassroots neighborhood work.[39]

Bambara also constantly promoted networking and community among the younger and older Black artists of Atlanta and the South, linking those artists to each other and to African American cultural activists elsewhere. In many respects, she played the same part that her friend Tom Dent did in New Orleans. She conducted writing classes in a wide range of venues, including Spelman, the NAC, and her apartment. She organized frequent gatherings of artists and intellectuals and brought writers together in less formal ways, often introducing local artists to more nationally known figures when they were in town. Pearl Cleage still remembers with a certain amount of amazement the time Bambara brought Toni Morrison over to her apartment for dinner when Morrison was in Atlanta so that Cleage found herself simultaneously face to face with two of her most idolized authors, the "two Toni's."[40] As mentioned earlier, Bambara was one of the chief organizers of SCAW, an organization that was in some ways parallel to SBCA but more strictly focused on Black southern writing as opposed to the arts generally.

Bambara's fusing of radical Black nationalist and feminist politics helped make Atlanta a comparatively friendly space for Black women with similar stances. She was one of the central figures of a feminist Black liberation group, Sojourner South, which also included Shirley Franklin, Patricia Daly, Janet Douglas, and Jualynne Dodson (research director at the AU School of Social Work and closely associated with IBW). Cleage recalls Bambara as someone to whom she could talk about her own combination of nationalism and feminism without having to explain herself.[41]

Bambara wrote her 1980 novel *The Salt Eaters* during her time in Atlanta as a member of the Spelman College faculty and a community political and cultural activist. One thing the novel does is meditate on the Black Arts and Black Power movements of the 1960s and 1970s from the perspective of an insider, an activist, Velma Henry, who has become deranged and uncentered by both the oppressive and racist system of capitalism in the United States and the material and ideological ways that the system has deformed the movement for the liberation of the oppressed, especially but not solely black women, especially herself. The novel is not a rejection of those movements. Rather, its radical Black feminist critiques come from the inside of the movements, seeking to strengthen them. That the novel should be set in Claybourne, Georgia, drawing heavily on Bambara's experience in Atlanta rather than, say, New York (which Bambara as a native New Yorker knew well) says something about the South in general and Atlanta in particular as a crucial site of Black Arts and Black Power. The novel also locates Black women and their struggle against male supremacy within the Black liberation movements at the center of this southern landscape, helping to generate a Black feminism that offered critical support for the Black Power and Black Arts movements, rather than marking them as irredeemably masculinist and misogynist, while seeking to change them from the inside:

> At some point in her life she was sure Douglass, Tubman, the slave narratives, the songs, the fables, Delaney, Ida Wells, Du Bois, Garvey, the singers, her parents, Malcolm, Coltrane, the poets, her comrades, her godmother, her neighbors, had taught her that. Thought she knew how to build immunity to the sting of the serpent that turned would-be cells, could-be cadres into cargo cults. Thought she knew how to build resistance, make the journey to the center of the circle, stay poised and centered in work and not fly off, stay centered in the best of her people's traditions and not be available to madness, not become intoxicated by the heady brew of digress and career and congratulations for nothing done, not become anesthetized by dazzling performances with somebody else's aesthetic, not go under. Though the

work of the Sixties had pulled the Family safely out of range of the serpent's fangs so the works of the Seventies could drain the poisons, repair damaged tissues, retrain the heartworks, realign the spine.[42]

While a sort of commonplace about the antagonism between feminism and Black nationalism still has wide circulation, the central role that Bambara, Cleage, Andrea Frye, Alice Lovelace, and other women played in the community cultural and political institutions of the city (and beyond) gave them a credibility and a base of support for their feminist nationalism (or nationalist feminism) that allowed them and these institutions to significantly avoid this antagonism. It did not seem to be a contradiction for Bambara and Cleage, say, to work at the NAC and other community-based Black institutions with Black male nationalists and Marxists (and nationalist Marxists) and be active in the circles anchored by the Charis and More bookstores, landmarks of feminism in the South.[43] Neither was it a problem for Cleage to articulate her feminist nationalism in columns published first in the alternative press and later in the *Atlanta Tribune*, one of the city's larger Black magazines. In fact, it was through these columns that Cleage initially gained a wide reputation as a writer in Atlanta—though it was her plays, and later her novels, that made the largest mark beyond Atlanta.[44]

As a result of the nationalist feminist participation in the leading African American intellectual, cultural, and political institutions of the city, Atlanta increasingly became a national locus of Black feminism. An example of the city's regional and national importance can be seen in the fact that the National Black Feminist Organization chose Atlanta as one of the three cities in which it held press conferences in 1974 to protest what it saw as the stereotypes of Black women in the ABC television show *That's My Mama*. Tellingly, the conference was very well received in the Atlanta African American press, especially the *Atlanta Daily World*—much better than in the mainstream *Atlanta Journal*.[45]

The push to build new African American cultural institutions in historic African American communities that one finds throughout the South today, and the desire to construct networks between these institutions within the region and like institutions elsewhere, owes much to a constituency significantly shaped by the SBCA's successful southern Black Arts network building project and the Atlanta model of using Black political and economic power to build public grassroots Black arts institutions and programs that not only bring art to African American communities but also bring art and artists out of the communities. One can see the plethora of national African

American arts events that now take place in the South, such as the Black Arts Festival in Atlanta and the National Black Theatre Festival in North Carolina (and even in its way, the New Orleans Jazz and Heritage Festival) and relatively recent institutions that have gained national attention, such as Project Row Houses in Houston, as descending in large part from the vision of Dent and the SBCA and the Atlanta Black Arts activists. Other artists from the FST/BLKARTSOUTH/SBCA network—including Kalamu ya Salaam, John O'Neal, and Chakula Cha Jua in New Orleans, Muntu Thomas Meloncon in Houston, the late Nayo Watkins in North Carolina, Shirley Richardson and Pat Williams in Miami, and Levi Frazier in Memphis, joined by migrants from the Black Arts movement elsewhere in the United States, such as the late Ebon Dooley, the late Toni Cade Bambara, and Ed Spriggs in Atlanta—served as influential arts elders in their communities and across the region as well as attracting attention to southern African American art and artists and helping make the region the powerhouse of Black cultural production in artistic spheres other than music that it is today.

Conclusion

The Decline of Black Arts in the South, the Persistence of Black Arts in the South

Though the southern Black Arts movement flourished longer and became more embedded in the grassroots infrastructure than in any other region in the United States, it, too, saw a marked diminishment in the 1980s. Its legacies were even more pointedly challenged in the 1990s. As elsewhere in the United States, Black Arts in the South declined for both internal and external reasons under material and ideological pressures that were interlinked.

As noted previously, Black Arts and Black Power in the South did not see the same degree of conflict between Marxists and cultural nationalists that decimated many of the national and local groups elsewhere. Still, the collapse or decline of national organizations that had had considerable purchase in the South, such as CAP, ALSC, and SOBU/YOBU, and the absence or increasing isolation of such political events as the National Black Political Assemblies (the last of which took place in Little Rock, Arkansas, in 1974), affected the South too. The disappearance of national radical Black journals such as *Black World*, the *Journal of Black Poetry*, *SoulBook*, *Black Theater*, and *Black Dialogue* also had a big impact on the movement in the South as elsewhere. With the exception of the *Black Scholar*, those journals that survived, notably *Callaloo* (a product of southern Black Arts), altered much in character in the 1980s, if not before, moving away from their Black Arts/Black Power origins.

Changes in the national and regional political climates also transformed the environment for Black cultural institutions, programs, and organizations in the South—indeed, all cultural groups and initiatives working in the public arts sector across the United States. The election of Ronald Reagan in 1980 marked the beginning of a long Republican war not only against "big government" generally but public support of the arts, especially Black art with any sort of political thrust, in particular. Of course, given that there was a tremendous grassroots support for public accessibility to the arts and arts institutions in many constituencies in the United States, such anti-public arts efforts have not been completely successful to this day. However, many crucial programs were shut down or curtailed. For example, CETA, through which many Black theaters and other arts organizations paid their staff, essentially lost its funding in 1981 and was replaced by the Job Placement Training Act in 1982, which did not really provide for the arts. As a result, programs and institutions significantly underwritten by CETA funds, such as the NAC, were thrown into crisis. Reductions in Community Block Grants that had also supported theaters and other community arts projects exacerbated the problems created by the abolition of CETA.

In some important ways, the success of Black Arts in building public support for arts initiatives created new pressures on radical Black cultural institutions and artists, especially as national and state governments moved to the right. For one thing, what might be seen as the more reformist or liberal wing of Black Power and Black Arts that had been previously willing to support radical efforts promoting Black political and cultural empowerment felt less inclined to do so after earlier efforts opened up new space for African American cultural and civic participation in a less revolutionary mode. In all fairness to those politicians, arts administrators, and cultural activists, they felt compelled to seek new sources of support and of political leverage to gain such support when the institutional and organizational base of Black Power and Black Arts largely fell apart or was isolated nationally as national radical Black institutions, organizations, journals, and so on collapsed or dwindled into a shadow of their former selves in the late 1970s and 1980s.

Public support for Black art (and Black Arts) initiatives and institutions proved particularly problematic on the state and national level where funding ultimately issued from largely conservative-dominated southern state houses and legislative bodies or agencies under heavy pressure from those political authorities. On the local level, particularly in large and midsized cities with large African American communities (which is to say, nearly all southern cities), it was easier for grassroots arts programs to engage with local Black politicians. Still, those locales generally had access to fewer resources than state and federal agencies, even in relatively prosperous cities like Atlanta, Raleigh, and Nashville, much less more economically challenged cities like Jackson, New Orleans, Memphis, and Birmingham. Consequently, African American arts activists were under constant pressure to tone down the politics of their programs and institutions. This is not to say that the community-based notion of serving the people disappeared—far from it. But there was a marked decline in what might be thought of as openly revolutionary African American arts initiatives and projects. Such challenges became even more pronounced in the 1990s when, after a period of relative political centrism in a number of southern state governments with the election of moderate Democrats as governors, such as Bill Clinton in Arkansas, Ray Mabus in Mississippi, and Jimmy Carter and Zell Miller (who was more liberal as a governor than in his subsequent career as a U.S. Senator) in Georgia, there was a marked turn to the right by many white southerners as the dominant industries of the South, especially textile production, went into sharp decline, producing new levels of social anxiety and racial resentment. This rightward shift had a marked ideological impact on state and local governments that became increasingly dominated by conservative white Republicans even as the number of elected Black officials in the South continued to rise.

The 1980s in Atlanta, for example, were a contradictory period for Black art and Black Arts institutions. While many of the most important independent, nongovernmental Black Arts and Black Power institutions collapsed or declined in that decade, in other ways Black political power allowed the institutionalization of the Black public art sector to continue and even thrive until it, too, ran into severe political headwinds in the 1990s. The rightward turn in the South (and elsewhere) took a toll on Atlanta's African American arts institutions that were a base of Black political power. In fact, Lomax's championing of the arts as chair of the Fulton County Commission was a prime target of the Right in what became known as the "tax revolt of 1991." In this "revolt," conservatives especially rallied white voters on Atlanta's North Side as well as in many of the suburbs against Lomax's leadership of the commission. While Lomax initially survived these attacks, they undermined his leadership and forced the commission to draw back in its support of the arts. The tax revolt also contributed to Bill Campbell's solid victory over Lomax in the 1993 mayoral campaign, effectively ending Lomax's political career.[1] The 1996 elimination of the NEA Expansion Arts Program, a program that had supported many community-based theaters, also had a negative impact on African American arts institutions in Atlanta. The 1990s saw financial crisis in and even collapse of some of the most prominent Black arts organizations and theaters in Atlanta, including the NAC, Jomandi Productions, New Jomandi Productions, and the Black Arts Festival. While some of these institutions, like New Jomandi and the Black Arts Festival, were able to regroup and survive their financial problems, others like the NAC vanished.[2] Of course, again, these sorts of problems were not just limited to Atlanta, but also true of some of the best-known Black arts institutions across the nation, such as New York's Negro Ensemble Company and New Jersey's Crossroads Theater. Also, as private and public funding dried up for independent artistic and intellectual endeavors at the same time that job opportunities opened up at predominantly white universities, there was a considerable exodus of artists and scholars from AUC and Atlanta.

Still, though most of the political and cultural institutions of the Black Power and Black Arts movements in Atlanta did not survive the 1990s, many of the individuals who sparked or were trained by those institutions, including Ebon Dooley, Ed Spriggs, Andrea Frye, Jim Alexander, Pearl Cleage, and Stephanie Hughley, remained at the heart of Black arts initiatives in the city. Even those such as Frye, Hughley, Carlton and Barbara Molette, and A. B. Spellman who left Atlanta for long periods of time (or even permanently) for brighter career opportunities, often returned to act in or direct plays, curate art shows, work on the National Black Arts Festival, or help gain support for Atlanta arts initiatives. Nowhere else was the issue of public support of the arts such a grassroots issue and so prominently tied up with Black political and economic empowerment and white backlash toward that empowerment. As a result, nowhere else have the long-term legacies and failures of the Black Arts and Black Power movements been so clearly displayed.

By the early 1980s (and even earlier in some cases), there was also a retrenchment in the Black arts (and Black Arts) institutions in New Orleans and elsewhere in what might be thought of as the SBCA archipelago. While the institutions affiliated with the SBCA often successfully reached community audiences, they were generally unable to figure out a way to attain the grassroots financial base that nearly all of them saw as one of their primary goals. Instead, like their counterparts elsewhere, they had depended on CETA, grants from the NEA (especially the Expansion Arts Program), and other national, state, and local public agencies. Tom Dent and Jerry Ward reflected on the funding contradictions that these institutions faced:

WARD: Although John O'Neal didn't have the funeral for the Free Southern Theater until November 1985, the institution seems to have died in the middle of the 1970s.

DENT: It did. It died at the same time that so many Black community theatres did. I see the death of the FST as a part of the national backlash against Black cultural activity which took a separatist, Black Pride direction and identified strongly with Black political and economic gains.

WARD: The concept of national backlash is interesting but debatable. The whole point of Black community theatre was independence.

DENT: Independence?

WARD: Yes, independent development. What was never resolved for many community theatres was the fact that they could not depend on foundations and other people to sustain them. Community people had to fund community theatre.

DENT: None of the Black community theatres which began in the 1960s and prospered for a while in the early 1970s were funded through communities. Almost all of them had some foundation or National Endowment for the Arts support. We wished that the communities would support theatre, but the Black communities were poor. Communities gave funding priority to churches and other organizations that had longer service histories than the new theatres. We were in a catch-22 situation. For instance, if we tried to support a theatre like the Free Southern Theater solely by charging admission, we would have had to charge something like 20 dollars a ticket. Once you begin to do that, of course, you've cut off the community.[3]

Part of the decline had to do, too, with a question of personnel. Relatively few people had the skills, contacts, and desire to build artistic networks that reached beyond their own institutions and locales. Some who did, such as Kalamu ya Salaam, spent their energies primarily in political and educational work. The 1990s saw the early deaths of two figures most active in the building of local and regional Black arts (and Black Arts) groups, Tom Dent and Wendell Narcisse. Dent spent much of the late 1970s, 1980s, and 1990s continuing to initiate new organizations, workshops, and so on, such as the Congo Square Writers, which nurtured such younger Black writers as Quo Vadis Gex Breaux, Chakula cha Jua, Felipe Smith, and Sharon Adams.[4] No one really replaced Dent as that sort of cultural organizer in New Orleans and the South generally after his sudden death in 1998. Narcisse, long central to the SBCA and to Black theater and cultural activities in south Florida, died in 1991.[5]

The Persistence of Black Arts in the South

Despite the losses of the SBCA, the FST and the Congo Square Writers Union in New Orleans, the NAC in Atlanta, the Afro Arts Theater in Miami, the Black Arts Center in Houston, and other Black Arts and Black Power cultural and political institutions, in many respects CAP and other Black Power activists' vision of the potential for radical Black political and cultural movements in the South has come to fruition. In fact, Black radical political and cultural movements in the region rebounded in the twenty-first century, in response to rightwing attempts to curtail Black citizenship and access to the ballot and to the increasingly dire state of majority-Black cities there. The South is home to many of the most exciting progressive political and cultural movements in the contemporary United States. These political movements include Moral Mondays and NAACP leader William Barber's "new fusion politics" in North Carolina, Randall Woodfin's mayoral administration in Birmingham, the Malcolm X Grassroots Movement and Black Power veteran Chokwe Lumumba's election as Jackson's mayor in 2013, and the subsequent victory of his son Chokwe Antar Lumumba in the 2017 Jackson mayoral vote following his father's untimely death in 2014.

Zandria Robinson perceptively notes, too, that southern cities have been incubators for what she calls "Dirty South bohemian" spaces and institutions:

> Municipal support and cultivation of the arts is central to the success and proliferation of all bohemian scenes, but certainly black political power and presence are especially essential to the success of black bohemian scenes.
>
> Southern cities in general are less segregated than their Northern counterparts, but Memphis's segregation index is often higher than that of other Southern cities. This signals two competing processes: a continuation of the separate city, a site of creative proliferation for black folks outside of the gaze and control of whites, and the marginalization of black bohemian cultures from access to arts resources and spaces that would sustain scenes and cultivate new generations of artists.[6]

Robinson views Memphis as somewhat anomalous in terms of the position of Black artists and arts institutions with respect to their extreme separation from the mainstream cultural institutions of the city compared to many other southern cities. Still, one can extend Robinson's argument to say that what southern cities, including Memphis, have in common is that they generate community-based Black cultural initiatives that provide a base which, along with Black political power, puts African Americans at the cultural center. Thus, in Atlanta, the existence and success of basically Black institutions like Hammonds House and the Black Arts Festival, as well as decades of Black leadership in city hall, exert major influences on the programming and leadership of the High Museum. Also, while "Dirty South bohemia" is a useful way of naming the new efflorescence of southern African American arts projects and organizations in the hip-hop era, it is worth noting that when one is talking about "Black bohemia" in the sense of an organized or quasi-organized counterculture, even though the term goes back to the early twentieth century, in terms of immediate antecedents, what one is talking about is really the Black Arts movement. If one digs a bit into the origins of many Black Memphis arts institutions, such as the Hattiloo Theatre and, as the name suggests, the Memphis Black Arts Alliance, one finds the roots of those institutions and their founders in Black Arts as well as in, as Robinson suggests, older spaces of Black clubs, juke joints, and TOBA theaters. Those sorts of institutions and spaces Memphis certainly shares with other southern cities.

To a considerable degree, these movements and institutions, especially those that seek to build Black community and advance African American political and economic power, are directly influenced by the Black Arts/Black Power notion of culture and the arts as a central arena of struggle for such efforts. Of course, many cities and communities across the United States that have suffered deindustrialization and job loss have sought to build the "creative economy" as a means of revitalizing their economic base. But for Black activists the "creative economy"—or as Cooperation Jackson in Jackson, Mississippi, calls it, "creative survival"—has a particular political valence as a means of Black empowerment.[7]

The new Black radical vision in Jackson, for example, is in many respects a combination of Black Power, Black Arts, anarchism, municipal socialism, and council communism, but with a decidedly contemporary eco-socialist twist. In many ways it is the direct descendant of the Left nationalism that was so influential in the southern Black Power/Black Arts movements, gaining much attention outside the region after the election of Chokwe Lumumba as mayor in 2013. Lumumba was a veteran of the RNA, a revolutionary Black nationalist group that advocated and attempted to lay the foundation of an autonomous communal Black society in the Mississippi Delta "Black Belt" that they called Kush. The RNA's plan was essentially crushed by state repression. However, after a hiatus, Lumumba returned to Jackson in the 1970s, working for decades as a people's lawyer, organizer, and a city councilperson, reviving the RNA's slogan of "Free the Land." Years of Lumumba and his family working for the Black community, allied community political activity through the Malcolm X Grassroots Organization, and the complete failure of more moderate political solutions for the problems of Jackson propelled Chokwe Lumumba's election as mayor.

Mississippi also housed a vital Black cooperative movement during the civil rights and Black Power eras, attempting to build African American economic, political, *and* cultural self-sufficiency instead of depending on white employers who often used their economic power against Black liberation struggles. Jackson's Farish Street, the historic center of Black community political, cultural, and economic life, was the home of the Liberty House Cooperative, an umbrella for sixteen African American handcraft co-ops from across Mississippi run by COFO veteran Jesse Morris with much help from FST founder and photographer Doris Derby. As is the case with Cooperation Jackson, Liberty House drew on other arts than handcrafts through its affiliation with the filmmakers of Southern Media and the selling and lending of books of Black poetry and other sorts of literature published by such Black Arts presses as Broadside and Drum and Spear.[8]

Jackson is also a hub of Black higher education through the presence in or near the city of Jackson State and Tougaloo, the birthplace of the FST. Tougaloo's connection to the network that grew out of FST and BLKARTSOUTH continued into the 1970s and 1980s, in large part through the efforts of faculty member, critic, and SBCA activist Jerry Ward. Through the work of Ward, Tougaloo hosted the 1979 conference of the SBCA.[9] Longtime Jackson State faculty member Margaret Walker, the poet and novelist, organized many important conferences, festivals, institutes, and symposia of the arts there, including institutes for Black Studies and for Black Culture in which Tom Dent and Doris Derby played leading roles and which brought such artists as painters Skunder Boghossian and Jeff Donaldson, writers John Killens and Alice Walker, and dramatist Loften Mitchell to Jackson.[10] These and other campus activities were joined by such community groups connected to SBCA as the Repertory Theatre of Mississippi (which produced Ntozake Shange's *for colored girls who have considered suicide/when the rainbow is enuf* in Jackson) and the Studio of Creative Arts run by Wanda Moncure.

In short, the current expression of Black radical politics in Jackson and surrounding Hinds County has a long foreground. While much of the publicity and journalism that has described the Jackson Project and Cooperation Jackson has emphasized the economic side of the project, the Lumumbas and the Malcolm X Grassroots Liberation Organization have insisted that the base of the project is cultural—that is to say, like Black Power and Black Arts, they are trying to build a new culture of Black cooperation and self-determination. Not surprisingly, along with cooperatives in such obviously commercial areas as Construction Worker/Skilled Labor, Solar Insulation/Green Retrofitting, Auto Repair, and Food Service/Catering, there is one in the Arts and Cultural Production, emphasizing the material and economic nature of culture and the arts as well as the cultural nature of areas that are often separated from ideas of culture: "Cooperation Jackson's Just Transition plan includes building community land trusts, worker owned cooperatives, food sovereignty, a network of eco-villages, and policy transformation on a municipal level. As Kali Akuno, a leader of Cooperation Jackson, emphasizes, the policy for a Green New Deal needs to be shaped by grassroots efforts, noting that 'it's often easier to act a new way of thinking rather than to think a new way of acting . . . this is intentional cultural development.'"[11]

Houston, too, was a major node of the SBCA circuit. Like other such centers, it suffered reverses in the late 1970s and 1980s with the loss of arts funding from public and private sources. The Black Arts Center in the Fifth Ward, for example, closed in 1976. At the same time, the networks created by the SBCA set in motion a series of initiatives, some long-lasting, some more transitory, that would change Houston into a national center of African American art. The Black Heritage Gallery was a bridge between Black Arts and the contemporary efflorescence of African American art in Houston. The gallery opened in 1978. It displayed visual art by such local visual artists as John Biggers, Bert Long, and Earlie Hudnall when there were few other spaces for them in Houston outside of Texas Southern. The Black Heritage Gallery continued well into the twenty-first century before a landlord sold the building in which it was housed in 2014, forcing the gallery to close.[12]

Project Row Houses was the most nationally prominent institution that picked up the torch from the Black Heritage Gallery, championing many of the same Black Houston artists. The 2007 documentary *Third Ward Texas* chronicles the creation and activities of Project Row Houses, which gained national attention, including several articles in the *New York Times*. The brainchild of a young Black artist, Rick Lowe, Project Row Houses was originally conceived in the mid-1990s as a guerilla art effort in about a block and a half of condemned shotgun houses in the historically African American Third Ward, one of the original six wards of Houston. The idea was that these houses would display various sorts of public art visible from the street. In this, Lowe says he was significantly inspired by the visionary paintings of John Biggers, which linked Third Ward shotgun houses and everyday Black Houston to a highly spiritualized rendering of West African cultures.[13]

However, Lowe's project soon evolved into a much more complex and permanent undertaking, ultimately enlisting the help of many younger and older artists and community leaders, such as activist Ernie Atwell, the painter Floyd Newsum, Bert Long, Earlie Hudnall, the photographer Ray Carrington, and the art historian and curator Alvia Wardlaw, many of whom are veterans of the Black Power/Black Arts era. Among the many aspects that Project Row Houses came to encompass were the displaying of art for neighborhood residents who would rarely, if ever, go to arts venues downtown; artist's studios for emerging as well as more established Black artists; housing for single mothers; community arts classes; the promotion of cultural and historical memory in the Third Ward, which was the cultural and political center of Black Houston for much of the twentieth century; and the resistance to the mix of decay, gentrification, and redevelopment that had largely displaced the African American community in the adjacent Fourth and Fifth Wards, also historically significant centers of Black life in Houston.

Third Ward Texas is quite fascinating but contains a strange gap. While John Biggers, his paintings of shotgun houses, and his work at Texas Southern are mentioned as inspirations, basically one would get the idea that Project Row Houses jumped off the canvases and walls of Biggers's art into the brain of Rick Lowe. However, anyone familiar with the Black Power and Black Arts movements of the 1960s and 1970s (and the Popular Front even) will recognize their sort of combination of guerilla art, performance center/school, the creation of affordable housing for the community, the promotion of local artists along with providing spaces for residencies and/or visits from outside artists with national reputations, and education in local and national African American culture and history. Houston was a vital locus of such activities in the 1960s and 1970s, significantly through the influence of John Biggers and the TSU Art Department and beyond, despite the absence of such a foreground in *Third Ward Texas*. The Third, Fourth, and Fifth Wards in particular were hotbeds of such Black cultural and political radicalism.

The South has been the region, too, where African Americans have come to possess (and expect) a place in the running and programming of mainstream cultural organizations and institutions unmatched elsewhere. As previously noted, Atlanta has been ground zero for this transformation as Black artists and arts administrators have increasingly moved to the center of the visual arts, theater, music, and literature there. As the important director and theater administrator Kenny Leon noted with respect to his work in the previously almost entirely white-oriented Alliance Theater, this change not only entailed the appearance of Black faces in the company's productions but also a new sense of Atlanta on the part of the Black community, a sense that they, too, had a sort of ownership of the institution:

> So, if America's problem is that deep, you know, how can one theater company solve that problem? We can only do what we can. So, for me, like if I say I'm not a racist or a sexist, and I know I've got to produce eleven plays and I say these are the eleven plays I want to do, and three of those plays happen to be by African American writers, but those people who've been affiliated with the theater for twenty years, they're like, "Wait a minute, you're doing three plays by black people. You're turning this into a black theater." I'm like, "No, I'm not." But, you have to understand. They think that you're taking something away, because three looks bigger than one, you know. And then you have black audience members who are new, and they're like, "Well, they don't want us to come to that theater, they just want to use us for that big gospel show, and that big road show coming in, but they don't want us to come to everything." And I said, "No, I want you to come to Ibsen, I want you to come to Shakespeare, I want you to come to 'Much Ado About Nothing', I want you to come to 'Ghosts', I want you to come to all of our plays." And for the black folks to buy on to, we're going to see the August Wilson and the Pearl Cleage, and also these other writers. That was ownership. They knew somebody gave them ownership of the building, of the theater, not just coming to one play. So, that's kind of hard, you know, for some people, because it's different.[14]

African Americans felt that they had ownership of mainstream and Black art institutions not only because they saw some number of Black faces and a certain percentage of African American programming, but also because a new kind of infrastructure was put into place, significantly supported by public and private funds enabled by Black political and economic power. In Michael Lomax's words,

> And today when you see in a black commercial arts community making films and TV shows and all that—that has its roots in the '70s opportunities that were created that began to attract that talent to the community. And writers like Pearl and others were the, the, so, you know, so that there was a—you know, Sam and LaTanya and Kenny and Pearl they were part of an early generation and, you know, and, and when Sam comes back, you know, in the '70s, later in the '70s to be in "School Daze," he isn't coming back as street theater, he's coming back as somebody else, I mean, this, the, the world is changing—or

"Jungle Fever." I mean, the, you know, the, so, the, these, these things happened because you created an environment where they could happen.[15]

At the same time that changes in the infrastructure of the arts institutions gave Black Atlanteans a new sense of ownership of those institutions, the longtime mass Black support maintaining a continuity with the Black Arts era made increased radical African American access to power in the arts possible. Photographer Jim Alexander put it succinctly:

> In other places [Black artists and activists] would not be over anything, because Michael Simanga [a radical former CAP leader who became head of the Fulton County Arts Council] would not be over anything—people who are in power have a high respect for Michael and artist-activists always have his back. Bill Edwards [then mayor of Atlanta]; Emma Darnell who is with Fulton County. He [Simanga] built a senior center with a fantastic arts program—murals—performing, etc. He built a grassroots constituency, especially among seniors.[16]

This sort of conscious continuity with the Black Arts era is exemplified by the 2017 mural *Journey to Freedom: Women of the Civil Rights Movement,* underwritten by Atlanta's Office of Cultural Affairs and featuring twenty-one images by photographer, writer, FST founder, longtime Mississippi political and cultural activist, and current Atlanta resident Doris Derby.

Despite the comparative neglect by scholars noted in the introduction of this book much of the grassroots success of Black Arts in the South grew in part out of a sense of regional neglect by the broader movement—though few in the SBCA, for example, seem to have doubted the legitimacy of their participation in this larger movement. One might, and some southern Black Arts veterans do, argue that this sense of neglect was in many ways a source of strength, producing a degree of unity within Black Power and Black Arts in the South that mitigated the factionalism that wracked the movements elsewhere, contributing to relatively long-lived institutions and allowing individuals with very different ideological outlooks to continue to work together in productive ways—even until this moment.

However, again, Black Arts in the South gave (and continue to give) much to Black expressive culture in general and the national Black Arts movement in particular. Whether one is speaking of the idea of a Black nation within a nation in a more general ideological sense or the demographic realities of where the institutionalization of Black political and cultural power had the most practical potential, the South was and is key. The work of BLKARTSOUTH and the SBCA; such community-based groups as SUDAN/Southwest, the Beale Street Repertory Theatre, the Theater of Afro-Arts, and the NAC; the campus-based workshops, institutes, and festivals; and the whole infrastructure of Black Arts organizations, institutions, and events in the South made the imagining of a viable Black nation possible—just as the Cooperation Jackson Project and Project Row Houses with their antecedents in Black Arts and Black Power can be said to make it palpable in the present moment.

The Black Arts movement in the South owed an enormous debt to the long and still living tradition of African American artistic, intellectual, and political activism in the city of New Orleans, a tradition that Tom Dent did much to make accessible first to the young artists attracted to the workshops of the FST and later to Black cultural workers throughout the South, especially through the SBCA. The work of Dent and the SBCA still reverberates today. Many of the stalwarts of the SBCA kept on at the center of the African American arts scene in their local communities long after the organization's demise. Both Tom Dent in New Orleans and Wendell Narcisse in Miami continued to form new groups to encourage young Black writers until their early deaths in the 1990s. The poet and critic Lorenzo Thomas migrated from New York to Houston in the 1970s, becoming not only a major participant in the SBCA and subsequent Black cultural institutions in Houston and elsewhere in the South but also one of the pioneering and most perceptive scholars of the Black Arts movement and African American poetry until his death in 2005. Dent, along with Jerry Ward and Charles Rowell, was responsible for the conception and early publication of *Callaloo* in the late 1970s, seeing it as fulfilling essentially the same function as *Nkombo* but with a greater openness to Black writers from outside the South (and, indeed, outside the United States). Ward recalls,

> *Callaloo* is an outgrowth of some very interesting discussions from the very early 1970s. Mainly discussions about publishing, creativity, writing, in the Southern Black Cultural Alliance. It actually grew out of a group that was interested in community theater, but involved a lot of people who were interested in other forms of writing as well. So I remember in 1975 a meeting that we had in Birmingham, that was where the group met that particular year, and we had this very long and intense discussion involving Rowell, Tom Dent, a lot of other people and me about what we might possibly do. And obviously Rowell

> said we need to have a publication, and of course Tom Dent and I agreed with that. So Dent, Rowell, and Ward became the earliest editors, co-editors of this.[17]

Though Rowell (who had the heaviest editorial and fundraising load on *Callaloo*) took the journal in a far more academic and far less specifically southern direction by the early 1980s, *Callaloo* remains a major legacy of the New Orleans–based southern Black Arts movement and the spirit of the SBCA.[18]

The push to build new African American cultural institutions in historic African American communities that one finds throughout the region today, and the desire to construct networks between these institutions within the South as well as with like institutions elsewhere, owes much to a constituency significantly shaped by the SBCA. One can see the plethora of national African American arts events that now take place in the South, such as the Black Arts Festival in Atlanta and the National Black Theatre Festival in North Carolina (and even in its way, the New Orleans Jazz & Heritage Festival) as descending in large part from the vision of Dent and the SBCA. Other artists from the FST/BLKARTSOUTH/SBCA network—including Kalamu ya Salaam, the late John O'Neal, Quo Vadis Gex Breaux, and Chakula Cha Jua in New Orleans, Doris Derby in Atlanta, Muntu Thomas Meloncon in Houston, the late Nayo Watkins in North Carolina, Shirley Richardson and Pat Williams in Miami, and Levi Frazier in Memphis, joined by migrants from the Black Arts movement elsewhere in the United States, such as the late Ebon Dooley and Ed Spriggs in Atlanta—became influential arts elders in their communities and across the region long after the heyday of Black Arts.

Coda: What It Means to Miss New Orleans

Very few of the Black Arts institutions and organizations of New Orleans survived into the twenty-first century—or past the 1980s, really. By 2000, the FST, BLKARTSOUTH, the SBCA, the Dashiki Project Theater (which faded away after the death of its founder Theodore Gilliam in 1991), and *Nkombo* were all gone. At the same time, there is a certain sense in which Black Arts, the communities it nurtured, and its sensibilities endure in New Orleans to the present. Until his death in 2019, John O'Neal and Junebug Productions long kept O'Neal's Junebug Jabbo Jones one-person shows as the core of its offerings.[19] Again, such people who were schooled by FST/BLKARTSOUTH/SBCA as Quo Vadis Gex Breaux, Chakula cha Jua, Mona

Lisa Saloy, Jerry Ward (who relocated from Jackson to New Orleans), and Kalamu ya Salaam remain at the heart of Black literature, art, and cultural memory in New Orleans. In fact, Salaam returned to cultural work in the 1990s to a degree that he hadn't done since the early 1970s. And, though many groups disappeared, others in New Orleans and the FST/BLKARTSOUTH/SBCA archipelago, such as the M-Ensemble of Miami, held on.[20] While many of these individuals remain in touch with each other, and new groups and institutions have arisen, what disappeared, especially after the deaths of Dent and Narcisse, is the organized regional umbrella that kept Black Arts institutions in the South in regular communication and cooperation.

In the summer of 2005, Hurricane Katrina (with human help) very publicly and rapidly did immense damage to the infrastructure, demography, and psyche of New Orleans, especially those of the city's long-standing Black communities, scattering Black residents across what sociologists Marcus Hunter and Zandria Robinson call the "chocolate maps," especially in the South.[21] As Jerry Ward observed, the natural disasters became "elements of a national tragedy."[22] Media images of the largely African American crowds in the Superdome and the Morial Convention Center and the inadequacy of the response by the Bush administration seemed to encapsulate a continuing animus toward Black people in the twenty-first century United States, prompting bitter artistic and media responses by such ideologically varied artists as Bruce Springsteen, Kanye West, and Li'l Wayne. In many respects, the damage the hurricane did provided the occasion for a very intentional existential challenge to the Black communities, their culture, and cultural memory in the city—really, the very identity of New Orleans itself.

The reconstruction of the city and privatization of public resources and public goods, including the virtual abandonment of the public schools, saw the wholesale demolition or abandonment of housing, educational institutions, community centers, and businesses in the Ninth Ward, Gentilly, and other Black neighborhoods. This also produced great debates about the relationship between politics and public support of the arts insofar as versions of African American culture have long been and continue to be at the center of the appeal of the tourist industry in New Orleans. The key question, then, was what does it mean to draw on versions of Black culture without Black people? These debates emerged from a particular place and moment, but raised issues likely to be of considerable duration as the questions of cultural legacies of the 1960s and 1970s and the public support of the arts in the United States continue to generate political debate in the public sphere.

Of course, Black artists, activists, and grassroots community members (and, often, people who were some combination of all three) emphatically tried with some considerable success to foreclose that question. While the demographics of New Orleans continue to remain less Black than before the hurricane, African American New Orleanians have persistently and forcefully returned to the city as they are able, reclaiming neighborhoods like Hollygrove and Gentilly so that their populations now approach something like their pre-Katrina levels—though the Black populations in some neighborhoods, particularly Tremé, remain threatened by gentrification. Almost immediately after the hurricane, when the future shape of New Orleans was very unclear, Black artists and activists like Kalamu ya Salaam in his Listen to the People Project set to work creating new sorts of popular archives recording Black life, history, and culture in New Orleans, as well as the life and culture of other groups. Organizations and institutions in the spirit of BLKARTSOUTH and the SBCA sprang up in the 1990s and the twenty-first century. For example, the Ashé Cultural Arts Center (better known locally as Ashé Cac), a cultural center founded in the heart of the old Central City Black commercial district, programs a wide range of Black visual art, theater, music, poetry, dance, and other forms of art with a deep sense of connection to the Black Arts movement's legacy. And, of course, longtime cultural traditions, practices, and groups, such as brass bands and Mardi Gras "Indians" have been maintained and revitalized at the grassroots level, often combined with newer forms, such as "bounce," a particularly New Orleans variant of hip-hop.

However, despite the persistence of a Black Arts sensibility and the struggle to maintain both the physical presence of Black people and African American culture and cultural memory rooted in Black communities, the hurricane and the reconstruction of the city after Katrina highlighted an issue that has often been neglected by cultural historians. That issue is the way that dramatic, and often quite planned, changes in the urban landscape of the United States have not only disrupted the cultural life of historically Black neighborhoods but also even our sense of grassroots arts activity in the United States, especially our sense of local audiences and artists who essentially remained known only regionally. While the destruction of older African American communities through neglect, so-called urban renewal, gentrification, and highway construction is a fact all across the nation, it has been particularly acute in the urban South—as seen in many chapters of this book. La Villa, the historic center of Black life in Jacksonville, Florida, for example, was levelled in the 1990s. A Black historical and cultural museum was later built in La Villa on the ruins of an old theater but was quite literally detached from the Black communities of the city, so much so that it almost appeared to rise out of an urban prairie. Much the same could be said about the tribulations of Beale Street in Memphis, Jefferson Street in Nashville, Farish Street in Jackson, Hayti in Durham, the Third, Fourth, and Fifth wards in Houston, Jackson Ward in Richmond, the West End in Louisville, and even, to a lesser degree, Auburn Avenue in Atlanta (the old Black center buffeted in recent years by decay, neglect, and, now, gentrification). In some ways, the destruction by Katrina was like a speeded-up, time-lapse version of a process going on all across the country, especially the South, for decades as economic and political hurricanes struck and continue to strike old Black neighborhoods and commercial and cultural centers.

Catherine Michna is one cultural historian much concerned with the destruction of Black neighborhoods, the displacement of their populations, and the subsequent impact of this planned urban mayhem on the culture of New Orleans. She observes that the building of a highway over Claiborne Avenue and the razing of what had been a major thoroughfare and public front yard of Black New Orleans resulted in tremendous damage to the vital street culture of parading, brass bands, second lining, and others sorts of local African American expression.[23] Similar destruction of key Black thoroughfares and commercial and cultural districts elsewhere has obtained much the same results. The population of those neighborhoods has been dispersed, and the old cultural, social, economic, and political institutions that anchored them have been similarly scattered or destroyed.

Speaking of my own personal experience in researching the larger history of the origins and development of the Black Arts movement, one result of this dispersal and destruction is that it is hard to find the people who patronized and participated in the small theaters, galleries, arts organizations, and so on in the 1960s and 1970s, but who never went on to any fame outside of those communities and that moment—which is to say the vast majority of those who worked in and supported Black Arts, especially in the South. Despite the pre-Katrina damage to physical and cultural infrastructure chronicled by Michna and Michael Crutcher, New Orleans before the hurricane was still something of an exception, a city where many of the better- and lesser-known participants in Black Arts remained and where if someone did not know about the theater that had been in her or his neighborhood, they could direct you to someone who did.[24] Such guidance is extremely difficult to find in many cities where the old neighborhoods have been built over (or simply left a collection of empty lots with a sprinkling of derelict or decaying buildings) and their old inhabitants moved elsewhere. Often in those cities if someone still in the old neighborhood does not know the answer to your question, they are unsure where the people who would know live or even if those people are still alive at all. Thus, the question of whether one should rebuild the old historically Black neighborhoods of New Orleans—a city where, in spite of much racism, neglect, and destruction of neighborhood infrastructure, there were stable African American neighborhoods with an incredible sense of tradition, as in the much maligned Ninth Ward—was and remains a crucial question of, among many other things, our cultural health, and an artistic legacy that has marked and continues to mark our national culture down to the present. The ability of people to have access to decent housing and return to (or remain in) communities in which they have a history and a deep personal and cultural stake is, of course, paramount. But, additionally, the question of "the archives" and developing or maintaining and making broadly available alternative archives beyond those found in Special Collections holdings and other repositories of research libraries is one of much concern to scholars in this moment. On another level, as the BLKARTSOUTH, NAC, and other southern Black Arts activists taught us, cultural memory and the ability to frame and interpret that memory is almost as important to the grassroots as a place to live.

So, ultimately, one major question that Katrina and its aftermath raised, and Black artists and activists sought to answer, is what is the relationship between housing/basic services and the access of people, especially Black people and people of color, to cultural memory, especially as expressed and framed by art? What happens to one when the other, like work, disappears? What is the consequence to scholarship, particularly in African American/Africana Studies? What is the import for the grassroots communities that we ultimately serve? What happens when whole communities vanish, whether the Desire Projects (one-time home of the FST) in New Orleans or Farish Street in Jackson, whether by catastrophic event, bulldozer and wrecking ball, or neglect or all of the above?

Notes

Introduction

1. Crawford, *Black Post-Blackness*, 107–36; Salaam, *The Magic of Juju*; Michna, "Hearing the Hurricane Coming"; Ward, "Southern Black Aesthetics"; Lorenzo Thomas, *Extraordinary Measures*; Smethurst, *The Black Arts Movement*, 319–66; Smethurst, "Black Arts South"; Smethurst, "The Black Arts Movement in Atlanta"; Smethurst, "Retraining the Heartworks"; Redmond, *Drumvoices*.

2. Tate, "Our Art Itself."

3. Rohmer, *Slavery in the Connecticut Valley*.

4. I don't wish to get into the argument over whether chattel slavery inculcated a true caste system in the United States, a debate that has been recently revived by Isabel Wilkerson's *Caste: The Origins of Our Discontent*. However, whether or not slavery produced a genuine caste system, it undoubtedly depended on racialized notions of slavery and freedom, of citizen and non-citizen, of human and subhuman that were transmitted through the generations.

5. Wilson, *Our Nig*.

6. Crawford, *Black Post-Blackness*, 111–12; Lesley Clark, "Can a Black Candidate Win Florida's Top Job?"

7. Lang, *Grassroots at the Gateway*, 7–12.

8. Ignatiev and Garvey, 9–14.

9. The Communist view of the "National Question" had its antecedents in the thinking of Lenin, Stalin, and the Bolsheviks as they theorized about how to build a successful revolution (and, after the October Revolution of 1917, successfully construct socialism) in the notoriously polyglot Russian Empire (the "prison house of nations"). The classic Bolshevik statement on what constituted a nation that had much influence on the Comintern's later formulation of nationalism is contained in Stalin's 1913 *Marxism and the National Question*, "A nation is a historically-constituted, stable community of people, formed on the basis of a common language, territory, economic life, and psychological life manifested in a common culture." Though Stalin came to be rejected by large sections of the Left (as evidenced by the fact that when I bought an English translation of *Marxism and the National Question* in the 1990s, it was only available new through an Albanian imprint), the stream of Marxism that comes out of Maoism, including that to which Baraka subscribed, did not renounce Stalin and his thinking in the same manner. It should be noted that the CPUSA after 1956, and even much of the anti-Stalinist Left, remained marked by the notion of African Americans as a people or nation, even if they did not support the idea of a "Black Belt Republic."

This definition could be (and often was) applied quite mechanically as a sort of checklist where if all the items were not checked off, the population in question was not a "nation." However, Black Marxists (including Baraka), especially from the Black Power/Black Arts era on, often did not follow the checklist and were extremely reluctant to separate Black people in the ghettoes from those in the Black Belt even if they did not share a contiguous territory.

10. Anderson, *Imagined Communities*.

Chapter One

1. Baraka, *Blues People*, x–xi.

2. *From Spirituals to Swing*.

3. Kelley, *Hammer and Hoe*, 229–30.

4. For an account of the setting up and functioning of the CPUSA southern headquarters in Chattanooga, see Stanton, *Red Black White*, 25–32.

5. Gellman, 189; Jackson, interview by the author.

6. As Anne Gessler notes, Albert Dent also had a considerable involvement in the cooperative movement in New Orleans, which she describes as being a part of the broader circles of the Popular Front there. She also argues that Albert Dent's connection to the cooperative movement was a major influence on his son Tom Dent and the FST, a claim that may be overstated—though certainly Albert Dent's connections to cooperative movement activists as well as to former southern Popular Front leaders like Esther and James Jackson influenced his son's sense of radical Black southern history and traditions (*Cooperatives in New Orleans*, 83–149).

7. Gellman, 213–54; Jackson, interview by the author; McDuffie, *Sojourning for Freedom*, 141–47; Haviland, *James and Esther Cooper Jackson*.

8. Letter from Edward Strong to W. E. B. Du Bois, December 2, 1956, W. E. B. Du Bois Papers, MS 312, University of Massachusetts Amherst; letter from W. E. B. Du Bois to Edward Strong, December 14, 1956, W. E. B. Du Bois Papers, MS 312, University of Massachusetts Amherst.

9. James Jackson, a political fugitive who was "underground" for several years during the Red Scare, was the southern secretary of the CPUSA in the 1950s and the editor of the CPUSA newspaper, *The Worker*, in the early 1960s. As a member of the CPUSA's Central Committee, James Jackson was able to defend *Freedomways* against charges of "bourgeois" Black nationalism that came from some quarters.

10. Cruse saw *Freedomways* as essentially a continuation of the Harlem Left of the 1940s and 1950s and such institutions and organizations as *Freedom*, the American Negro Theatre, the Committee for the Negro in the Arts, and the Harlem Writers Guild. While this characterization has its points, it misses the roots of *Freedomways* in SNYC and the South and SNYC's spirit of building Black political and cultural institutions run by African Americans. (Cruse, *The Crisis of the Negro Intellectual*, 240–52).

11. Many Black Arts and Black Power activists, especially those active on the West Coast in the 1960s, have spoken to me of the importance of the Black Bay Area CPUSA leader Roscoe Proctor as well as the longtime Black national CPUSA leader William L. Patterson in advising the BPP in the practical aspects of organizing a national defense movement in support of Huey Newton in 1967 following Newton's indictment for murder, assault, and kidnapping. See also Horne, *Black Revolutionary*, 196.

12. Jackson, interview by the author.

13. Killens, "Lorraine Hansberry: On Time!," 335–39.

14. Salaam, *The Magic of Juju*, 65.

15. McDuffie, *Sojourning for Freedom*, 202–3.

16. Morton, *Complete Library of Congress Recordings*.

17. Woods, *Development Drowned and Reborn*, 157–58.

18. Fairclough, *Race & Democracy*, 54–57.

19. Denning, *The Cultural Front*.

20. Smethurst, "The Street Ran through Cities," 27–28.

21. Fairclough, *Race and Democracy*, 87–99.

22. Knight, *The Essential Etheridge Knight*.

23. Salaam, "Enriching the Paper Trail," 327–44.

24. Sanchez frequently made this point in 2014 and 2015 book events for *SOS: Calling All Black People: A Black Arts Movement Reader* (edited by Bracey, Sanchez, and Smethurst).

25. For a discussion of the Herndon case and the CPUSA efforts to organize the unemployed in Atlanta, see Lorence, "Mobilizing the Reserve Army," 57–80.

26. For example, Lester Maddox, who in many respects embodied the segregationist resistance to civil rights in Georgia during the 1960s and 1970s for his resistance, sometimes physical, to serving Black customers in his fried chicken restaurant in Atlanta, was elected governor in 1966. While Maddox was a lifelong Atlanta resident (despite sometimes being described as a backwoods demagogue), he was not really part of the city's political elite, losing two elections for mayor to "moderate" establishment candidates before being elected governor.

27. Donald F. Davis, "Hale Woodruff," 149.

28. Davis, "Hale Woodruff," 149–52; Morgan, *Rethinking Social Realism*, 42–170; Woodruff, Oral History Interview.

29. Hill and Hatch, *A History of African American Theatre*, 258–61.

30. Sullivan, *Days of Hope*, 249–75.

31. Washington, "Disturbing the Peace," 1–23.

32. Catlett initially studied at Taller de Gráfica Popular supported by a Rosenwald grant. She basically lived in Mexico for the rest of her life, in no small part to avoid political persecution during the McCarthy era. *The Negro Woman* series never ran in the journal due to some disputes between Catlett and the editors. For a listing of all the linoleum cuts and reproductions of some of them, see http://nationalhumanitiescenter.org/pds/maai3/segregation/text5/catlettnegrowoman.pdf.

33. For an excellent, concise discussion of Jones's work and its relation to Black feminism and Black Left nationalism, see Higashida, *Black Internationalist Feminism*, 20–24.

34. Theisen, 13.

35. Fowler, "Photographer Earlie Hudnall."

36. "Inspired by both American artist Dr. John Biggers and the German artist Josef Beuys, PRH is a unique experiment in activating the intersections between art, historic preservation, affordable and innovative housing, community relations and development, neighborhood revitalization, and human empowerment. John Biggers once

commented on shotgun houses, saying 'I see them as I walk the Third Ward of Houston, the rhythm of their shadows, the square of the porch three over four like the beat of a visual gospel.' Through our partnership and collaborative efforts with the Rice Building Workshop, PRH expands its perspective on the shotgun house design and the community it creates." Project Row House: http://projectrowhouses.org/about-us/.

37. Fosl, *Subversive Southerner*, 89–96; Gilpin, "A Louisville Union"; Gilpin, *The Long Deep Grudge*, 151–226.

38. Wilson, "Underknown," 55.

39. Golden and Whitney, *Bob Thompson*, 34–36.

40. Cunningham, "A Part Of," 19.

41. Douglas, "The History of Louisville's African American Artists."

42. Douglas, "The History of Louisville's African American Artists."

43. Douglas, "The History of Louisville's African American Artists."

44. Douglas, "The History of Louisville's African American Artists."

45. Salaam, interview by the author, 2000; Salaam, *The Magic of Juju*, 295.

46. For a discussion of Washington's public and private actions in the civil rights struggles of the late nineteenth and early twentieth centuries, see Alexander, *An Army of Lions*.

47. In many ports, especially but not solely in the South, the ILA had dual segregated Black and white locals. While this worked to the disadvantage of Black stevedores in the sense that the white locals got the best jobs, it also guaranteed that the Black locals had Black leadership, giving organized labor an influence in southern Black communities that was relatively rare elsewhere in the early twentieth century. Even to this day, despite the relative conservatism and, often, corruption of the national ILA leadership, the ILA remains a stronghold of African American organized labor and, even radicalism, in the South. When the CIO's Left-led International Longshore and Warehouse Union (ILWU) sought to bring workers of the port of New Orleans into its orbit, it ultimately failed. This failure was in part because of redbaiting intimidation against the ILWU and dubious union elections. However, a major factor was that Black longshoremen were reluctant to give up the institutions they already controlled. It did not help that some of the West Coast ILWU locals (such as those in Portland and Los Angeles) were notoriously hostile to Black workers, something that the generally Left national leadership of ILWU was unable to successfully change for many years due to the union's strong tradition of local autonomy. However, the ILWU did successfully organize some warehouses in New Orleans, giving it a presence in the city.

48. Harold, *The Rise and Fall of the Garvey Movement*, 29–60.

49. Harold, *The Rise and Fall of the Garvey Movement*, 57–58.

50. McDuffie, *Sojourning for Freedom*, 78–83, 207–208; Harold, *The Rise and Fall of the Garvey Movement*, 120–121; Audley Moore FBI file.

51. Vought, "Racial Stirrings," 65.

52. Vought, "Racial Stirrings," 57–58.

53. Harold, *The Rise and Fall of the Garvey Movement*, 72–74.

54. Rose, *The Struggle for Black Freedom in Miami*; Lichtenstein, "Putting Labor's House in Order," 7–23.

55. Lorenzo Thomas, *Extraordinary Measures*, 138.

56. FBI report on the Nation of Islam.

57. One of the leaders of the CPUSA and the Popular Front in the Tidewater area was the leading Black Arts critic and scholar Addison Gayle Jr.'s father, Addison Gayle Sr.; FBI Report on the NOI. One of the chief characters in the novel, though not a Muslim, has taken on the name of "Robert X"—in this case, to mark his immediate abandonment by his father, the protagonist Phillip Martin who also stands in for the rupture in Black history and family caused by slavery and the Atlantic slave trade.

Chapter Two

1. McWhorter, *Carry Me Home*, 427–37.

2. National Center for Education Statistics, *The Traditionally Black Institutions*, 13–15; Biondi, *The Black Revolution on Campus*, 143.

3. It is worth noting that there were some significant exceptions in this regard. Langston Hughes, for one, continued to read his work at Black schools, churches, and so on in the South. Also, Black public art, such as John Biggers's murals in Houston, continued to exist, be created, and seen in community institutions. And while one might say that high-level shows of art, concerts, theater, and so on were often restricted to HBCUs, the appreciation of such art was taught by Black teachers in Jim Crow schools and discussed in the Black press, among other places, so it was not as though Black people beyond the campus were unaware of and completely unfamiliar with such art even if they did not attend cultural events at HBCUs.

4. O'Neal, "Motion in the Ocean," 71.

5. O'Neal, interview by the author, 2005.

6. Gelber's play both drew on and critiqued Becket's *Waiting for Godot*, situating the action in an interracial group of heroin addicts waiting for their dealer. Among the cast members were reed player Jackie McLean, drummer Larry Ritchie, bassist Michael Mattos and pianist Freddie Redd, who composed the score for the play. As McLean noted, the dynamic between the musicians, who actually played the score in *The Connection*, and the other actors changed from night to night. Sometimes the music was the focus of the performance and not the script (Spellman, 226–27).

7. O'Neal, interview by the author, 2005.

8. O'Neal, "Do You Smell Something Stinky?" 145.

9. Derby interview, Southern Oral History Program, 32; O'Neal, interview by the author, 2013; talk by O'Neal, Free Southern Theater Fiftieth Anniversary, Tulane University, October 18, 2013.

10. O'Neal, interview by the author, 2005; Dent, Schechner, and Moses, *Southern Theater*, 3, 164–67; Fabre, "The Free Southern Theatre," 56.

11. O'Neal, interview by the author, 2005; Dent, Schechner, and Moses, *Southern Theater*, 10.

12. Talk by O'Neal, Free Southern Theater Fiftieth Anniversary, Tulane University, October 18, 2013.

13. O'Neal, interview by the author, 2005, 2005; Salaam, interview by the author, 2005.

14. O'Neal, "Motion in the Ocean," 72.

15. Nicholas, interview, *The HistoryMakers*.

16. O'Neal, interview by the author, 2005.

17. Author's conversation with Derby; Myrick-Harris, "Behind the Scenes," 224; McMillon, "Hidden Voices," 77.

18. Bellafante, "Liberty House."

19. Dent, Schechner, and Moses, *Southern Theater*, 111–34; O'Neal, interview by the author, 2005; Salaam, interview by the author, 2005.

20. O'Neal, interview by the author, 2005; Salaam, interview by the author, 2005; Dent, Schechner, and Moses, *Southern Theater*, 10.

21. O'Neal, interview by the author, 2005; Salaam, interview by the author, 2005; Dent, Schechner, and Moses, *Southern Theater*, 13.

22. O'Neal, interview by the author, 2005; O'Neal, interview by the author, 2013.

23. Hamer saw parallels between the characters Vladimir and Estragon who wait futilely for Godot and poor Black people in the rural South who wait for something to change and it never does. Her conclusion was that Black people in the South could not wait for Godot but needed to take action. Larocco, "COFO Is Not Godot," 509–10.

24. Nicholas, interview, *The HistoryMakers*.

25. McMillon, "Hidden Voices," 57.

26. O'Neal, interview by the author, 2005; O'Neal, interview by the author, 2013.

27. O'Neal, interview by the author, 2005; O'Neal, interview by the author, 2013.

28. It is worth noting that though some might (and did at the time) view O'Neal and his supporters as elitist and opposed to building local Black theater institutions with real roots in the community, O'Neal worked more or less continuously in Black New Orleans neighborhood theater for the rest of his career.

29. Thomas, interview by the author, 2001.

30. Thomas, *Extraordinary Measures*, 137–38.

31. Thomas, *The Collected Poems*, 299.

32. Despite her commitment to SNCC and the movement in Mississippi, Derby, like O'Neal, saw the center of her artistic discipline, painting, in New York City and so spent part of the year up North. Author's conversation with Derby; O'Neal, interview by the author, 2005; Salaam, "Enriching the Paper Trail," 332–33.

33. Thomas, *Extraordinary Measures*, 141–42.

34. Dent, "Marcus B. Christian," 22–26; Salaam, "Enriching the Paper Trail," 327–44.

35. Salaam, interview by the author, 2000; Thomas, "Tom Dent and the Umbra Workshop."

36. Dent, *Magnolia Street*, 29.

37. Letter from Harold Battiste III to Tom Dent, n.d., Folder 7, Box 5, Tom Dent Papers, Amistad Research Center.

38. The following are in Tom Dent Papers, Amistad Research Center: letter from Langston Hughes to Tom Dent, January 26, 1966, Box 1, Folder 6; letter from Joe Goncalves to Tom Dent, October 8, 1969, Box 2, Folder 4; letter from Esther Jackson to Tom Dent, November 20, 1970, Box 2, Folder 5; letter from Toni Cade Bambara to

Tom Dent, n.d. 1970, Box 2, Folder 5; letter from Amiri Baraka to Tom Dent, December 29, 1967, Box 2, Folder 2.

39. Salaam, "Enriching the Paper Trail," 335–36.

40. Moses became a successful theater and television director in New York, winning an Obie for the direction of Amiri Baraka's *Slave Ship* in 1969 and a Tony nomination for a Broadway production of *Ain't Supposed to Die a Natural Death* in 1971. Nicholas became best known for her role in the television series *Room 222*. Orman, who took over as artistic director of the FST immediately after Moses's departure, became most familiar to a national audience through his long-term role as Gordon Robinson on *Sesame Street*.

41. Salaam, "Enriching the Paper Trail," 333–36; Salaam, interview by the author, 2000; Salaam, interview by the author, 2005; Ward, "Southern Black Aesthetics," 143–50.

42. Salaam, interview by the author, 2000; Salaam, interview by the author, 2005; Salaam, "Enriching the Paper Trail"; O'Neal, interview by the author, 2005.

43. Letter from Tom Dent to the Free Southern Theater Board, October 23, 1970, Box 188, Tom Dent Papers, Amistad Research Center.

44. Salaam, interview by the author, 2000; Salaam, interview by the author, 2005.

45. Crawford, *Black Post-Blackness*, 110–16.

46. Michna, "Hearing the Hurricane Coming," 99.

47. Salaam, interview by the author, 2000; Salaam, interview by the author, 2005; O'Neal, interview by the author, 2005; Michna, "Hearing the Hurricane Coming," 95–96.

48. Interestingly, one result of the success of the Black Arts movement in Southern urban centers, especially but not solely in Atlanta, is that it is now possible to be a successful actor, playwright, or director and be based in the South—though New York and Los Angeles still exert a great pull on Black film and theater workers.

49. O'Neal, "As a Weapon Is to Warfare," 68.

50. Watkins, interview by the author.

51. Dent, editorial comment, 3.

52. Dolphy can be heard saying after the tune "Miss Ann" finishes on the 1964 recording *Last Date*, "When you hear music, after it's over, it's gone in the air; you can never recapture it again." *Last Date*, Limelight Records, 1964.

53. Crawford, *Black Post-Blackness*, 143.

54. Michna, "Hearing the Hurricane Coming," 83.

55. Crawford, *Black Post-Blackness*, 133–36.

56. Salaam, interview by the author, 2000; Salaam, interview by the author, 2005; Watkins, interview by the author.

57. Frazier, interview by the author; King, interview by the author.

58. Frazier, interview by the author.

59. Salaam, interview by the author, 2000; Salaam, interview by the author, 2005.

60. Of course, as Ashley Farmer has convincingly argued, even in the hardcore Kawaidaist strongholds of the United States itself, such as US and the early Committee for a Unified Newark/CAP in Newark, which more or less publicly accepted Maulana Karenga's precepts on gender roles, Black women struggled against those roles

even as they appeared to accept them, significantly changing both organizations so that even Karenga openly apologized for his earlier positions on this issue. *Remaking Black Power*, 93–126.

61. "History of SUDAN," 15–16; Salaam, interview by the author, 2005; Thomas, "Neon Griot," 313.

62. Though a complete script of *Second Line Funeral for Uncle Tom* has not been discovered, Michna describes it as "a multi-voiced poetry show about an escaped slave's journey that captured the interplay between the historic specificity of individual Black experiences and the shared consciousness of African diasporic identities." Also according to Michna, the play was structurally based around Robert Hayden's poem, "Runagate, Runagate" but also "included shorter poems by workshop members and Dent." Michna, "Hearing the Hurricane Coming," 113.

63. "History of SUDAN," 1971.

64. Salaam, interview by the author, 2005; Salaam, *Magic of Juju*, 49–51.

65. "History of SUDAN," 15–16; Salaam, interview by the author, 2005.

Chapter Three

1. Bush, *We Are Not What We Seem*, 211.

2. Baraka, "Coordinator's Statement," 115.

3. Dent and Ward, "After the Free Southern Theater," 121.

4. Salaam, *Magic of Juju*, x–xi.

5. Black vaudeville (musical/comic/theatrical revues) continued long after white vaudeville expired, largely due to the continuing lack of television roles for Black performers and the related paucity of television programming aimed at Black audiences in the late 1950s and early 1960s.

6. Hobson, *Legend of the Black Mecca*, 215–27.

7. Molette, interview by the author.

8. Grady-Willis, *Challenging U.S. Apartheid*, xvii–viii.

9. Ture and Thelwell, *Ready for Revolution*, 515–19; Joseph, *Stokely*, 184–87.

10. King interview.

11. Ahmad, interview by the author; Touré, interview by the author; Grady-Willis, *Challenging U.S. Apartheid*, 67.

12. SNCC Vine City Project, *Black Power*, 4.

13. Ture and Thelwell, *Ready for Revolution*, 567–70; Grady-Willis, *Challenging U.S. Apartheid*, 79–113; Touré, interview by the author.

14. SNCC Vine City Project, 5.

15. Spellman, interview by the author, 2000; Spellman, interview by the author, 2006; Alkalimat, interview by the author; Lefever, *Undaunted by the Fight*, 161–64.

16. As will be discussed at more length in chapter 5, the presence of Spelman College in Atlanta meant that there was a tradition of hiring Black women as artists-in-residence, something that was relatively rare in most places, even in the South. Those Black women artists who were employed by HBCUs outside of Spelman were generally writers, such as poet and novelist Margaret Walker, who were not there primarily as artists but as instructors in literature and expository writing.

17. Early, "Memory of Black Arts Spirits," 27.

18. Dooley, interview by the author.

19. "Statement of Purpose," 1.

20. Molette, "Theater Round-Up: Atlanta," 90.

21. Salaam, interview by the author, 2000; Salaam, interview by the author, 2005.

22. Dooley, interview by the author; Spellman, interview by the author, 2000; Spellman, interview by the author, 2006.

23. "Statement of Purpose," 1.

24. Strickland, interview by the author; Vincent Harding, "History of the Institute of the Black World," 145; Rachel Harding, "Biography, Democracy, and Spirit," 691; Strickland, "Critik," 168–70.

25. Grady-Willis, *Challenging U.S. Apartheid*, 143–68; Vincent Harding, "History of the Institute of the Black World," 146–147; Strickland, "Critik," 170–72; Rachel Harding, "Biography, Democracy, and Spirit," 691. For another short history of the inception and early days of the Institute of the Black World, see Stephen Ward, "Scholarship in the Context of Struggle," 42–53.

26. Rachel Harding, "Biography, Democracy, and Spirit," 692.

27. Institute of the Black World, "Statement of Purpose and Program," 576.

28. "Black World Institute in Operation at A.U.," 1.

29. *IBW: The First Year*, October 1, 1970, 6–7, Box 21, Folder 10, Vincent Harding Papers, Woodruff Library, Emory University; *Celebration of Blackness* (program of the formal opening of IBW), Doris Derby Papers, Box 24, Woodruff Library, Emory University.

30. Early, 29–30. The following are in Vincent Harding Papers, Woodruff Library, Emory University: letter from Hoyt Fuller to Vincent Harding, September 16, 1970, Box 14, Folder 6; letters from Haki Madhubuti to Sharon Bourke, February 12 and February 14, 1972, Box 15, Folder 5; letter from Sterling Plumpp to Vincent Harding, April 6, 1972, Box 15, Folder 7; letter from Kalamu ya Salaam to Vincent Harding, n.d., Box 18.

31. Lomax, interview, *The HistoryMakers*.

32. Molette, interview by the author; Molette, "Atlanta," 90–92.

33. Letter from John O'Neal to Vess Harper (Clark College Drama Department), February 21, 1964, Box 2, Doris Derby Papers, Woodruff Library, Emory University.

34. Molette, interview by the author.

35. Woodard, *A Nation Within a Nation*, 159–218; Simanga, *Amiri Baraka and the Congress of African People*, 33–48.

Chapter Four

1. Parker, "The Historical Role," 3–14.

2. For a study of the rise of the impulse toward Black schools, first in K-12 and then in higher education, see Rickford, *We Are an African People*.

3. Biondi, *The Black Revolution*, 3.

4. For example, at the University of Massachusetts Amherst in the early 1970s, the W. E. B. Du Bois Department of Afro-American Studies, located then (as now) in New Africa House (a former dormitory converted to academic space), contained faculty

from a wide range of disciplines in the humanities and the social sciences, including such artists as percussionist and composer Max Roach, saxophonist Archie Shepp, painter Nelson Stevens, textile artist Femi Richards, sculptor Dorrance Hill, dancer Diane Ramos, poet Amus Mor, playwright Paul Carter Harrison, and playwright Shirley Graham Du Bois. (James Baldwin and Chinua Achebe, too, would be closely affiliated with the department a bit later.) What might be thought of as the New Africa House complex also included a "minority" mentoring program, a restaurant, a theater group, and an art gallery.

5. Biondi, *Black Revolution*, 243–53.

6. Conversation with John Bracey.

7. To the great embarrassment of the Kennedy administration, diplomats from newly independent African nations were denied service in restaurants as they traveled between New York and Washington, D.C.

8. Baraka, interview by the author; Thelwell, interview by the author; Thelwell, "The Professor," 617–38; Joseph, *Stokely*, 26. For the best account of the *Dasein* group and their work to date, see Nielsen, *Black Chant*, 59–77.

9. Thelwell, interview by the author; Ture and Thelwell, *Ready for Revolution*, 133–35.

10. Miller, *Fathering Words*, 96–97.

11. Ahmad, interview by the author; Thelwell, interview by the author; Ture and Thelwell, *Ready for Revolution*, 114–16.

12. Gillette, *Between Justice and Beauty*, 151–69.

13. Nielsen, "Now Is the Time," 33.

14. "3-Day African Festival," B4.

15. The Marion Brown Quintet included percussionist Rashied Ali, bassist Reggie Johnson, and trumpeter Alan Shorter, brother of saxophonist and composer Wayne Shorter. Kenny Fisher, a leading jazz musician in Pittsburgh, would later play tenor saxophone in one of drummer Max Roach's groups.

16. "Three Excellent Examples," 5.

17. Wheatley and Valentine, *Under the Radar*. As noted in chapter 3, Lumumba's urging to form a new cultural center and school echoed portions of the SNCC Atlanta Project's Black Power statement. Since a number of the Atlanta Project's staff were in or close to RAM, this suggests that the establishment of such cultural institutions/schools was a part of the RAM program.

18. Ahmad, interview by the author; Baraka, *Autobiography*, 289–290.

19. McQuirter, "16 October 1968," https://www.dc1968project.com/blog/2018/10/17/16-october-1968-amp-new-school-celebrates-anniversary.

20. Jenkins, "Bill Brower," 83. According to some observers, the Washington-based Piedmont "folk" blues musician received a mixed response from the crowd at the opening, with those observers suggesting something about the narrow vision of blackness, Black culture, and Black history by Black Power and Black Arts activists and supporters. Yet it is worth noting that Neal and other members of the Cardozo Area Arts Committee felt it important to include the blues, including more rural "folk" blues as part of the offering at the opening, again attesting to the wide vision of at least those who put the program together.

21. Estada, "Activist and Poet," B7.
22. Campbell, "'It All Comes from the Soul.'"
23. West, "Black Avant Garde," 42; West, "Jazz Gets New Stage," B11.
24. Markle, "'Book Publishers," 16–26.
25. Markle, "Book Publishers," 18.
26. Gilmore, "Drum & Spear Bookstore."
27. Gilmore, "Drum & Spear Bookstore."
28. Cox, interview, Southern Oral History Program, 41.
29. The politics of Black Power and Black Arts and their relationship to Israel and Zionism are complicated, as Nadia Alahmed demonstrates. On the one hand, many Black nationalists of the 1960s and 1970s saw the creation and success of Israel as evidence that it was possible to forge a nation with a new common language out of culturally and linguistically diverse people. (The German payment of reparations to the state of Israel for the crimes of the Holocaust, also, some felt, set a precedent for the payment of reparations to a new Black state.) On the other hand, as previously noted, solidarity with the resistance to Israel and to the displacement of Palestinians, was a widely held, practically ubiquitous, feature of Black Arts and Black Power—causing a number of moments of crisis for the movement as criticism of Israel and support of Palestinians was equated by some outside Black Arts/Black Power as a form of anti-Semitism. Perhaps the most famous incident in this vein was John Johnson's closing of *Black World*, ostensibly for publishing an "anti-Semitic" article about Israel and Zionism. Alahmed, "Black Intifada." See also Feldman, *A Shadow Over Palestine*, 59–102.
30. Markle, "Black Publishers," 19–20.
31. Kelley, "Introduction," 7–8.
32. James, *A History*, 1969.
33. Kelley, "Introduction," 19.
34. Rogers, "Remembering the Black Campus Movement," 30–41.
35. The 1967 play, which takes its name from Amiri Baraka's poem "State/meant," blames the oppression and emasculation of Black men in part on a perceived matriarchal domination of the Black community. It ends with the mentally liberated protagonist's murder of his overbearing, accommodationist mother who psychically killed his father and was doing the same to him. The two Black women (especially "Old Sister") in Sonia Sanchez's play *The Bronx Is Next* (1968), which features a character named Jimmy, can be seen as in part in critical dialogue with *And We Own the Night*.
36. Rickford, *We Are an African People*, 201–3.
37. Cobb, interview by Davis, 12.
38. "Black Studies Purpose," B7.
39. Cobb, interview by Davis, 11–13; Rickford, *We Are an African People*; Ridley, "There Must Be a Way," 19.
40. "Black Artists to Appear," 8.
41. Nashville Christian Leadership Council, *Toward the Beloved Community*.
42. Solomon, *The Cry Was Unity*, 249–50.
43. Killens, "The Artist," 63.
44. Killens, "The Artist," 63.
45. Killens, "The Artist," 63.

46. Gilyard, *Liberation Memories*, 113–37.

47. For an account of the 1966 Fisk conference, see Llorens, "Writers Converge," 54–68. For a brief description of the Hayden-Tolson debate at the conference, see Farnsworth, *Melvin B. Tolson*, 297–98.

48. For a short description of the 1967 Fisk conference, see "On the Conference Beat," 90–93.

49. Madhubuti, interview by the author; Gilyard, *Liberation Memories*, 128. Killens also inaugurated a series of Black Writers Conferences at Medgar Evers College, a campus of the City University of New York in Brooklyn, during a stint there as a writer-in-residence near the end of his career. The first conference at Medgar Evers took place in 1986 (Killens died in 1987) and is still held there every few years.

50. Rickford, *We Are an African People*, 216; Benson, "Black Power."

51. Alkalimat, interview by the author.

52. Alkalimat, interview by the author.

53. Alkalimat, interview by the author.

54. "Notes on . . . Art and Liberation," 6.

55. Alkalimat, interview by the author.

56. Karenga, "Black Cultural Nationalism," 51–52.

57. Alkalimat, "The When of It," 1; Alkalimat, interview by the author.

58. Alkalimat, "The When of It," 6.

59. Alkalimat, interview by the author.

60. Greene, *Women and the Black Freedom Movement*, 74–77, 88–95.

61. Goldston, "Your Own Thing Theatre," 3A.

62. Davis, "History: Durham's Soul Scene Spins Again."

63. Irwin, "A Black Voice in Durham," 114–22; Belvin, "Malcolm X Liberation University," 27.

64. Irwin, "A Black Voice in Durham," 118.

65. Belvin, "Malcolm X Liberation University," 21–39.

66. Smurthwaite. "Black Week Approaches," 1, 12.

67. Rickford, *We Are an African People*, 169–70.

68. Belvin, "Malcolm X Liberation University," 29–32.

69. Belvin, "Malcolm X Liberation University," 32–34.

70. Bourne, "Malcolm X Liberation University."

71. Ford, *Liberated Threads*, 7.

72. Waller, *Love and Revolution*, 54–60.

Chapter Five

1. Salaam, interview by the author, 2000; Salaam, interview by the author, 2005.

2. Dooley, interview by the author.

3. Frazier, interview by the author; King, interview by the author.

4. Salaam, interview by the author, 2005.

5. Coleman, "Dashiki Project Theatre," 64–65.

6. Frazier, interview by the author.

7. Ward, interview by the author, 2005.

8. Salaam, "Enriching the Paper Trail," 338.

9. Salaam, "Enriching the Paper Trail," 338.

10. Ward, interview by the author, 2001; Salaam, "Enriching the Paper Trail," 338–39; Salaam, interview by the author, 2005.

11. Salaam, "Enriching the Paper Trail," 338–39.

12. Salaam, "Enriching the Paper Trail," 338–39; Salaam, interview by the author, 2005.

13. Frazier, interview by the author; Ward, interview by the author, 2001; Ward, interview by the author, 2005.

14. SBCA flyer, 1982.

15. Frazier, interview by the author; Ward, interview by the author, 2001; Ward, interview by the author, 2005.

16. Ward, interview by the author, 2001; Ward, interview by the author, 2005.

17. Watkins, "The Partnering of Artists," 39–40.

18. Thomas, interview by the author.

19. Letter from Ahmos Zu-Bolton to Tom Dent, December 1976, Folder 12, Box 5; letter from Ahmos Zu-Bolton to Tom Dent, n.d., Folder 9, Box 5; letter from Jerry Ward to Tom Dent, March 1, 1974, Folder 1, Box 4; all from Tom Dent Papers, Amistad Research Center.

20. Lorenzo Thomas, *Don't Deny My Name*, 44–63.

21. Author's email exchange with Ahmos Zu-Bolton; letter from Jerry Ward to Tom Dent, March 1, 1974, Folder 1, Box 4, Tom Dent Papers, Amistad Research Center.

22. Miller, *Fathering Words*, 70–71.

23. Alexander, interview by the author.

24. "Executive Summary," Neighborhood Arts Center Archives, Box 1, Folder 1, 7, Auburn Avenue Library, Atlanta, Georgia; Lomax, interview by the author.

25. Strickland, "Critik," 176–77.

26. Lomax, interview by the author.

27. Letter from Ebon Dooley to Mike Clark, October 24, 1973, Box 17, Folder 5, Vincent Harding Papers, Woodruff Library, Emory University. Clark was an official at the We Shall Overcome Foundation at the Highlander Research and Education Center in New Market, Tennessee, which gave "The Great Black Music" a $500 grant, apparently facilitated by IBW director Vincent Harding—though Harding's precise role is not entirely clear from his papers.

28. Alexander, interview by the author.

29. Dooley, interview by the author; "Executive Summary," Neighborhood Arts Center Archives, Box 1, Folder 1, 5, Auburn Avenue Library, Atlanta, Georgia.

30. "Tentative Programming for 1981–82," Neighborhood Arts Center Archives, Box 3, Folder 1, Auburn Avenue Library, Atlanta, Georgia; Gaffney, "The Neighborhood Arts Center."

31. Lovelace, "It Was a Time of Hope," 53–54.

32. News Release from the Department of Cultural Affairs, Box 7, Maynard Jackson Records, Woodruff Library, Special Collections, Clark Atlanta University.

33. Lomax, interview by the author; Alexander, interview by the author.

34. Brock, "NBAF Looks to 2000,"11L; Flannery, "A Black Arts Festival," 8, 30.

35. Fox, "Seeking an Artful Transition," Arts 1L; Spriggs, interview by the author.

36. Fenderson, *Building the Black Arts Movement*, 134–46. My colleague John Bracey has spoken to me on several occasions of a meeting with Johnson he attended after *Black World*'s demise in which Johnson defended his decision by citing his support of Black Power and Black Arts. Johnson claimed that he had lost many thousands of dollars on *Black World*, demanding to know who else had contributed that kind of money to the movement.

37. Historian Robert Harris Jr. recalls attending a 1976 meeting of the National Committee of Concern Over the Demise of *Black World* at John Henrik Clarke's apartment in New York City to discuss the creation of a new journal to replace *Black World* that helped lead to the founding of *First World*. Robert Harris Jr., Comments, Modern Cultural Politics panel, Organization of American Historians annual meeting, Memphis, Tennessee, April 3, 2003. Harris was the secretary of the steering committee of the national committee, which consisted almost entirely of African American academics, primarily from various institutions of the Black Studies movement. Haki Madhubuti remembers similar meetings in Chicago (Madhubuti, interview by the author). It is quite likely that other meetings occurred elsewhere.

38. Tate, "Our Art Itself," 183–87. For a study of the role of Spelman students and faculty in the civil rights movement, see Lefever, *Undaunted by the Fight*.

39. Letter from Lorenzo Thomas to Toni Cade Bambara, October 6, 1975, Box 1; letter from John O. Killens to Toni Cade Bambara, November 11, 1982, Box 1; letter from Hoyt Fuller to Toni Cade Bambara, October 20, 1978, Box 2; all from Toni Cade Bambara Papers, Spelman College Archives.

40. Cleage, interview by the author; Lovelace, interview by the author; Grady-Willis, *Challenging U.S. Apartheid*, 199–204.

41. Cleage, interview by the author.

42. Bambara, *The Salt Eaters*, 258.

43. Cleage, interview by the author.

44. Cleage, interview by the author. For a collection that contains many of Cleage's column's in Atlanta's alternative and Black press, see *Deals with the Devil*.

45. Springer, *Living for the Revolution*, 41.

Conclusion

1. The mayoral campaign of 1993 was complicated. Both Campbell and Lomax were Black Democrats. Maynard Jackson (who had fallen out with Lomax when the latter challenged him in a bitter 1989 mayoral race) endorsed Campbell. Andrew Young supported Lomax. However, Campbell, tarnished by charges of corruption, was seen as a post-civil rights movement leader more friendly to business. The largely-white "tax revolt" was a major factor in building support for Campbell and diminishing Lomax's appeal.

Lomax, interview by the author. For an example of the attack on Lomax by one of the tax revolt's leaders, see Skandalakis, "Lomax's Use of Tax Dollars," A11. For the response of Lomax (who went on to become president of Dillard University and the head of the United Negro College Fund) to the revolt and his subsequent political defeat by Campbell, see Pomerantz, "Lomax on Leaving Atlanta," 02E.

2. Spellman, interview by the author, 2006; Molette, interview by the author; Landon Thomas, "Saving the Black Arts Festival," A14; Sabulis, "Exit of Theater," Features 1E; Hulbert, "Jomandi's JAM," Arts 1.

3. Dent and Ward, Jr., "After the Free Southern Theater," 120.

4. Breaux, "Tom Dent's Role," 341.

5. Community and educational advocate D. C. Clark, for example, describes how Narcisse, along with cultural activists Marshall Davis, Altine Baki, and Gene Tinney, held an annual Kwanzaa celebration in Miami for many years (Clark, *Lessons from the Other Side*, 229).

6. Robinson, "Space, Time, and Race," 225–26.

7. Akuno and Nangwaya, *Jackson Rising*; Gutterplan, "Is This the Most Radical."

8. Doris Derby Papers, Special Collections, Woodruff Library, Emory University, Boxes 2 and 21.

9. Letter from Jerry Ward to Wendell Narcisse, April 7, 1979, Jerry Ward Papers, Mississippi State Department of Archives and History, Jackson, Mississippi.

10. Doris Derby Papers, Special Collections, Woodruff Library, Emory University, Box 11.

11. Cooperation Jackson, "Science Facts, Science Fictions," September 6, 2019, https://cooperationjackson.org/blog/2019/9/6/sciencefactssciencefictionsgndusdac.

12. Claudia Feldman, "African American Art."

13. Garrison, *Third Ward Texas*; Kimmelman, "In Houston," AR1.

14. Leon, interview, *The HistoryMakers*.

15. Lomax, interview, *The HistoryMakers*.

16. Alexander, interview by the author.

17. Ward, interview by Cleophus Thomas, 6, 27.

18. Letter from Jerry Ward to Lance Jeffers, November 6, 1976, and letter from Jerry Ward to Lance Jeffers, August 30, 1978, Folder 5, Box 2, Lance Jeffers Papers, Mississippi State Department of Archives and History, Jackson, Mississippi; letter from Tom Dent to Jerry Ward, August 24, 1978, Folder 9, Box 3, Jerry Washington Ward Papers, Mississippi State Department of Archives and History, Jackson, Mississippi.

19. For a collection of O'Neal's Junebug Jabbo Jones work, see O'Neal, *Don't Start Me*.

20. Fields, "M Ensemble Theater."

21. Hunter and Robinson, *Chocolate Cites*, 117.

22. Ward, *Katrina Papers*, 20.

23. Michna, "Hearing the Hurricane Coming," 32–35.

24. Crutcher, *Tremé*.

Bibliography

Archival Sources

Amherst, Massachusetts
- University of Massachusetts Amherst, W. E. B. Du Bois Library, Special Collections
  - W. E. B. Du Bois Papers

Atlanta, Georgia
- Auburn Avenue Library
  - Neighborhood Arts Center Archives
- Clark Atlanta University, Woodruff Library, Special Collections
  - Hoyt Fuller Papers
  - Maynard Jackson Records
- Emory University, Woodruff Library, Special Collections
  - Doris Derby Papers
  - Vincent Harding Papers
- Spelman College Archives
  - Toni Cade Bambara Papers

Jackson, Mississippi
- Mississippi State Department of Archives and History
  - Lance Jeffers Papers
  - Jerry Washington Ward Papers

New York, New York
- Schomburg Center for Research in Black Culture
  - John Henrik Clarke Papers
  - Julian Mayfield Papers
  - Larry Neal Papers
  - Records of the Institute of the Black World

Washington, D.C.
- Howard University, Moorland-Spingarn Research Center
  - Amiri Baraka Collection
- Smithsonian Institution, Archives of American Art
  - Oral History Interviews

Interviews

Ahmad, Muhammad. Interview by the author, telephone, August 20, 2002.

Alexander, Jim. Interview by the author, Atlanta, April 16, 2011.

Alkalimat, Abdul. Interview by the author, Zoom, June 17, 2020.
Baraka, Amiri. Interview by the author, Newark, New Jersey, July 15, 2000.
Cleage, Pearl. Interview by the author, telephone, August 8, 2007.
Cobb, Charlie. Interview by Joshua Clark Davis, October 16, 2015, Veterans of the Civil Rights Movement, https://www.crmvet.org/nars/cobb2015.pdf.
Cox, Courtland. Interview, July 8, 2011, Southern Oral History Program, Smithsonian Institution's National Museum of African American History and Culture and the Library of Congress.
Derby, Doris. Interview, April 26, 2011, Southern Oral History Program, Smithsonian Institution's National Museum of African American History and Culture and the Library of Congress.
———. Conversation with the author, New Orleans, October 18, 2013.
Dooley, Ebon. Interview by the author, Atlanta, August 16, 2001.
Frazier, Levi, Jr. Interview by the author, telephone, December 26, 2005.
Jackson, Esther and James. Interview by the author, Brooklyn, New York, July 8, 2002.
King, Martin Luther, Jr. Interview with Mike Wallace, *60 Minutes*, CBS, September 27, 1966.
King, Woodie. Interview by the author, New York City, January 3, 2004.
Leon, Kenny. Interview, *The HistoryMakers*, September 9, 2007, https://www.thehistorymakers.org/biography/kenny-leon-41.
Lomax, Michael. Interview by the author, Cambridge, Massachusetts. August 28, 2007.
———. Interview, *The HistoryMakers*, January 31, 2017, https://www.thehistorymakers.org/biography/michael-lomax.
Lovelace, Alice. Interview by the author, telephone, March 4, 2007.
Madhubuti, Haki. Interview by the author, telephone, August 22, 2003.
Molette, Carlton. Interview by the author, telephone, December, 8, 2006.
Nicholas, Denise. Interview, *The HistoryMakers*, May 19, 2007, https://www.thehistorymakers.org/biography/denise-nicholas-41.
O'Neal, John. Interview by the author, Amherst, Massachusetts, December 5, 2005.
———. Interview by the author, New Orleans, October 19, 2013.
Salaam, Kalamu ya. Interview by the author, New Orleans, April 23, 2000.
———. Interview by the author, Cambridge, Massachusetts, December 6, 2005.
Spellman, A. B. Interview by the author, Washington, D.C., December 28, 2000.
———. Interview by the author, telephone, November 11, 2006.
Spriggs, Edward. Interview by the author, Atlanta, August 16, 2001.
Strickland, William. Interview by the author, Amherst, Massachusetts, November 6, 2002.
Thelwell, Ekwueme Michael. Interview by the author, Pelham, Massachusetts, February 20, 2003.
Thomas, Lorenzo. Interview by the author, Chicago, December 28, 1999.
Touré, Askia. Interview by the author, Cambridge, Massachusetts, December 2, 2000.

Ward, Jerry. Interview by the author, New Orleans, December 28, 2001.
———. Interview by the author, telephone, December 6, 2005.
———. Interview by Cleophus Thomas, Documentary and Oral History Studio, Loyola University, New Orleans, January 21, 2016, https://loyoladohs.files.wordpress.com/2016/10/transcript-of-jerry-w-ward-jr-interview-corrected-06-23.pdf.
Watkins, Nayo. Interview by the author, telephone, January 14, 2002.
Woodruff, Hale. Interview, Smithsonian Institution Archives of American Art, November 18, 1968.

Books, Chapters, Essays, Articles, Broadsides, Films, Pamphlets, Phonographic Recordings, and Dissertations

Akuno, Kali, and Ajamu Nangwaya. *Jackson Rising: The Struggle for Economic Democracy and Black Self-Determination in Jackson, Mississippi*. Montreal: Daraja, 2017.
Alahmed, Nadia. "'Black Intifada': Black Arts Movement, Palestinian Poetry of Resistance and the Roots of Black and Palestinian Solidarity." Ph.D. diss., University of Massachusetts Amherst, 2019.
Alexander, Shawn. *An Army of Lions: The Civil Rights Struggle Before the NAACP*. Philadelphia: University of Pennsylvania Press, 2013.
Alkalimat, Abdul. *The When of It Is Now: Art and Revolution for the Black Man*. Nashville: People's College, 1973.
Anderson, Benedict. *Imagined Communities: Reflections on the Origins and Spread of Nationalism*. New York: Knopf Doubleday, 1983.
Bambara, Toni Cade. *Gorilla, My Love*. New York: Random House, 1972.
———. *The Salt Eaters*. New York: Random House, 1980.
Baraka, Amiri. *Autobiography of LeRoi Jones*. New York: Lawrence Hill, 1997.
———. *Blues People: Negro Music in White America*. New York: Morrow, 1963.
———. "Coordinator's Statement." In *African Congress: A Documentary History of the First Pan-African Congress*, edited by Amiri Baraka, 115–22. New York: Morrow, 1972.
Bellafante, Ginnia. "Liberty House and the Shifting Focus of Political Style." *New York Times*, April 16, 2017.
Belvin, Brent. "Malcolm X Liberation University: An Experiment in Independent Black Education." Master's thesis, North Carolina State University, 2004.
Benson, Richard. "Black Power, Education, and the History of the People's College." *Black Perspectives*, May 17, 2017. https://www.aaihs.org/black-power-education-and-the-history-of-the-peoples-college/.
Biondi, Martha. *The Black Revolution on Campus*. Berkeley: University of California Press, 2012.
"Black Artists to Appear." *The Hilltop*, November 15, 1968.
"Black Studies Purpose: To 'Africanize' Students." *Washington Post*, March 13, 1969.

"Black World Institute in Operation at A.U." *Atlanta Daily World*, January 20, 1970.
Bourne, St. Clair, dir. "Malcolm X Liberation University." WNET *Black Journal*, 1969.
Breaux, Quo Vadis Gex. "Tom Dent's Role in the Organizational Mentoring of African American Southern Writers: A Memoir." *African American Review* 40, no. 2 (Summer 2006): 339–44.
Brock, Wendell. "NBAF Looks to 2000 and a New Cadre of Artists." *Atlanta Constitution*, June 28, 1988.
Bush, Rod. *We Are Not What We Seem: Black National and Class Struggle in the American Century*. New York: New York University Press, 2000.
Campbell, Emahunn. "'It All Comes from the Soul:' The New School of Afro American Thought, Washington, D.C., and Black Arts." 38th Annual Conference on D.C. Historical Studies, November 2011.
Carmichael, Stokely (Kwame Ture), and Ekwueme Michael Thelwell. *Ready for Revolution: The Life and Struggles of Stokely Carmichael (Kwame Ture)*. New York: Scribner's, 2003.
Clark, D. C. *Lessons from the Other Side*. Bloomington, IN: IUniverse, 2004.
Clark, Lesley. "Can a Black Candidate Win Florida's Top Job? Andrew Gillum Bids to Make History." *Miami Herald*, November 2, 2018. https://www.miamiherald.com/news/politicsgovernment/election/article220860635.html.
Cleage, Pearl. *Deals with the Devil and Other Reasons to Riot*. New York: Ballantine, 1993.
Coleman, Stanley. "Dashiki Project Theatre: Black Identity and Beyond." Ph.D. diss., Louisiana State University, 2003.
Crawford, Margo. *Black Post-Blackness: The Black Arts Movement and Twenty-First Century Aesthetics*. Urbana: University of Illinois Press, 2017.
Cruse, Harold. *The Crisis of the Negro Intellectual*. New York: Morrow, 1967.
Crutcher, Michael E. *Tremé: Race and Place in a New Orleans Neighborhood*. Athens: University of Georgia Press, 2010.
Cunningham, Wesley Sawyer. "'A Part Of, Rather Than Apart From': Louisville's Black Arts Scene in the Mid-twentieth Century." Master's thesis, University of Louisville, 2016.
Davis, Donald F. "Hale Woodruff of Atlanta: Molder of Black Artists." *Journal of Negro History* 69, no. 3-4 (Summer-Autumn 1984): 147–54.
Davis, Joshua Clark. "History: Durham's Soul Scene Spins Again." *News and Observer*, August 13, 2014. https://www.newsobserver.com/news/local/community/durham-news/dn-opinion/article10032212.html.
Denning, Michael. *The Cultural Front: The Laboring of American Culture in the Twentieth Century*. New York: Verso, 1996.
Dent, Thomas C. Editor's comment. *Echoes from the Gumbo* (December 1968): 3.
———. *Magnolia Street*. New Orleans: Self-published, 1976.
———. "Marcus B. Christian: An Appreciation." *Black American Literature Forum* 18, no. 1 (Spring 1984): 22–26.

———. *New Orleans Griot: The Tom Dent Reader*. Edited by Kalamu ya Salaam. New Orleans: University of New Orleans Press, 2018.
Dent, Thomas C., Richard Schechner, and Gilbert Moses, eds. *Southern Theater, by the Free Southern Theater. A Documentary of the South's Radical Black Theater, with Journals, Letters, Poetry, Essays, and a Play Written by Those Who Built It*. Indianapolis: Bobbs-Merrill, 1969.
Dent, Tom, and Jerry Ward. "After the Free Southern Theater: A Dialog." *The Drama Review: TDR* 31, no. 3 (Autumn 1987): 120–25.
Dolphy, Eric. *Last Date*. Limelight Records, 1964.
Douglas, Robert. "The History of Louisville's African American Artists Since 1958," July 16, 2013. http://bobdouglasart.com/?p=911.
Du Bois, W. E. B. *Behold the Land*. Birmingham, AL: Southern Negro Youth Congress, 1946.
Early, James. "Memory of Black Arts Spirits: Kofi Bailey and Atlanta in the 1960s." *International Review of African American Art* 15, no. 1 (1998): 27–30.
Estada, Louis. "Activist and Poet Gaston T. Neal Dies" *Washington Post*, October 22, 1999.
Fabre, Genevieve. "The Free Southern Theatre, 1963–1979." *Black American Literature Forum* 17, no. 2 (Summer 1983): 55–59.
Fairclough, Adam. *Race & Democracy: The Civil Rights Struggle in Louisiana, 1915–1972*. Athens: University of Georgia Press, 1995.
Farmer, Ashley. *Remaking Black Power: How Black Women Transformed an Era*. Chapel Hill: University of North Carolina Press, 2017.
Farnsworth, Robert. *Melvin B. Tolson, 1896–1966: Plain Talk and Poetic Prophecy*. Columbia: University of Missouri Press, 1984.
Feldman, Claudia. "African American Art Institution Shutters after 37 Years." *Houston Chronicle*, February 28, 2014. https://www.houstonchronicle.com/entertainment/arts-theater/article/African-American-art-institution-shutters-after-5279266.php.
Feldman, Keith. *A Shadow over Palestine: The Imperial Life of Race in America*. Minneapolis: University of Minnesota Press, 2015.
Fenderson, Jonathan. *Building the Black Arts Movement: Hoyt Fuller and the Cultural Politics of the 1960s*. Urbana: University of Illinois Press, 2019.
Fields, Dorothy Jenkins. "M Ensemble Theater Finds a Permanent Home in Liberty City." *Miami Herald*, October 20, 2016. https://www.miamiherald.com/news/local/community/miami-dade/community-voices/article109413172.html.
Flannery, James. "A Black Arts Festival—And More." *New York Times*, July 31, 1998.
Ford, Tanisha. *Liberated Threads: Black Women, Style, and the Global Politics of Soul*. Chapel Hill: University of North Carolina Press, 2015.
Fosl, Catherine. *Subversive Southerner: Anne Braden and the Struggle for Racial Justice in the Cold War South*. New York: Palgrave Macmillan, 2002.
Fowler, Gene. "Photographer Earlie Hudnall: 'Art Is Life.'" *Glasstire (Texas Visual Art)*, November 12, 2018. https://glasstire.com/2018/11/12/photographer-earlie-hudnall-art-is-life/.

Fox, Catherine. "Seeking an Artful Transition: Hammonds House at Crossroads as Gallery's Longtime Director Retires." *Atlanta Journal-Constitution*, August 4, 2002.

From Spirituals to Swing: The Legendary 1938 & 1939 Carnegie Hall Concerts Produced by John Hammond. Vanguard 169/71-2, 1999.

Gaffney, Nicholas. "The Neighborhood Arts Center, Cultural Pride, and Community Self-Awareness: Black Power and Black Arts in Atlanta, 1975–1985." College of Charleston Black Power Conference, September 2012. http://avery.cofc.edu/wp-content/uploads/2012/08/Gaffney_Avery-Center-Conference_NAC.pdf.

Garrison, Andrew, dir. *Third Ward Texas*. Welcome Home Productions, 2007.

Gellman, Erik. *Death Blow to Jim Crow: The National Negro Congress and the Rise of Militant Civil Rights.* Chapel Hill: University of North Carolina Press, 2012.

Gessler, Anne. *Cooperatives in New Orleans: Collective Action and Urban Development*. Jackson: University Press of Mississippi, 2020.

Gillette, Howard. *Between Justice and Beauty: Race, Planning, and the Failure of Urban Policy in Washington, D.C.* Philadelphia: University of Pennsylvania Press, 2006.

Gilmore, Brian. "Drum & Spear Bookstore." *Beltway Poetry Quarterly* 11, no. 2 (Spring 2010). http://washingtonart.com/beltway/drum&spear.html.

Gilpin, Toni. *The Long Deep Grudge: A Story of Big Capital, Radical Labor, and Class War in the American Heartland*. Chicago: Haymarket Books, 2020.

———. "A Louisville Union Built Its Strength as Blacks, Whites Took on International Harvester." *Leo Weekly*, August 30, 2017. https://www.leoweekly.com/2017/08/louisville-union-built/.

Gilyard, Keith. *Liberation Memories: The Rhetoric and Poetics of John Oliver Killens*. Detroit: Wayne State University Press, 2003.

Golden, Thelma, and Judith Whitney. *Bob Thompson*. Berkeley: University of California Press, 1998.

Goldston, Leon. "Your Own Thing Theatre Opens at Regal." *Carolina Times*, July 26, 1969.

Grady-Willis, Winston. *Challenging U.S. Apartheid: Atlanta and Black Struggles for Human Rights, 1960–1977*. Durham, NC: Duke University Press, 2006.

Greene, Christina. *Women and the Black Freedom Movement in Durham, North Carolina*. Chapel Hill: University of North Carolina Press, 2005.

Gutterplan, D. D. "Is This the Most Radical Mayor in America?" *The Nation*, November 17, 2017. https://www.thenation.com/article/archive/is-this-the-most-radical-mayor-in-america/.

Harding, Rachel. "Biography, Democracy, and Spirit: An Interview with Vincent Harding." *Callaloo* 20, no. 3 (Summer 1997): 682–98.

Harding, Vincent. "History of the Institute of the Black World." In *Education and Black Struggle: Notes from the Colonized World,* edited by the Institute of the Black World. Cambridge: Harvard Educational Review, 1972.

Harold, Claudrena. *The Rise and Fall of the Garvey Movement in the Urban South, 1918–1942*. New York: Routledge, 2007.

Haviland, Sara Rzeszutek. *James and Esther Cooper Jackson: Love and Courage in the Black Freedom Movement*. Lexington: University of Kentucky Press, 2015.

Higashida, Cheryl. *Black Internationalist Feminism: Women Writers of the Black Left, 1945–1995*. Urbana: University of Illinois Press, 2013.

Hill, Errol, and James Hatch. *A History of African American Theatre*. New York: Cambridge University Press, 2003.

"The History of SUDAN (in Texas?)." *Nkombo* 3, no. 2 (March 1971): 15–16.

Hobson, Maurice. *The Legend of the Black Mecca: Politics and Class in the Making of Modern Atlanta*. Chapel Hill: University of North Carolina Press, 2017.

Horne, Gerald. *Black Revolutionary: William Patterson and the Globalization of the African American Freedom Struggle*. Urbana: University of Illinois Press, 2013.

Hulbert, Dan. "Jomandi's JAM Black Theater's in Fight for Its Life." *Atlanta Constitution*, November 13, 1994.

Hunter, Marcus Anthony, and Zandria F. Robinson. *Chocolate Cites: The Black Map of American Life*. Berkeley: University of California Press, 2018.

Ignatiev, Noel, and John Garvey. "Abolish the White Race by Any Means Necessary." In *Race Traitor*, edited by Noel Ignatiev and John Garvey, 9–14. New York: Routledge, 1996.

Institute of the Black World. "Statement of Purpose and Program." In *New Black Voices: An Anthology of Contemporary Afro-American Literature*, edited by Abraham Chapman, 575–578. New York: New American Library, 1972.

Irwin, Carolyn K. "A Black Voice in Durham." *Ebony*, June 1973.

James, C. L. R. *A History of Pan-African Revolt*. Oakland: PM Press, 2012 (1938, 1969).

Jenkins, Willard. "Bill Brower: Notes from a Keen Observer and Scene Maker." In *DC Jazz: Stories of Jazz Music in Washington, DC*, edited by Maurice Jackson and Blair A. Ruble, 75–90. Washington: Georgetown University Press, 2018.

Joseph, Peniel. *Stokely: A Life*. New York: Basic *Civitas* Books, 2014.

Karenga, Maulana. "Black Cultural Nationalism." In *SOS: Calling All Black People, A Black Arts Movement Reader*, edited by John Bracey, Sonia Sanchez, and James Smethurst, 51–54. Amherst: University of Massachusetts Press, 2014.

Kelley, Robin D. G. *Hammer and Hoe: Alabama Communists During the Great Depression*. Chapel Hill: University of North Carolina Press, 1990.

———. "Introduction." In C. L. R. James, *A History of Pan-African Revolt*, 1–33. Oakland: PM Press, 2012 (1938, 1969).

Killens, John O. "The Artist and the Black University." *Black Scholar* 1, no. 1 (November 1969): 61–65.

———. "Lorraine Hansberry: On Time!" In *Freedomways Reader*, edited by Esther Cooper Jackson, 335–39. New York: Dodd, Mead, 1980.

Kimmelman, Michael. "In Houston, Art Is Where the Home Is." *New York Times*, December 17, 2006.

Knight, Etheridge. *The Essential Etheridge Knight*. Pittsburgh: University of Pittsburgh Press, 1986.

Lang, Clarence. *Grassroots at the Gateway: Class Politics and Black Freedom Struggle in St. Louis, 1936–1975*. Ann Arbor: University of Michigan Press, 2009.

Larocco, Christina. "'COFO Is Not Godot': The Free Southern Theater, the Black Freedom Movement, and the Search for a Usable Aesthetic." *Cultural and Social History* 12, no. 4 (2015): 509–510.

Lefever, Harry. *Undaunted by the Fight: Spelman College and the Civil Rights Movement, 1957–1967*. Macon, GA: Mercer University Press, 2005.
Lichtenstein, Alex. "Putting Labor's House in Order: The Transport Workers Union and Labor Anti-Communism in Miami during the 1940s." *Labor History* 39, no. 1 (1998): 7–23.
Llorens, David. "Writers Converge on Fisk University." *Negro Digest* 15, no. 8 (June 1966): 54–68.
Lorence, James. "Mobilizing the Reserve Army: The Communist Party and the Unemployed in Atlanta, 1929–1934." In *Radicalism in the South Since Reconstruction*, edited by Chris Green, Rachel Rubin, and James Smethurst, 335–339. New York: Palgrave Macmillan 2006.
Lovelace, Alice. "It Was a Time of Hope—It Was a Time of Change." *High Performance* (Winter 1993): 53–54.
Markle, Seth. "Book Publishers for a Pan-African World:Drum and Spear Press and Tanzania's Ujamaa Ideology." *Black Scholar* 37, no. 4 (Winter 2008): 16–26.
McDuffie, Erik. *Sojourning for Freedom: Black Women, American Communism, and the Making of Black Left Feminism*. Durham, NC: Duke University Press, 2011.
McMillon, Kim. "Hidden Voices: The Women of the Black Arts Movement and the Rise of the Ancestors." Ph.D. diss., University of California, Merced, 2019.
McQuirter, Marya. "16 October 1968 & New School of Afro-American Thought's 3rd Anniversary." DC1968 Project. https://www.dc1968project.com/blog/2018/10/17/16-october-1968-amp-new-school-celebrates-anniversary.
McWhorter, Diane. *Carry Me Home: Birmingham, Alabama, the Climactic Battle of the Civil Rights Revolution*. New York: Simon & Schuster, 2001.
Michna, Catherine. "Hearing the Hurricane Coming: Storytelling, Second-Line Knowledges, and the Struggle for Democracy in New Orleans." Ph.D. diss., Boston University, 2011.
Miller, E. Ethelbert. *Fathering Words: The Making of an African American Writer*. Baltimore: Black Classics, 2000.
Molette, Barbara. "Theater Round-Up: Atlanta." *Black World*, April 1973.
Morgan, Stacy. *Rethinking Social Realism: African American Art and Literature, 1930–1953*. Athens: University of Georgia Press, 2004.
Morton, Jelly Roll. *Complete Library of Congress Recordings*. Rounder Records, 2005.
Myrick-Harris, Clarissa. "Behind the Scenes: Doris Derby, Denise Nicholas and the Free Southern Theater." In *Women of the Civil Rights Movement: Trailblazers and Torchbearers, 1941–1965*, edited by Vicki Crawford, Jacqueline Anne Rouse, and Barbara Woods, 219–32. Bloomington: Indiana University Press, 1993.
Nashville Christian Leadership Council. *Toward the Beloved Community: Story of the Nashville Christian Leadership Council*. Nashville: Nashville Christian Leadership Council, n.d.
National Center for Education Statistics, *The Traditionally Black Institutions of Higher Education, 1860–1982*. Washington, DC: NCES, 1985.
Nielsen, Aldon. *Black Chant: Languages of African American Postmodernism*. New York: Cambridge University Press, 1997.

———. "Now Is the Time: Voicing against the Grain of Orality." In *People Get Ready: The Future of Jazz Is Now!*, edited by Ajay Heble and Rob Wallace, 31–43. Durham, NC: Duke University Press, 2013.

Notes on . . . Art and Liberation. Nashville: People's College, 1971.

O'Neal, John. *Don't Start Me to Talking . . . : Plays of Struggle and Liberation*. New York: Theatre Communications Group, 2016.

———. "'Do You Smell Something Stinky?' Notes from Conversations about Making Art while Working for Justice in Racist, Imperial America in the Twenty-First Century." In *Acting Together II: Performance and the Creative Transformation of Conflict*, edited by Cynthia E. Cohen, Roberto Gutiérrez Varea, and Polly O. Walker, 125–57. New York: New York University Press, 2011.

———. "Motion in the Ocean: Some Political Dimensions of the Free Southern Theatre." *The Drama Review: TDR* 12, no. 4 (Summer 1968): 70–77.

"On the Conference Beat." *Negro Digest* 16, no. 9 (July 1967): 90–93.

Parker, Patsy. "The Historical Role of Women in Higher Education." *Administrative Issues Journal: Connecting Education, Practice, and Research* 5, no. 1 (Spring 2015): 3–14.

Pomerantz, Gary. "Lomax on Leaving Atlanta." *Atlanta Journal*, May 2, 1997.

Redmond, Eugene B. *Drumvoices: The Mission of Afro-American Poetry: A Critical History*. Garden City, NY: Anchor, 1976.

Rickford, Russell. *We Are an African People: Independent Education, Black Power, and the Radical Imagination*. New York: Oxford University Press, 2016.

Ridley, Ike. "There Must Be a Way to Legitimize Black Thought." *Baltimore Afro-American*, March 19, 1969.

Robinson, Zandria F. "Space, Time, and Race in Dirty South Bohemia." In *The Bohemian South: Creating Countercultures, from Poe to Punk*, edited by Shawn Bingham and Lindsey Freeman, 224–41. Chapel Hill: University of North Carolina Press, 2017.

Rogers, Ibram. "Remembering the Black Campus Movement: An Oral History Interview with James P. Garrett." *Journal of Pan African Studies* 2, no. 10 (June 2009): 30–41.

Rohmer, Robert. *Slavery in the Connecticut Valley of Massachusetts*. Amherst, MA: Levellers Press, 2009.

Rose, Chanelle. *The Struggle for Black Freedom in Miami: Civil Rights and America's Tourist Paradise, 1896–1968*. Baton Rouge: Louisiana State University Press, 2015.

Sabulis, Tom. "Exit of Theater Pioneer Jolts Jomandi, Community." *Atlanta Constitution*, January 5, 2001.

Salaam, Kalamu Ya. "Enriching the Paper Trail: An Interview with Tom Dent." *African American Review* 27, no. 2 (Summer 1993): 327–44.

———. *The Magic of Juju: An Appreciation of the Black Arts Movement*. Chicago: Third World, 2016.

Simanga, Michael. *Amiri Baraka and the Congress of African People: History and Memory*. New York: Palgrave Macmillan, 2015.

Skandalakis, Mitch. "Lomax's Use of Tax Dollars to Fund Arts is Politically Motivated." *Atlanta Constitution*, April 15, 1993.

Smethurst, James. "The Black Arts Movement in Atlanta." In *Neighborhood Rebels: Black Power at the Local Level*, edited by Peniel Joseph, 173–90. New York: Palgrave Macmillan, 2010.

———. *The Black Arts Movement: Literary Nationalism of the 1960s and 1970s*. Chapel Hill: University of North Carolina Press, 2005.

———. "Black Arts South: Rethinking New Orleans and the Black Arts Movement in the Wake of Hurricane Katrina." In *Radicalism in the South since Reconstruction*, edited by Christopher Green, Rachel Lee Rubin, and James Smethurst, 129–48. New York: Palgrave Macmillan, 2011.

———. "Retraining the Heartworks: Women in Atlanta's Black Arts Movement." In *Want to Start a Revolution: Radical Women in the Black Freedom Struggle*, edited by Dayo Gore, Jeanne Theoharis, and Komozi Woodard, 205–22. New York: New York University Press, 2009.

———. "The Street Ran through Cities: Faulkner and the Early African American Migration Narrative." In *Faulkner and the Black Literatures of the Americas*, edited by Jay Watson and James G. Thomas Jr., 20–35. Jackson: University Press of Mississippi, 2016.

Smurthwaite, Richard. "Black Week Approaches." *Bufee Chronicle*, January 30, 1969.

SNCC Vine City Project. *Black Power: A Reprint of a Position Paper for the SNCC Vine City Project*. Washington, DC: United States Student Association, n.d.

Solomon, Mark. *The Cry Was Unity: Communists and African Americans, 1917–1936*. Jackson: University Press of Mississippi, 1998.

Spellman, A.B. *Four Lives in the Bebop Business*. 1967. Ann Arbor, MI: University of Michigan Press, 2011.

Springer, Kimberly. *Living for the Revolution, Black Feminist Organizations, 1968–1980*. Durham, NC: Duke University Press, 2005.

Stalin, J.V. *Marxism and the National Question*. Moscow: Co-operative Publishing Society of Foreign Workers in the U.S.S.R., 1935 (1913).

Stanton, Mary. *Red Black White: The Alabama Communist Party, 1930–1950*. Athens: University of Georgia Press, 2020.

Strickland, Bill. "Critik: The Institute of the Black World (IBW), the Political Legacy of Martin Luther King, the Intellectual Struggle to Rethink America's Racial Meaning." In *Radicalism in the South Since Reconstruction*, edited by Chris Green, Rachel Rubin, and James Smethurst, 167–89. New York: Palgrave Macmillan 2006.

Sullivan, Patricia. *Days of Hope: Race and Democracy in the New Deal Era*. Chapel Hill: University of North Carolina Press, 1996.

Tate, Candy. "'Our Art Itself Was Our Activism': Atlanta's Neighborhood Arts Center, 1975–1990." Ph.D. dissertation, Clark-Atlanta University, 2012.

Theisen, Olive Jensen. *A Life on Paper: The Drawings and Lithographs of John Thomas Biggers*. Denton: University of North Texas Press, 2006.

Thomas, Landon. "Saving the Black Arts Festival." *Atlanta Constitution*, August 15, 1992.

Thomas, Lorenzo. *The Collected Poems of Lorenzo Thomas*. Edited by Aldon Lynn Nielsen and Laura Vrana. Middletown, CT: Wesleyan University Press, 2019.

———. *Don't Deny My Name: Words and Music and the African American Intellectual Tradition*. Ann Arbor: University of Michigan Press, 2008.

———. *Extraordinary Measures: Afrocentric Modernism and Twentieth-Century American Poetry*. Tuscaloosa: University of Alabama Press, 2000.

———. "Neon Griot: The Functional Role of Poetry Readings in the Black Arts Movement." In *Close Listening: Poetry and the Performed Word,* edited by Charles Bernstein, 300–323. New York: Oxford University Press, 1998.

———. "Tom Dent and the Umbra Workshop." American Studies Association Annual Meeting, Washington, DC, 2001.

"3-Day African Festival of Music Stated Here." *Washington Post,* March 6, 1966.

"Three Excellent Examples." *Baltimore Afro-American,* April 2, 1966.

Vought, Kip. "Racial Stirrings in Colored Town: The UNIA in Miami During the 1920s." *Tequesta* 1, no. 60 (2000): 65.

Waller, Signe. *Love and Revolution: A Political Memoir*. Lanham, MD: Rowman & Littlefield, 2002.

Ward, Jerry. *The Katrina Papers: A Journal of Trauma and Recovery*. New Orleans: University of New Orleans Press, 2008.

———. "Southern Black Aesthetics: The Case of *Nkombo* Magazine." *Mississippi Quarterly* (Spring 1991): 143–150.

Ward, Stephen. "'Scholarship in the Context of Struggle': Activist Intellectuals, the Institute of the Black World (IBW), and the Contours of Black Power Radicalism." *Black Scholar* 31, No. 3-4 (Fall-Winter 2001): 42–53.

Washington, Mary Helen. "Disturbing the Peace: What Happens to American Studies If You Put African American Studies at the Center?" *American Quarterly* 50, no. 1 (March 1998): 1–23.

Watkins, Nayo. "The Partnering of Artists and Communities: New Methods Evolving in the Durham CAPP." *High Performance* (Winter 1993): 39–40.

West, Hollie I. "Black Avant Garde." *Washington Post,* December 7, 1970.

———. "Jazz Gets New Stage." *Washington Post,* March 7, 1969.

Wheatley, Lorenz, and Valca Valentine, dir. *Under the Radar: The New School for Afro-American Thought*. Produced by Donald Freeman (Mamadou Lumumba). Community Research, Inc., 2010.

Wilkerson, Isabel. *Caste: The Origins of Our Discontent* (New York: Random House, 2020).

Wilson, Harriet E. *Our Nig; Or, Sketches from the Life of a Free Black, in a Two-Story White House, North*. Boston: Rand & Avery, 1859.

Wilson, Judith. "Underknown: Bob Thompson." *Archives of American Art Journal* 46, no. 3/4 (2007): 55.

Woodard, Komozi. *A Nation Within a Nation: Amiri Baraka (LeRoi Jones) and Black Power Politics*. Chapel Hill: University of North Carolina Press, 1999.

Woods, Clyde. *Development Drowned and Reborn: The Blues and Bourbon Restorations in Post-Katrina New Orleans*. Athens: University of Georgia Press, 2017.

Index